THE
U.K. BUSINESS
INTERNET STARTER KIT

THE U.K. BUSINESS INTERNET STARTER KIT

2000 edition

NAOMI LANGFORD-WOOD
& BRIAN SALTER

with

ROB YOUNG

An imprint of PEARSON EDUCATION

Harlow, England · London · New York · Reading, Massachusetts · San Francisco · Toronto · Don Mills, Ontario · Sydney
Tokyo · Singapore · Hong Kong · Seoul · Taipei · Cape Town · Madrid · Mexico City · Amsterdam · Munich · Paris · Milan

PEARSON EDUCATION LIMITED

Head Office:
Edinburgh Gate
Harlow CM20 2JE
Tel: +44 (0)1279 623623
Fax: +44 (0)1279 431059

London Office:
128 Long Acre
London WC2E 9AN
Tel: +44 (0)207 447 2000
Fax: +44 (0)207 240 5771

First published in Great Britain 2000

© Pearson Education Limited 2000

ISBN 0-13-020886-8

British Library Cataloguing in Publication Data
A CIP catalogue record for this book can be obtained from the British Library.

Library of Congress Cataloging in Publication Data
Available from the publisher.

10 9 8 7 6 5 4 3 2 1

Typeset by Pantek Arts, Maidstone, Kent.
Printed and bound in Great Britain by Biddles Ltd, Guildford & Kings Lynn.

The Publishers' policy is to use paper manufactured from sustainable forests.

CONTENTS

Chapter 9: Newsgroups – The Human Encyclopaedia 113

Chapter 10: Chat & Talk Without Moving Your Lips 133

Chapter 11: Grabbing The Goodies With FTP 149

Part Three: Using The Internet

Chapter 12: Shaking The Software Tree 161

Chapter 13: Safety On The Internet 175

Chapter 14: FAQs – Internet Questions & Answers 185

Appendices

INTRODUCTION

As far as business is concerned, the Internet really hit the headlines in 1994. People started talking about it, journalists started writing articles about it, and those weird-looking addresses full of dots and dashes started popping up at the end of TV shows and adverts. *Ah yes*, everyone said, knowingly. *Hype. It'll be something different next year.* But something unexpected happened…

Unlike most other objects of media hype in recent years, millions of people are still using the Internet every day – to communicate with others, for business, for entertainment, for leisure, to learn or research, to buy goods… the list is almost endless. And every day the number of people using the Internet grows by thousands. If these people weren't finding it useful or enjoyable, that number would, instead, be getting smaller.

In fact, you don't have to be a technical genius to use the Internet. As long as you're reasonably comfortable with using a PC and Windows – now an industry standard – it's no more tricky than anything else you use your computer for. That's the thing that really happened in 1994: although the Internet has been around since the 1960s, this was when software suddenly started to appear that made it friendly and easy to use.

But that's history, and we're not going to bore you with lengthy history lessons, or throw a lot of impressive but unnecessary jargon at you. The aim of this book is twofold – first, to help you connect your computer to the Internet and find your way around it, and second, to point you towards the practical and useful things that the Internet enables *all* businesses of all sizes and shapes to do. To that end, any technical detail that you won't need straight away has been banished to the back of the book. In fact, you may never need all that technical detail at all!

Why Do We Need A *UK* Business Guide To The Internet?

In the UK, businesses use the Internet differently from American organisations: different providers offer the services we need, charge different prices for them, and give us different options to choose from. And once we're connected, we want to find the information that matters to *us* and *our* firms, so we need to look in different places to find it. In addition, because we're not from the USA (or France, or Italy, etc.), our interests, habits, laws, environment, and whole way of life differ enormously. These affect both the way we use the Internet, and what we use it for.

▶ Most American users have access to free local phone calls, which means that they can stay connected to the Internet all day long for no extra charge. In the UK, where we still have to pay to get online, to follow some of the suggestions given in an American guide could end up costing a small fortune! Throughout this book, it's assumed that you want your time on the Internet to have as little impact as possible on the size of your phone bill, commensurate with the benefit your business gains from it.

▶ As a UK business user, you are likely to want to find information with a UK slant. In addition, your British customers will want to read home-grown newspapers and magazines; see local weather forecasts; check local TV listings and sports results; find out what's showing at their nearest cinemas; use UK travel agents, hotels, airlines and trains; plan days out at UK theme parks and museums, and so on.

▶ Many Internet sites give support, help and advice on any subject you can imagine. Although some American Internet books can point you towards valuable information, they won't tell you where to get the best UK business, legal or consumer advice, or discuss financial matters with other businessmen.

▶ You can now order almost anything from 'cyberstores' on the Internet. But do you really want to pay in dollars and wait for the goods to be shipped from America when there are plenty of UK sites just a couple of mouse clicks away? In fact, if you want to use the Internet to dynamise your business, you'll have to find the right sites in the UK!

How Is This Book Organised?

This book is split into six major parts to help you find the answers you want quickly and easily.

Part One, *Getting Online*, introduces all the basic concepts and services of the Internet, helps you choose the type of Internet account that suits you best, and tells you what you need to know to get online.

Part Two, *Finding Your Way Around*, shows you the main services you can use on the Internet, and the software you'll need to access them. Much of this software can be found on the CD-ROM in the back of this book (as well as on the Internet itself), and these chapters explain how to set it up and how to use it.

Part Three, *Using The Internet*, gives an in-depth guide to using your connection and software to accomplish something on the Internet, such as doing research, reading online newspapers and magazines, shopping, planning days out, finding computer software, managing your finances, or any of the 101 other business uses of the Web.

Part Four, *Business On The Web*, introduces the business opportunities and new ways of doing business that the Internet can provide, including research, online sales, security and payment systems.

Part Five, *Building Your Site* concentrates on the things you need to consider when thinking about planning, setting up and maintaining a company website. It gives examples of multimedia on the Internet, and leads you to some of the weird, wonderful, and exotic locations on the World Wide Web. You'll also learn how to design your own World Wide Web pages and publish them for the rest of the world to see.

The *Appendices* section includes handy references, lists and glossaries, and a 'JargonBuster Super Reference' to help you decipher what everyone's talking about!

The *Directory* is a useful collection of contact details for companies that provide access to the Internet, as well as a list of useful business addresses.

How Should We Use It?

This book is organised in such a way that you can read it from cover to cover if you want to, but you certainly don't have to. We write books in a chatty style so that you can dip into them and learn something new from reading just a couple of paragraphs, because we know you're busy. You'll find plenty of cross-references to tempt you towards other parts of the book. However, we do have a few suggestions:

▶ If you haven't yet connected to the Internet and you don't have an Internet account, we recommend that you read the first two parts of the book, which will help you get online and give you all the basic information in a sensible order.

▶ If you already have an Internet connection, you can cheerfully skip Part 1 and begin with Part 2, which will get you started on the road to mastering the Internet's services and software.

▶ If you've been using the Internet's tools and services for a while and you know the basics, skip about the book all you like. You might still find some things you didn't know in Part 2, but we suggest taking a look at Parts 3, 4 and 5 – you'll find plenty of great sites to visit, together with information and tips to help you get the most out of the Internet, to have your own website designed and published, to explore virtual worlds online, and lots more.

Icons & Conventions

Throughout the book we've used a few special features and conventions that make it easier to find your way around. In particular you'll notice that chapters are split up into bite-sized chunks with subheadings. If something looks a bit too complicated or irrelevant, just skip to the next heading.

You'll also find some icons and text in boxes containing extra information that you may find useful:

 A question-and-answer format highlighting questions or problems that might present themselves while you're reading about something or trying it out yourself.

A selection of handy hints, tips and incidental notes that might save you some time, point you in a new direction, or help you avoid a few pitfalls.

 Explains any technical terms that couldn't be avoided, or any related jargon that you may encounter when dealing with a particular area of the Internet.

We've also used different type styles and keyboard conventions to make particular meanings clear, as shown below.

Convention	Description
bold type	Indicates a new term being encountered, an Internet address, or text that you'll type yourself.
bold-italic type	Means that you'll type this text yourself, but we don't know exactly what it will be. For example, if you have to type the location of a file you want to open, you'll see something like ***open directory/filename***.
Ctrl+C	A key-combination, saving frequent mouse excursions to pull-down menus. The keys to press will be separated by '+' signs. This example means press and hold the 'Ctrl' key while pressing 'C' once.
File | Open	Means that you should open the software's 'File' menu, and select its 'Open' option. You might see something longer, such as View | Options | General: in this case you'll open the 'View' menu, select the 'Options' entry and then click on something that says 'General' – it may be a button or a tabbed page, but it will always be obvious when you get there.
Enter	Although we've referred to the 'Enter' key throughout, on your keyboard this key might be labelled 'Return' instead.
Directories	To users of Windows 95 and later, these are better known as 'folders'. On the Internet they're known as 'directories', but the meaning is the same.

A Few Basic Assumptions

Finally, we're assuming that you know how to use a computer and you're reasonably familiar with the different parts of Windows. By that, we mean that you know how to use the mouse, you understand what directories and files are, you're comfortable with using menus and dialog boxes, and you know how to start programs and switch between windows. If you get stuck, you can usually find the answers in Windows' Help files.

If you have an Apple Mac, or a RISC-PC or some other type of personal computer then you will find that the principles are the same. We've stuck to the Windows operating system since in the main that is the system most preferred by businesses in this country.

1

GETTING ONLINE

In This Part...

MEET THE INTERNET

Before you can really get excited at the prospect of getting on the Internet, it helps to have some idea of what it really is, what you can use it for, and (we hate to say it) how it works. So let's kick off by looking at how the Internet is organised, and at some of the ways you can use it. We're also going to introduce most of the technical-sounding stuff you'll need to know in this chapter. It's all quite painless, though, and we hope that this appetiser will leave you hungry for the main course.

What Is The Internet?

This is the obvious first question, but let's try and skip through its literal answer as quickly as possible. The technical explanation is that it's a giant, worldwide computer network made up of lots of smaller computer networks. As with any network, these computers are connected to one another so that they can share information. Unlike most networks, though, the vastness of the Internet means that this information has to be passed around using modems, telephone lines and higher capacity cables such as ISDN and optical fibre, as well as satellites, rather than an office full of cables.

But all that's just hardware, and it's probably not making your mouth water. Instead, let's zoom in on that word 'information', the key to the *real* Internet. The types of information these computers can share covers a huge (and expanding) range – pictures, sounds, text, video, applications, music, and much more – making the Internet a true multimedia experience. Any business can connect their computer to the Internet and gain instant access to millions of files, browse around, or search for some specific item, and grab as much as they want while they're there.

GOOD QUESTION

How big is the Internet?

When it comes to numbers, no-one knows. A lot of informed guesswork goes on, but it doesn't look terribly well informed when you compare results. It's safest just to say that millions of computers are serving tens of millions of people, and leave it at that. To be honest, even if we could give you the exact numbers right now, they'd be wrong by the time you had completed the Times crossword.

People Power

The other aspect of the real Internet is people. All the information you'll find is put there by real people, often simply because they want to share their knowledge, skills, interests or creations with anyone who's interested. The people themselves may be in companies just like yours, keen to have a business web presence to promote their products; organisations such as universities, charities and governments; or individual users.

Along with people, of course, comes communication, and the Internet is a great communications system. You can exchange messages (e-mail) with other users, hold conversations or online meetings by typing messages back and forth, or actually send your voice over the Internet using a microphone instead of a telephone. You can take part in any of 30000 discussion groups on any subject you'd care to mention and this can be an ideal medium for market and product research. Add to this the wealth of human knowledge and experience that lies at its heart, and the Internet is, quite simply, a very big place that makes the world seem much smaller and global trading more achievable even for the tiniest of companies.

What Can My Business Use It For?

Once you're armed with a connection to the Internet, the possibilities for using it are almost limitless. Here's just a tiny sample of the things you can do on the Net, all of which you'll be learning about later:

▶ Virtualise your business processes.

▶ Research your chosen market without your competitors even knowing and without having to wait.

▶ Reduce your costs.

▶ Give information to customers and prospective customers – 24 hours a day, 365 days a year.

▶ Get paid faster and help your cash flow.

▶ Get into export without huge start-up costs.

▶ Improve your customer relations.

▶ Improve your communication processes with customers, suppliers and distributors.

5

▶ Control robots and movie cameras on other continents while the live camera footage is beamed straight to your desktop.

▶ Book travel online with up-to-the-minute prices and weather reports.

▶ Hold conversations with people on the other side of the world by typing on your keyboard or talking into a microphone, for the price of a local call.

▶ Manage your company finances, and pay bills at any time of the day or night.

▶ Read magazines and newspapers online, along with books, dictionaries, encyclopaedias, thesauri, and every type of reference you could dream of.

▶ Download the latest versions and updates of your software long before they hit the shops.

JARGON BUSTER

Download

The act of copying a file from one distant computer across a network of computers and telephone lines to your own hard disk. The opposite term is 'upload' – copying a file from your own disk to a remote computer.

The Most Popular Internet Services

What you've just read is a general taste of what's on offer on the Net, but all the things you want to do (or get, or see) will be scattered around the world on different computers. In other words, these computers offer the *services* you want to use. The Internet is made up of a bundle of different services, but here's a quick look at the six most popular:

▶ **E-mail.** E-mail is the oldest and most used of the Internet services with well over 40 million messages whizzing around it every day. The majority of e-mail messages are just ordinary text, but you can attach almost any type of computer file you want to send along with it (such as a spreadsheet or a small program), and encrypt the message so that no-one except the intended recipient will be able to read it.

▶ **The World Wide Web.** This service, often known simply as the Web, has had so much publicity and acclaim that you may think it *is* the Internet. In fact, it's the Net's new baby, born in 1992. It's a very lively, gurgling baby though, packed with pictures, text, video, music, and information about every subject under the sun. Any of the pages on the Web can be linked together, so that a page you're viewing from a computer in Bristol could lead you to a page in Tokyo, Brisbane or Oslo with a single mouse-click. Multinational companies, small and medium sized enterprises (SMEs), micro businesses, political parties, universities and colleges, football teams, local councils, to name but a few, have their own pages on the Web, as well as very many individual users.

▶ **Newsgroups.** A newsgroup is a discussion group that focuses on one particular subject area. The discussion itself takes place through a form of e-mail, but the big difference is that these messages are posted for the whole group to read and respond to. You can join any group you like from a choice of over 30 000, and subjects range from the specific, such as a certain type of camellia, to more general discussions, such as how to deal with difficult people in the workplace.

▶ **Chat.** This isn't chat as in 'yakety-yak'; more 'clickety-click'. You can hold conversations with one or more people by typing messages back and forth which appear instantly on the screens of everyone involved. Some chat programs allow 'whiteboarding' (drawing pictures and diagrams in collaboration), private online conferences, and control of programs running on someone else's computer.

▶ **Voice on the Net.** This *is* chat as in 'yakety-yak'. As long as you've got a soundcard in your computer, and a microphone plugged into it, you can talk to anyone in the world just as you do with the telephone. So why not use the telephone? Your Internet connection will be a local call, letting you hold these conversations for as little as 60p per hour. Compare that with the cost of a direct-dialled call to New York (£6 plus) and you've got a pretty good reason for using the Net!

▶ **FTP.** The computers that make up the Internet hold a combined library of millions upon millions of files. The FTP system lets you look inside directories on some of these computers and copy files straight to your hard disk just as if you were copying files between your own directories.

Although other services exist, these are almost certainly the ones you'll be using most (and you may use nothing but e-mail and the World Wide Web – the services are there if you want them, but you don't have to use them).

Understanding Internet Addresses

So the Internet is big, the computers that form the Internet are counted in millions, and yet somehow all that information manages to get wherever it's supposed to go. But how does that tiny, helpless file find its way from deepest Ohio to your own office computer all by itself?

The answer is in much the same way that an ordinary letter manages to arrive at your office: it has an address attached to it that identifies one single office in the whole world. Every single computer on the Internet has a unique address, called its **IP address**, which consists of four numbers separated by dots, such as 158.152.123.241 (for Topspin Group on Demon Internet).

JARGON BUSTER

IP address

'IP' stands for Internet Protocol. IP works with its best friend, TCP, to handle the tricky job of sending computer files down telephone lines, and part of this job is knowing which computer is asking for the file and which is sending it. Is it really as exciting as it sounds? Yes, almost exactly. But if you still want to know more about TCP, IP and protocols in general, skip ahead to the Jargonbuster Super Reference on page 343.

Domain Names – The Easier Way

Of course, if you need to connect to one of these computers you'll need to know its address. But don't panic! You don't have to remember streams of meaningless numbers; there's an easy way. As well as this numerical IP address, each computer is given a much friendlier **domain name**. Going back to those IP addresses we mentioned just now, instead of having to remember 158.152.123.241, the domain name is simply **topspin-group.com**. Best of all, most of the Internet programs you'll be using will store these addresses for you so that you can recall them with just a couple of mouse clicks.

Talking in dots

If you're ever in that awkward situation where you have to say a domain name out loud, use the word 'dot' to replace the dot itself. The rule applies to every dot in the address, such as 'demon dot co dot uk' for **demon.co.uk** or even 'bbc dot co dot uk' for **bbc.co.uk**.

The function of the domain name is simply to make life less complicated for Internet users. The computers themselves still use that numerical IP address. Whenever you want to connect to a computer somewhere on the Internet, you'll type its domain name into your software (or perhaps select it from a list of your favourites). The domain name is sent to another computer called a **domain name server** (DNS). The job of the DNS is to find the 'numbers and dots' IP address of the computer that uses that nickname and send it back to your computer. It might sound cumbersome, but this conversation between computers should happen very quickly. You probably won't be aware that it's happening, but you'd certainly be aware if it stopped happening!

Dissecting Domain Names

Apart from being a lot easier to remember than numbers, domain names can also tell you whose computer you're connected to, what type of organisation they are, and where the computer is located. The 'who' part is usually easy: given an address like **www.channel4.com**, the computer almost certainly belongs to the Channel 4 television company. It's the bits that come after that (known as **top-level domains**) that can be interesting, so here's a few to look out for:

Domain	Used by
.co	a commercial company
.com	originally an American company; now also used for companies outside the States
.ac	an academic establishment (college, university, etc.)
.edu	another college or university domain
.gov	a government agency
.mil	a military establishment
.net	normally an Internet access provider or some other organisation involved with organising the Net
.org	normally a non-profit-making organisation

Room for more on top

BY THE WAY

In 1997 a plan was announced to add a few more top-level domains to the list. Although little has actually happened so far, at the time of writing agreement has been reached on the setting up of a 15-strong international board to control the Web's domain names. The result is that we should soon be seeing businesses using suffixes such as **.firm** and **.bank**, information services using **.info**, consumer retailers using **.store**, and individuals using **.nom**, among others.

American domain names stop at this point (that's one way to tell they are American at the moment). Most of the domain names in other countries have an extra dot and a country code tagged onto the end. For example, you'll see **.uk** for United Kingdom, **.se** for Sweden, **.fr** for France, **.jp** for Japan, and **.fi** for Finland.

However, there are big moves afoot which will put domain names through the kind of renumbering that we all remember with the renumbering of BT's phone numbers throughout the country (when, for instance, 01 for London became 071 and 081 and then 0171 and 0181 – and now, within a very short timescale, it's changed yet again to the consternation of all those businesses that have had to reprint their stationery each time).

Getting Everything To Work Together

At this point there are just three more elements that should be mentioned – **clients**, **servers** and **protocols**. These are the vital ingredients that, when mixed together, give you access to all the Internet's services.

▶ The **client** is a software program that your office has chosen to run on your computer to access a particular service. For example, if you want to send and receive e-mail messages you'll need an e-mail client; if you want to browse the World Wide Web you'll need a Web client. These all look and work in much the same way as any other program you already use on your computer, and you can pick, choose and swap programs until you find the ones you're most comfortable using.

▶ The **server** is a computer that provides your Internet access; servers work in a similar way to clients. When you're dealing with e-mail, your e-mail client will contact the mail server; when you want to look at a page on the World Wide Web, your Web client will ask the Web server to fetch it from wherever it is in the world and send it 'down the line' to you.

▶ The word **protocols** popped up a couple of pages back. They're the vital link in the chain that makes everything work. These protocols (as goes with the territory) are known by bunches of initial letters like HTTP, SMTP, NNTP, IMAP4 and TCP/IP.

Protocol

JARGON BUSTER

When two computers need to communicate but don't speak the same language, they follow a set of rules called a 'protocol', just as a Czech and a Swede who don't speak each other's language may still be able to communicate in German. For example, your e-mail program may talk to the mail server in a language called SMTP (Simple Mail Transfer Protocol) whenever you want to send an e-mail message.

You may need to know which protocol is which when you're setting up your Internet connection or installing new client programs, but the rest of the time it's all just technical jargon. If you do need to know, you'll find it all explained in the 'JargonBuster Super Reference' in Appendix D and on the CD-ROM.

2

HOW CAN WE GET ONLINE?

In This Chapter...

▶ **Read about the different ways to get on the Internet**

▶ **Find out what you need to surf the Net**

▶ **Get top performance from your modem**

▶ **Learn the differences between online services and Internet access providers**

▶ **Get those phone charges sorted out**

Congratulations – you've waded through all the technical stuff and emerged unscathed! In this chapter you'll find out about the different ways you can go online and surf the Net, the decisions you'll need to make about how you want to do it, and the pros and cons of the two connection options.

Where Can We Get Internet Access?

There are several ways to get access to the Internet, and before we even consider setting up a connection for your business let us instead concentrate on the basics so that you can make reasonable decisions as to your business needs. You can get online almost immediately:

▶ **Set up your own Internet connection.** This is the most obvious option and, with your own computer connected to the Internet, you can use all its services whenever you want to. Better still, there are now a number of free Internet service providers allowing you to get online purely for the cost of a local call. We'll be looking at some of these free service providers later in the book.

▶ **Visit a cybercafé.** Some of these cafés and bars, which started to appear all over the place in the past few years, offering drinks and snacks... and Internet access, are still around, although very much on the wane as more and more people are getting connected. If you're not convinced that the Internet is for you, cybercafés offer valuable hands-on experience. Expect to pay around £6 per hour, and try to book time in advance (especially at lunchtimes, evenings and weekends).

▶ **Talk to one of your friends or business colleagues** – or even one of their children (or perhaps your own!). It's almost impossible to find a street-wise kid who has *not* surfed the Net.

What Do We Need?

That's the first decision taken care of – you want your own basic business Internet connection. The next step is to consult the checklist and see which of the required bits and pieces you're missing. Actually, it's a very short list: you'll need a telephone line, a computer, a modem, and an Internet access account. Let's look at each one in a little more detail.

Telephone Line

Just an ordinary phone line, with a socket fairly close to your computer so
that you can plug your modem into it. Depending on the level of use of your
fax machine, for a pound or two you can buy an adapter to let you plug a
modem into the same phone line socket, which might be a worthwhile option
at this early stage. If you find yourself spending a lot of time online, you may
want to consider installing a second phone line just for Internet access so that
people can still fax you while you're surfing, but that's a decision for later.

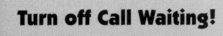

BY THE WAY

Turn off Call Waiting!

Depending on your phone system you could find that some of the ancillary
services such as Call Waiting or Divert on Busy can interrupt the signals to and
from your modem. If you have these facilities on your phone line, make sure you turn them off
every time you go online and back on again when you've finished, otherwise an incoming call
at the wrong moment could disconnect you and cancel anything you were doing (particularly
irritating if you were waiting for a huge file to download and were just seconds from
completion!). This will not apply to most larger businesses using a dedicated line for Internet
and e-mail usage.

Computer

A common misconception is that you've got to have a fast, powerful
computer to surf the Net. In fact, almost *any* computer will be up to the task.
We do have a few suggestions that will ease the way for your business:

▶ Windows 95 and 98 have built-in support for Internet connections that
make all the setting-up and connecting happen smoothly and simply. If
your business is still using Windows 3.x, this might be a good time to
review your computer installation as this older software will cause you
no end of frustration instead of easing the path.

▶ To hear the Internet's musical offerings and use Voice On The Net
software (see page 144) you'll need a soundcard.

▶ To enjoy the World Wide Web at its graphical, vibrant best, you'll be happiest with an absolute minimum of a 256-colour, 800 × 600 display. On modern computers it's the minimum standard setup anyway, so don't worry if that's all gobbledygook!

▶ Finally, a large hard disk. It's not vital – you'll have to install a few new programs, but they won't take more than a few megabytes – but you might be surprised how many files people start to send you once they know your business has an internet connection!

Modem

The modem is the device that converts the digital information on a computer into analog sound that can be sent down a phone line, and converts it back to meaningful information when it gets to the other end. The most important thing to look at when buying a modem is its *speed* – how much information it can move around per second. The faster your modem (in theory, at least), the quicker you'll get everything done that you planned to do, cutting your phone bill and any online charges as a result.

GOOD QUESTION

Is a fast modem really worth the extra money?

Generally speaking, yes it is. But you've heard the term 'superhighway' used to describe the Internet. Like any highway, there's a lot of people all trying to get to the same place and things can get jammed solid, so while the person with the slow modem is gazing at his screen for some sign of information arriving, the person with the fast modem is doing just the same. But, when everything's running smoothly, a 56Kbps modem is streets ahead of a 28.8.

At the moment, the fastest modems shift data around at a maximum speed of 56Kbps (56 thousand bits per second). The slowest (and therefore cheapest) modem you might still be able to find is 14.4Kbps, with a 28.8 and a 33.6 sitting in between. A 14.4 or 28.8Kbps modem really is a false economy – if you connect to the Net for more than a few minutes a week at this speed you'll be miserable. If your computer doesn't already have a modem installed (and most new PCs do), we strongly recommend buying a 56Kbps modem, with models starting at around £50.

Finally, on the subject of modems, you can choose between an internal or an external model. Although the external modem is slightly more expensive we'd go for it every time (assuming, of course, that you haven't got one installed already!). It's much easier to install than an internal one (just plug in the phone cable, serial cable, and mains plug). With an internal one, you have to get to grips with IRQs and jumpers as well as play around with screwdrivers.

BY THE WAY

Turbo-charge your modem

Data passing into and out of your computer through the modem is compressed, so make sure you squeeze the most out of it. Find the settings for the serial (COM) port that your modem is plugged into, and change the port speed to at least double your modem's rated speed (e.g. 115 000 for a 56Kbps modem).

Internet Access Account

With all the necessary hardware bits and bobs in place, the final thing you need is a way to connect to a computer that's a part of the Internet. There are hundreds of companies in the UK who specialise in selling dial-up links to the Internet via their own computers, so the next step is to choose one of these companies and set up an account with them. When selecting these it is important to note that the majority of these providers are not geared toward the business user.

This leads to the final decision you have to make: do you want an account with an **Internet access provider** (often just called an IAP) or with an **online service**? Which will provide you with the best business option?

Online Services & Internet Access Providers – What's The Difference?

The most important thing that access providers and the major online services have in common is that they both let you connect to the Internet. It's the way they do it and what else they have to offer that makes them different, along with their methods of deciding how much you should pay. In fact, this whole area is becoming greyed around the edges as the two are merging closer and closer together. Many providers are turning themselves into so-called 'portals' – one stop shops that provide both the initial access as well as content to grab your attention. We'll take a look at portals a little later on, but for the moment we'll round off this chapter by taking a look at the options and the pros and cons of each.

Online Services

You will probably have heard of the 'big three' online services, **AOL** (formerly known as America Online), **CompuServe** (CSi), and the **Microsoft Network** (MSN). In fact, if you buy computer magazines, you're probably snowed under with floppy disks and CD-ROMs inviting you to sign up to one or other of these. One of the main plus-points about these online services is the speed and ease with which you can sign up: just this one disk and a credit or debit card number is all you need.

But it's important not to confuse online services with the Internet itself. An online service is rather like an exclusive club: once you subscribe you'll have access to a range of members-only areas such as discussion forums, chat rooms and file libraries. Although you can 'break out' to the Internet from here, non-members can't get in. You won't find much in the members-only areas that you can't find on the Internet itself, but online services do have the combined benefits of ease of use, online help if you get lost, and an apparently friendly all-in-one program from which you can reach everything you need.

In late 1998, AOL bought up CompuServe, and although the two are still operating under their own banner, it is not beyond the realms of possibility that eventually they will present one image. A few months later, still on the acquisitions trail, AOL bought Netscape and now they account for some 40 per cent of subscribers to the Internet world-wide.

Although the Internet certainly isn't the chamber of horrors that some newspapers would have you believe, there's little control over what gets published there; online services carefully filter and control their *members-only* content, making them the preferred choice for some in getting the whole family online. However, in our experience we would have to say that we were shocked at the sheer volume of unsolicited 'hot-sex' e-mails received during a one month trial of AOL when we have had no such e-mails at all during four years of connection through a UK-based IAP. We believe that part of the problem lies with the fact that AOL's subscriber list can be so easily hacked into and therefore provides a ready target for unsolicited mailings.

How 'easy' is it to connect to an online service?

GOOD QUESTION

Typically it takes about 12 minutes from inserting the CD-ROM to officially 'arriving online'. Probably the most difficult thing you would have to do is read those shiny numbers on your credit card.

Online services provide the Internet, and a bit more. So what counts against them?

First and foremost, when trying to present your business well you need a good name and a good address. *Bank Chambers* is a good business address, whereas *Laburnum Cottage* is not. So it is with the Web. We'll be looking at Web addresses in more detail later, but the majority of online service providers insist on you having an address with your name incorporated into it, whereas your business would appear to have more virtual substance if it were just, for instance, www.mycompany.com.

Secondly, the time and the price. Most online services charge a low monthly subscription fee which includes only a few free hours online. This is ideal for a light user, but once your free hours are used up you'll be paying extra for subsequent hours, so the online service could be an expensive option. Most services offer alternative pricing plans though, so try to gauge how much time you're likely to spend online as you use your free first month, and change to a different plan if necessary before the second month begins. Online services tend to offer Internet access as an 'extra' – when you step out onto the Net itself you may find that you don't get the information as quickly as you would with a direct Internet connection.

Another negative point of OSPs is that the majority insist on pushing adverts at you before you can even access their most basic services. You can see why they want to do this, of course. With the large user bases that most of them enjoy, they can attract advertising revenue faster than a ray of light, but you have to quantify the cost of having your people sitting through the reception of these advertisements before they can get on with their work.

Internet Access Providers

An Internet Access Provider gives you access to the Internet, plain and simple – unless they have metamorphosed into portals. When you dial in to your access provider's computer, a message on the screen tells you you're connected. You can start your e-mail program or your Web software and begin doing whatever it is you want to do.

The IAP account has a number of valuable points in its favour. First, you'll only pay a single monthly charge (plus your telephone bill, of course) – unless you are signed up to a 'free' subscription service – with no restrictions or charges for the time you spend online. Second, you'll have far greater flexibility in your choice of software. Most access providers will give you a bundle of programs when you sign up, but you don't have to use them – try some of the programs on the free CD-ROM accompanying this book, or others mentioned in later chapters, until you find the ones that you're most comfortable with.

As just mentioned, there is now an increasing number of IAPs that offer their services entirely free of charge. The Dixons group was the first to make the big time in this way with their Freeserve service, signing up over a million 'subscribers' in only six months (compared with AOL taking three years to net the same number in the UK). Although free Web access is obviously highly attractive to the home user, once again the business user has to weigh up the pros and cons of having an address such as www.mycompany. freeserve.co.uk. In addition, because the service is free (the IAP actually makes its money by sharing some of the phone revenue with BT, or whichever telephone company you use) you have no comeback if your address is removed or given to someone else. Nor do you get some of the extra visitor tracking facilities that proper business accounts normally receive as standard. However, as we write, Dixons is now starting to target Freeserve at the business community with free Web management and e-commerce facilities on offer to small and medium sized firms.

Whilst some companies may not want to use free IAPs to run mission-critical applications, the services could be used in parallel to a main network as a low-cost solution to enable staff who would not normally have automatic e-mail access to be able to get online.

At the time of writing there are a few intrepid IAPs experimenting with free call access via 0800 dialling codes. In the main these restrict access to evenings and weekends, but expect to see a lot happening in this area over the coming months.

Phone Calls & Connections

Whether you've chosen to hook up with an IAP or an online service, you'll have to dial in to that company's computer every time you want to go online. This means that if you connect for 20 minutes you'll pay for a 20-minute phone call. So how much are these phone calls going to cost?

The good news is that you should always be able to connect through a local phone number. At the time of writing, British Telecom's local domestic call rate (per minute) is 4p peak, 1.7p cheap, and 1p at weekends. If you're setting this up in your home office you can add your access number to your 'Friends & Family' list and you'll save at least 10 per cent. And if your phone bill is high enough to qualify for the PremierLine scheme you'll be able to knock off another 15 per cent. Business rates, of course, are totally different and the deals you can get are so varied that we will have to leave this to your best judgement. Some cable telecom companies even offer free local call access, so keep checking with your business telephone providers in case you can strike a better deal.

Are There Any Other Options?

Yes indeed. For a standard dial-up account the humble modem probably offers the cheapest way of getting online. However, there are certainly much faster ways of accessing the Internet, a few of which are listed below.

▶ **ISDN line.** An ISDN line replaces your modem with a device called a Terminal Adapter, and gives you a maximum speed of 128Kbps (over twice that of the fastest modem). Apart from the cost of the Terminal Adapter (£50–£300), you'll need to get an ISDN line installed and pay a quarterly rental of around £150. Connection charges range from £250 to £600 according to the quantity of 'free' call time you want included in the deal. Call prices themselves are unchanged, and you can use this single line for up to eight devices at the same time and make phone calls or send faxes while surfing the Net.

Dig deeper

BY THE WAY

If you're seriously considering an ISDN line, make sure you check access providers' charges too. Some Internet access providers charge a higher monthly subscription for an ISDN connection than for a modem connection.

▶ **ADSL**, or Asynchronous Digital Subscriber Line, is what many are pinning their hopes on for much faster Internet access, and it is widely believed that ADSL will form the natural successor to ISDN. The maximum download speed is around 8Mbps (megabits per second) and the maximum upload speed around 1Mbps (hence asymmetric). ADSL needs a special modem, but the beauty of it is that it can use the same telephone line for voice calls and broadband Internet services. BT and other European telecoms providers have run trials on the viability of using ADSL, but since these same providers have invested a great deal in ISDN there may well be resistance to investing yet more money in radical changes to the way data is transmitted across the existing telecoms infrastructure. One of the first to bite the bullet is Kingston Communications in Humberside who provide ADSL to business users. There are alternatives to ADSL itself – such as UADSL which is said to be cheaper and easier to install and major players such as Microsoft, Intel and Compaq are throwing their weight behind this. There is also VDSL (Very high speed Digital Subscriber Line), which can offer speeds of up to 52Mbps.

BY THE WAY

Although we have not yet covered Internet addresses, you might like to return to this section at a later date if you are interested in finding out more about these technologies. For information on ADSL point your browser at **http://www.adsl.com**. Frequently asked questions on VDSL can be found at **http://www.adsl.com/ vdsl_faq.html**. Universal ADSL has a site at **http://www.uawg.org**.

▶ **Leased line**. There are a variety of leased lines available which offer fast direct connection to the Internet. A leased line will set you back anything from £7500 to £250 000 and gives you permanent connection and instant access to the Net.

▶ **Satellite**. There are now a number of providers offering Internet delivery via satellite downlinks. Some work on the back of broadcast TV signals, whilst others have satellite channels devoted solely to their use. In the coming months there will be many more such systems available, but one of the most popular with businesses at the time of writing is Easat which offers a download speed four times faster than ISDN using the Eutelsat 13° East (known as HotBird 3) satellite. Another provider, Telstra, uses Inmarsat. Major projects under development are Skybridge, which will require some 80 low earth-orbiting (LEO) satellites and will deliver 20Mbps; and Teledisc, which aims to offer, by 2002, 64Mbps using no fewer than 288 LEO satellites. Further information can be found at **http://www.telstra.com**, **http://www.skybridgesatellite.com**, and **http://www.teledisc.com**.

▶ **Wireless Leased Line Access**. Firms such as Tele2, which serves the Thames Valley area – although it is extending across the country – are offering access from 128Kbps up to 2Mbps. Users use wireless links to Tele2's communications infrastructure. Apart from a one-off connection fee of £4565, there is a charge of £650 per month, but Tele2 claims that users will typically save £7000 per year against prices charged by traditional leased line suppliers such as BT.

CONNECTING TO AN ACCESS PROVIDER

In This Chapter...

▶ **How to pick the best IAP for your needs**

▶ **The five essential questions to ask before subscribing**

▶ **Choose your business e-mail address**

▶ **Make sense of all the technical info your IAP gives you**

Now that you've made the all-important decisions, this is where things start to happen – after following the instructions in this chapter you'll be online and ready to start exploring the Internet. Right now you're just two steps away from connecting: you need to choose and subscribe to an access provider (IAP), and configure your version of Windows to make the connection. It may look a bit involved on first sight, but remember – you should only have to do it once!

Choosing An Access Provider

There are countless IAPs in the UK, and more are starting up all the time. The first step is to make a shortlist of half a dozen or so, using these tips as a guide:

▶ **Are they local?** You need to know the location of the computer you're dialling in to, which is sometimes called a 'node' or a PoP (Point of Presence). You **must** be able to dial in using a local phone number otherwise your phone charges could become astronomical! Most IAPs use 0345, 0645 or 0845 numbers, which means that wherever in the UK you are dialling from you will be charged local call rates.

▶ **Did someone recommend them?** If a particular IAP can offer you local access and you've also heard positive things about them (in terms of reliability of connection, good telephone support, etc.), they're definitely worth adding to your shortlist. Many popular Internet and computer magazines regularly review and rate IAPs and chart the current 'Top 10' in terms of service and reliability, but don't forget to view them from a business perspective!

The next step is to get on the phone. Any company that takes itself seriously will be happy to answer your questions, so pick a promising candidate from your shortlist and give them a ring. If you can't get straight answers to the following questions, either press the point harder or cross them off the list (and don't let them blind you with jargon either!).

Asking Questions – Five Of The Best

First, check any details from the list of IAPs at the back of this book, and any that were given to you by another subscriber, to make sure they're accurate and up-to-date. Then work your way down this list:

1 **What is your monthly subscription fee?** Prices for business users vary enormously from 'free' to hundreds of pounds. It's vital to dig deep and ask precisely what you are getting for your money. It can be as complicated as selecting tariffs on a mobile phone! So ask what they provide that other companies don't, and compare like with like. Look in some of the business Internet magazines for the best current offerings around.

2 **Do you charge extra for the time I spend online?** The correct answer to this is 'No we don't'. If they get this one wrong, go no further!

3 **What is your fastest modem connection speed?** All IAPs who want to be taken seriously should be able to offer connections at 56Kbps these days. Accept nothing less.

4 **When is telephone support available?** You'll almost certainly need telephone support sometime, so make sure it'll be available when you're most likely to be using the Internet. With the recent increase in IAPs providing a free subscription service, it is a good idea to check the cost of any telephone support line, as many IAPs now charge 50p or £1 per minute to call their support lines.

5 **Do you provide preconfigured connection software for my computer?** Many companies will ask you questions about your computer and operating system, and then send you software that's ready to install with all the tricky stuff taken care of. (The software may be on CD-ROM, so be sure to check this if you don't have a CD-ROM drive!) Find out if the connection will be easy to set up on your computer, and whether the technical support phone line will be able to talk you through the process if you get stuck.

When you've found a suitable access provider, you're almost ready to subscribe. But first…

Choosing Your Username

When you start a subscription with an access provider, you'll be identified by your choice of **username** (some companies refer to it as a user ID, logon name or member name). You'll need to quote this when you call the support line with a question, and when you log on to the provider's computer to surf the Internet. More importantly, it forms the unique part of your e-mail address. If you were to start an account with **mycompany.co.uk**, your e-mail address would be *username***@mycompany.co.uk** and this is the address you'd give out to people so that they can send you e-mail. As an example,

Naomi's username is **nlw** and her company account is **topspin-group.com**. So, her e-mail address is **nlw@topspin-group.com**.

GOOD QUESTION

Do I have to use my own name?

No, you can use just about anything you want. It'll be easier for you (and other people) to remember if it doesn't contain numbers, but there's nothing to stop you having whatever username you like, so long as your IAP does not already have it on its subscriber list. There again, (we know we're flogging this point to death, but…) think of your company image. This is the only way that other people can judge you until they do business with you.

The rules on usernames vary a little between providers. In general, they can't contain spaces (in common with any Internet address), but dots, dashes and underscores are usually acceptable. Most importantly, it must be a username that hasn't already been scooped by another subscriber to your chosen access provider, so it's worth putting a bit of thought into a second and third choice in case your first is unavailable.

For instance, one of our clients manufactures removable covers for mattresses etc. They trade globally and their name is Sidebottom. But **www.sidebottom.com** had already been taken, and so the options they also considered were **www.sidebottom-covers.com**, **www.cover-the-world.com** and **www.sidebottom-leeds.com**. (We'll look at the meanings of **www** and **.com** a little later on.)

And Now... Subscribe!

It's time to get back on the telephone to your chosen provider and tell them you'd like to subscribe. The provider will set up an account for you, but exactly what happens next will depend on the individual access provider:

▶ You may receive a disk in the post that's preconfigured for your computer, operating system and account. If so, follow the instructions that accompany it and it ought to be as easy to install as any other program.

▶ You might receive a disk of software and some documentation that tells you how to install it and how to configure your computer yourself.

▶ You might already have a browser such as Microsoft Internet Explorer installed on your machine (Windows 98 has IE4 or IE5 as part of the operating system itself), so your IAP will need to supply you only with the wherewithal to configure it yourself.

You should also receive a list of IP addresses, domain names and so on, to accompany the software package. Even if your software is preconfigured for quick and easy installation, make sure you hang on to this list for reference – you'll need to enter some of these settings into other software you use in the future. Included on the list will be most (though not necessarily all) of the following items:

Local dial-up phone number. The number your modem will dial to connect to the provider's computer.

Username and password. Confirmation of your chosen username, and a personal password. You'll enter both of these into your dial-up software so that you can log on to the provider's computer.

E-mail address. As mentioned above, this will be consist of your username, your company and your provider's domain name, looking something like **username@company.accessprovider.co.uk**.

E-mail account username and password. If you have a POP3 e-mail account, you'll use these to retrieve your e-mail messages. An SMTP e-mail account will use your normal logon details. (We'll look at these two types of account in Chapter 8.) Another protocol called IAP4 is also in use by some providers.

JARGON BUSTER

Log on/logon

The first of these is a verb; the second is usually a noun, but from time to time you might see a phrase like 'When you logon to the system…' Logging on simply means sending your username and password to your access provider's computer (just as you would log on to your own computer if you're on a company network) so that it can check that you're really entitled to connect to it. Once these details are entered into your software, the logon should happen automatically after dialling.

Mail server address. The domain name of the computer you'll connect to when you want to send and receive e-mail. You'll probably have addresses for **SMTP mail server** and **POP3 mail server** – we'll explain these in Chapter 8, but they'll usually both be something like **post.accessprovider.co.uk** or **pop3.accessprovider.co.uk**.

News server address. The domain name of the computer that handles newsgroup messages, which is usually **news.accessprovider.co.uk**.

Domain name server (DNS). This will be an IP address (you remember those four numbers separated by dots?) for the computer that translates friendly domain names into something that computers can understand and mere mortals can't. You may also be given an **alternative DNS** that your computer will try to connect to if the first one fails.

Other bits and pieces. The address of your company's Web site in case you want to take a look at it **(www.mycompany.co.uk** or **www.mycompany. com)**; the address of your provider's FTP server if it has one **(ftp.accessprovider.co.uk)**; and the telephone number and e-mail address of the provider's technical support services.

Now that your account has been set up, it's time to get that connection working. Your provider should have included instructions telling you how to install the software, so this should be a pretty painless step. All the same, keep that support line number handy, just in case! If you need a bit more help, you can head for the back of the book where all the technical stuff is gathered together. If you're using Windows 95 or 98, turn to Appendix A; if you're still using Windows 3.x, go to Appendix B, but you really should be considering upgrading by now. Windows 3.x will give you nothing but grief when you get online.

4

CONNECTING TO AN ONLINE SERVICE

In This Chapter...

▶ **Discover the differences between four popular online services**

▶ **Follow the simple sign-up routines to get connected**

▶ **Start exploring the member-areas and the Internet**

Choosing An Online Service

As we mentioned in Chapter 2, most business users will probably find that accessing the Internet via an IAP makes more business sense than using an OSP. However, very small businesses, or those wishing to dip their toes in the water for the first time, might find them a useful starting point.

Most offer a free 30-day trial, so you've got nothing to lose by picking one at random. All the same, it's better to make an informed choice if you can, so let's take a slightly closer look at the most popular online services, **CompuServe**, **AOL**, **The Microsoft Network**, and the UK-only service, **Virgin Net**.

Before we dive in to look at what the OSPs are offering, it is worth noting a relatively new phenomenon – the development of so-called *portals*. Whereas until now, the OSPs saw their main raison d'être as being a one-stop-shop for everything that was useful online, a number of Internet sites have now been set up to offer access to 'all the information you're likely to need' in one place. The presence and purpose of these portals further undermine the usefulness of OSPs for the business community, especially when you also take into account that the big names in OSPs have also set up portals, as we shall see later.

CompuServe

CompuServe has over 1000 different areas covering just about every conceivable subject including finance, news, TV listings, articles from popular magazines, travel information, movie and music previews, along with interactive chat rooms. Many retail companies have their own forums offering advice and product support, and business users will probably find more to interest them on CompuServe than the other services. UK-specific content is sparse for a company with so many UK users, but CompuServe are trying to improve things in this area. You can download a program called Cyber Patrol to restrict access to areas of CompuServe itself or the Internet, and limit the time your staff can spend online. In the autumn of 1998, CompuServe was bought by its arch-rival AOL, and it seems only a matter of time before the two services combine.

GOOD QUESTION

Do I have to use an online service to control my staff's access to the Internet?

Not at all. There are many good programs available that you can use with any Internet access provider or online service provider account to restrict access to different areas of the Net, or to particular types of information. We'll return to this in Chapter 14. However, in business terms, you have to ask yourself if using software is the best way of dealing with what is essentially a management problem.

AOL

In comparison with CompuServe, AOL has a very sunny, friendly and informal feel to it, making it a good choice for inexperienced computer-users. The content provided is very similar to that of CompuServe, with a couple of differences: business content, although growing, is still far from comprehensive, but you will find plenty of UK content. One major bonus is that AOL allows an account-holder to have up to five different member-names (AOL calls them Screen Names), which means that you can have five e-mail addresses; for small businesses, this allows everyone to receive their own personal e-mail. More importantly perhaps, you can set different restrictions for the different Screen Names, allowing you to bar access to areas of the service by your staff without affecting your own access to the same areas. At the start of 1999, AOL had half a million UK users and when it bought Netscape, many predicted that AOL would become the number one player on the Internet in the months to come.

The Microsoft Network

The Microsoft Network (or MSN) has a very stylish and modern appearance, contrasting massively with CompuServe's formality and AOL's friendliness. It also requires Windows 95 or later in order to run. MSN is 'cool', and unashamedly American in style, and this follows through to its content which is geared more towards entertainment than information. The service is split primarily into four main areas, OnStage, Essentials, Communicate, and Find. The first of these splits into sub-areas called 'channels', with each

▶ The main AOL desktop lets you click on a button to access the Internet or to use one of its own private services.

channel aimed at users with particular interests. Also in contrast with CompuServe and AOL. MSN is an Internet-based service: when you decide to explore the rest of the Net's offerings you'll generally find that the information travels much more speedily than with AOL or CompuServe.

Virgin Net

Virgin is a bit of a hybrid in the OSP world, positioning itself halfway between IAPs and online services. Although a limited range of online content is included (chiefly information and entertainment rather than business – but this simply reflects its main areas of business), Virgin's aim is to provide the easiest possible access to the Internet, which includes a 24-hour telephone support line. Like MSN, Virgin Net is an Internet-based service, so you'll notice no difference in speed when you move from the members-only areas to the Net itself. Being a UK-only company, the included content is UK-specific, with news, sport, chat rooms, and ready-sorted links to places of interest on the Internet.

◀ Virgin Net's
Internet Portal.

How Do We Sign Up?

The first job is to get your hands on the free connection software. These disks
are regularly glued to the covers of computer magazines so you may have
dozens of them already. If you have, make sure you pick the most recent. If you
haven't, either take a trip to your newsagent or phone the services and ask
them to send you the correct software for your computer and operating system.

GOOD QUESTION

What's to stop me using free 30-day trials forever?

Don't think that online services haven't thought of this one! The setup routines for
most online services will recognise your personal details. They might even find a trace of
previous trial software in your computer's system registry. You would also have to register with
a different name each time and how do you think your business will be regarded if it changes
like a chameleon every month?

Somewhere on the disk you'll be told how to start the program that signs you up, and the whole process will advance in simple steps. The exact routine will vary from one service to another, so we can't tell you exactly what to expect, but here are a few tips to bear in mind:

▶ Somewhere on the disk packaging you'll find a reference number (perhaps on a small label, or perhaps on the disk itself). Don't lose it – you'll have to enter this into the software to start the sign-up procedure.

▶ Make sure you've got your credit card or debit card handy. Although you won't be charged for the first 30 days' access, you'll have to enter the card number and its expiry date when you sign up.

▶ You may be asked to choose a dial-in phone number from a list covering the whole country. If so, make sure you choose a local number. (In some cases, the software will work out the best dial-in point for you, based on your own phone number, or it may use a local rate 0345, 0645 or 0845 number.)

▶ After you've entered all the necessary personal details, the program will dial up the service's computer and automatically set up your subscription. Within a minute or two you'll receive a username and password. These are your entry-ticket, so write them down and keep them safe.

BY THE WAY

Don't pass on your password

Keep your password private. Never include it in an e-mail message, don't type it in front of anyone, and make sure you change it at least once a month (you'll find instructions for this online). If possible, use a combination of letters and numbers at least five characters in length. And don't even consider using the word 'password' as your password!

How Do We Use An Online Service?

When you dial-in to your online service and log on using your username and password (which should happen automatically), you'll find plenty of assistance if you get lost, both in help files and online support areas.

Access to the Internet itself will be marked as one of the areas you can visit, and you'll probably see a big friendly button marked 'Internet' that will take you there. In most cases any extra software needed for Internet access was installed when you signed up, but you might be told that you need to download it yourself. If so, another friendly button will probably appear in front of you and all the spadework will be done for you while you sit back and wait.

Because this is a book about the Internet we're not going to dwell on the members-only areas of online services. But once you've clicked that big friendly button you're surfing the same Internet as everyone else, so the rest of the book is just as relevant to you. One of the few differences is in the way that e-mail is handled when it's sent to and from some online service accounts, and you'll learn how to work with e-mail in Chapter 8.

2

FINDING YOUR
WAY AROUND

In This Part...

5

EXPLORING THE WORLD WIDE WEB

In This Chapter...

▶ **Discover the breadth of the World Wide Web**

▶ **Learn to use your Web browser and start surfing**

▶ **Keep track of where you've been and where you're going**

▶ **Find out what else your multi-talented browser can do**

How would you describe television to someone who's never seen it? Somehow you've got to convey its variety, its entertainment value, and its potential as a learning tool. You've got to explain that some of the content is staggeringly good, and some is mindless twaddle, but sometimes the mindless twaddle can be more entertaining than the 'good' stuff. How do you describe a whole amazing new experience?

A First Look At The Wonders Of The Web

You wouldn't even *try* to describe it – you'd switch on the TV and say 'Just watch!' To describe the World Wide Web experience on paper isn't as easy – we can't show you the colour or the animation, nor can you hear the sounds and although it's interactive, you won't be able to interact with it. Nevertheless, a picture paints a thousand words, so here's the Web equivalent of a few photos of your TV screen.

Wokingham Online

http://www.wokingham.com

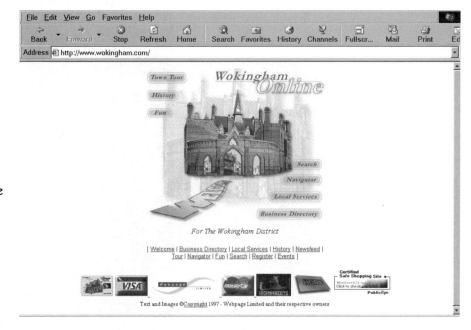

▶ Many towns are now promoting themselves as being attractive for business and provide information in a pain-free manner.

Nasdaq In The UK

http://www.nasdaq-uk.com

◀ We all think of Nasdaq as being US-based, but this exchange is making a blatant appeal to UK investors by providing a UK-oriented site.

British Library

http://www.bl.uk/collections/newspaper/

◀ The British Library's Newspaper Library is a superbly comprehensive archive of the UK's newspapers.

General Aviation Manufacturers And Traders Association

http://www.gamta.demon.co.uk

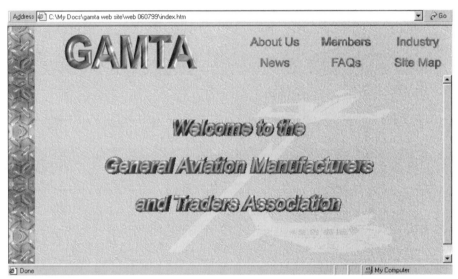

▶ GAMTA is a trade body that represents general and business aviation companies across the UK. This site aims to give answers to many of the frequently asked questions it receives daily.

Jaguar Cars

http://www.jaguar.co.uk/uk/

▶ The Jaguar cars' site is beautifully constructed, and captures the mood of luxury that you would expect from one of Britain's finest cars.

MathEngine

http://www.mathengine.com

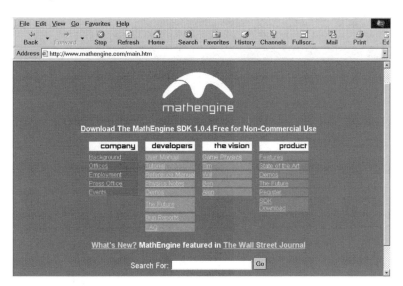

◀ The Web is an ideal place to promote new products. MathEngine is British, but is aimed at a world market.

Winkworth Estate Agents

http://www.winkworth.co.uk

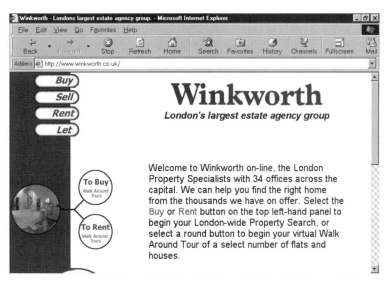

◀ Estate agents are springing up all over the Web. This site is customer-focused by letting the visitor choose easily what he or she wants to see.

DOCTA

http://www.docta.com

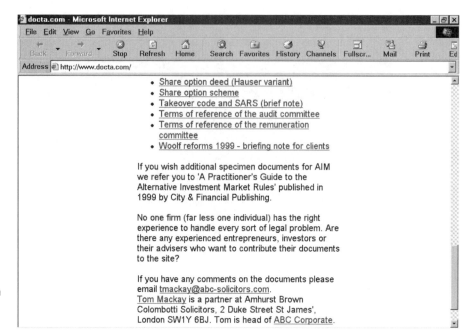

▶ Remember those legal documents that used to cost you an arm and a leg? Well, now you can download them for free!

Understanding The Web

The World Wide Web is the jewel in the Internet's crown, and the whole reason for the 'Internet explosion'. A large part of the Web's popularity lies both in its simplicity and its breadth: you don't have to be a Networking genius or a computer whiz to use it; you just point and click. The 'pages' you find on the Web contain a scattering of words that are underlined and highlighted in a different colour from the text around them. Just move your mouse-pointer onto one of these words or phrases (you'll see it change into a hand with a pointing finger as you do so) and click. Hey presto, another page opens. The entire 'web' of pages is being 'spun' by millions of people at the rate of several million new pages per day, and every page includes these point-and-click links to many other pages.

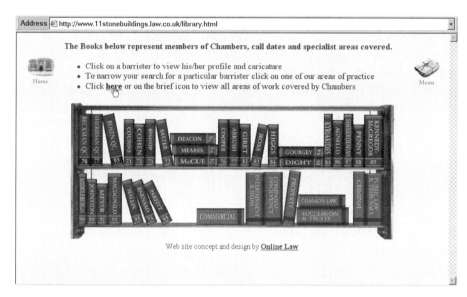

◄ To jump
between pages,
move the pointer
over the coloured
hypertext or over
one of the book
images and click
to open the
related document.

Web page

JARGON BUSTER

A 'page' is a single document that can be any length, like a document in a word processor. Pages can contain text, graphics, sound and video clips, together with clever effects and controls made possible by programming languages such as Java and ActiveX (we'll tell you more about these languages in Chapter 15.)

This system of clickable text is called **hypertext**, and you've probably seen it used in Windows help-files and multimedia encyclopaedias as a neat way to make cross-references. The Web takes the system a few stages further:

▶ These links aren't restricted to opening a document stored on the same computer: you might see a page from the other side of the world.

▶ A hypertext link doesn't have to be a word or phrase: it might be a picture that you click on, or it might be a part of a larger picture, with different parts linking to different pages.

▶ The link doesn't necessarily open a new Web page: it might play a video or a sound, download an application, display a picture, run a program … the list goes on.

The Web is made up of millions and millions of files placed on computers called Web servers, so no one person or company actually owns the Web itself. The Web servers are owned by many different companies, and they rent space (or give it away for free) to anyone who wants to put their own pages on the Web. The pages are created using a text-based language called **HTML** (HyperText Markup Language), which you'll learn more about in Chapter 22.

Once the newly created pages are placed on the Web server, anyone who knows their address can look at them. This partly explains why the Web became such an overnight success: a simple page can be written in minutes, so a Web site can be as up-to-date as its creator wants it to be. Many Web sites with news or business information are updated daily, and some may even change every few minutes.

JARGON BUSTER

Website

'Website' is a loose term that refers to the pages belonging to an individual or company. A site could be just a single simple page that your Auntie Ethel wrote to share a tasty fruitcake recipe, a virtual store selling riding saddles, or hundreds of complex pages belonging to a multinational.

What Do We Need?

To view pages from the World Wide Web you'll need a program called a **browser**. In fact, this single program will be the most powerful weapon in your Internet arsenal, and not just because you'll be spending so much time on the Web – you can use this program to handle many of your other Internet-related tasks as well. Although there are many different browsers available, the three most popular and capable are Microsoft's **Internet Explorer**, Netscape's **Navigator**, and now **Opera**.

If you're connected through one of the online services you'll usually be able to use these instead of their own proprietary software.

If you've recently bought a copy of Windows 98 (or a new computer with Windows 98 as its operating system), Internet Explorer is already installed - in fact, it's the program you've been using to 'surf' the contents of your own disks and directories. If you're using Windows 95, a version of Internet Explorer is included; it may be installed on your system already, or you might have to install it yourself using the **Add/Remove Programs** applet in Windows' Control Panel. If you haven't got at least version 4 of Internet Explorer it is worth upgrading straight away as it allows you to do so many more things than previous versions. As an alternative, Netscape Version 4 onwards is similarly endowed.

GOOD QUESTION

I'm using Netscape Navigator. Will I understand this chapter?

Netscape Navigator's buttons and menus differ from those in Explorer, but both tools were designed to do the same job so the methods are very similar. For simplicity, we're going to assume that you're using Explorer throughout this book, but you'll find the equivalent Netscape options listed in Appendix C.

Start Browsing

When you open Internet Explorer, and get online, the first thing you'll see is the **home page**. By default, Explorer is set to display the first page of Microsoft's Internet site, whilst Netscape – unsurprisingly – will try to lead you to their home page.

For now this is just a matter of idle curiosity – you've just arrived online, and you're eager to explore, so we'll forget about it for a while. But it could start to get irritating later on: every time you start Explorer you'll have to wait for this page to download before you can go anywhere else. In the *Customising Your Browser* section of Chapter 6, we'll explain how to swap this page for a different one or replace it with a document or picture on your own disk.

Time to go Home

BY THE WAY

On Internet Explorer's toolbar you'll see a button with the word 'Home' beneath it. Wherever your Web-wanderings lead you, you can just click the **Home** button to return to your home page anytime you want to.

Anatomy Of A Web Page

Now it's time to get acquainted with the basic workings of the browser and with the Web itself. If you look at the home page you should see several hypertext links (which are usually underlined, and in coloured text). Move your mouse-pointer onto any link that looks interesting and click. When you do that, your browser sends a message to the server requesting the page you want. If everything goes according to plan, the server will respond by sending back the requested page so that your browser can display it.

Spend a little time following links to see where they lead. Don't limit yourself to clicking textual links alone, though – many of the pictures and

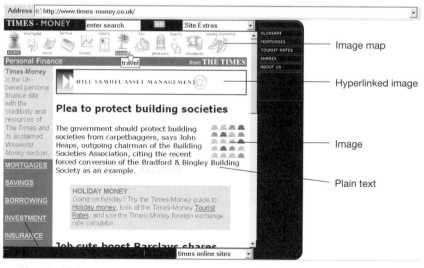

Image map

Hyperlinked image

Image

Plain text

▶ Some of the main elements that make up a Web page.

Hypertext link

graphics you see on a page will lead somewhere too. Take a look at the page shown in the screenshot opposite for a few clues to the type of thing you'll find on a Web page.

▶ **Plain text.** Ordinary readable text. Click it all you like – nothing will happen!

▶ **Hypertext link.** A text link to another page. Hypertext links will usually be underlined, but their text colour will vary from site to site.

▶ **Image.** A picture or graphic that enhances a Web site. Like most pictures, it paints a thousand words, but it won't lead anywhere if you click it.

▶ **Hyperlinked image.** Clicking this image will open a new page. In most cases a hyperlinked image will look no different to an ordinary image, but it may have a box around it that's the same colour as any hypertext links on the page.

▶ **Image map.** An image split up into small chunks, with each chunk leading to a different page.

GOOD QUESTION

How can I tell an ordinary image from a linking image?

Watch your mouse pointer! When you move the pointer onto any link (image or text), it will turn into a hand shape with a pointing finger. In a well-constructed image map, the different areas of the picture itself should make it clear where each link will lead. Finally, keep an eye on the status bar at the bottom of the browser – as you move over a link of any sort you'll see the name of the linked document or file appear.

Links & Colours

On the home page you were viewing, the text you clicked may well have been blue. If you go back and have another look you'll see it's changed colour (possibly to purple). This little indicator helps you keep track of pages you've seen before as you flit from one page to another. These links will return to their original colour after a few days, but it's worth noting that writers of Web pages can make their own colour choices, so the colours of visited and unvisited links will vary from one site to another.

Charting Your Course On The Web

By now you should be cheerfully clicking links of all descriptions and skipping from page to page with casual abandon. The problem is, you can only move forwards. If you find yourself heading down a blind alley, how can you retrace your steps and head off in a different direction? This is where the browser itself comes to your rescue, so let's spend some time getting acquainted with its toolbars and menus.

▶ Internet Explorer's button bar and address bar.

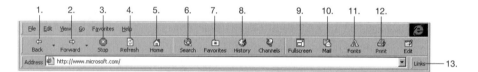

1 **Back.** Clicking this button will take you back to the last page you looked at. If you keep clicking you can step all the way back to the first page you viewed this session.

2 **Forward.** After using the Back button to take a second look at a previously-viewed page, the Forward button lets you return to pages you viewed later. This button will be greyed-out if you haven't used the Back button yet.

3 **Stop.** Stops the download of a page from the server. This can be useful if a page is taking a long time to appear and you're tired of waiting, or if you clicked a link accidentally and want to stay where you are.

4 **Refresh.** Clicking this tells your browser to start downloading the same page again. See Sometimes Things Go Wrong... on page 59 for reasons why you might need to Refresh.

5 **Home.** Opens your Home Page, explained on page 62.

6 **Search.** Opens a small frame in the browser window from which you can choose a Web search site and search for pages by subject or keyword. You'll learn about searching for information on the Web in Chapter 7.

7 **Favorites.** Displays the contents of your Favorites list (see below).

8 **History.** Opens a list of the sites you've visited recently, letting you revisit one with with a single click (see Retracing Your Steps with History, later in this chapter).

9 **Fullscreen.** Expands the browser window to fill the screen, covering the Windows Taskbar and everything else, and leaving just a tiny toolbar visible.

10 **Mail.** Opens a menu from which you can run your e-mail or newsreader software, or open a blank form to send an e-mail message.

11 **Fonts.** Clicking repeatedly enlarges or reduces the size of text on the page. (You can do this in a more controlled way by selecting View | Fonts).

12 **Print.** Prints the current page. You can choose your printer and page setup from the File menu.

13 **Links.** If you double-click on this word a new button bar will slide across revealing links to Microsoft's own site and some useful jumping-off points for your Web travels. To hide the Links bar again, double-click the word 'Address' to the left of the screen.

Increase your viewing space

BY THE WAY

In the best traditions of toolbars, you can find all these options on Explorer's menus as well, and most have keyboard shortcuts. If you'd like to see more of the pages themselves in Explorer's window, head off to the **View | Toolbars** menu and click any entry with a check mark beside it to hide it. Or switch back and forth between Fullscreen and Normal view by pressing F11.

One useful extra tool is a facility to search the page you're viewing for a particular word or phrase. Open the **Edit** menu, choose **Find (on this page)...** (or press Ctrl+F), and type the word you're looking for.

Many Happy Returns – Using Favorites

One of the most powerful Explorer tools is the Favorites system (known as Bookmarks or Hotlists in other browsers). Any time you arrive at a page you think might be useful in the future, you can add its address to your list of

Favorites and return to it by opening the menu and clicking the relevant shortcut. To add the current page to the list, click the **Favorites** toolbar button and click **Add to Favorites**. A small dialog box will appear giving a suggested title (you can replace this with any title you like to help you recognise it in future). To place the shortcut directly on the menu, click **OK**.

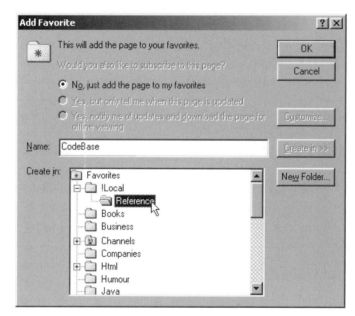

▶ Add a new shortcut to a **Favorites** submenu by clicking the submenu's folder followed by the OK button.

You can also organise your shortcuts into submenus to make them easier to find. Click the **Create in...** button and **New Folder**, then type a name for the folder. Click the folder into which you want to save the new shortcut and click the **OK** button to confirm. (If it ends up in the wrong place, don't worry! Select **Organize Favorites** from the Favorites menu and you'll be able to move, rename and delete folders and shortcuts, and create new folders.)

When you want to reopen a page that you added to your **Favorites** list, either select Favorites from the menu bar and click the name of the site   on the menu, or click the **Favorites** toolbar button to open a clickable list in a small frame in the left of the browser's window (see screenshot below).

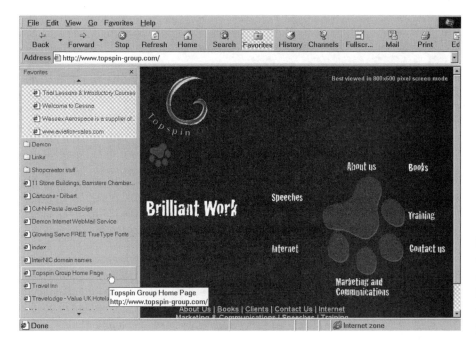

◀ Click the **Favorites** button on the toolbar and your Favorites list stays within easy reach while you surf.

Retracing Your Steps With History

The History list provides a handy way of finding an elusive site that you visited recently but didn't add to your Favorites list. Internet Explorer maintains this list automatically, and you can open it by clicking the **History** button on the toolbar. The sites are sorted by week and day with links to the various pages you visited on each site placed into folders. (In MS Explorer 5 they can also be sorted in many other ways that you specify.) You can revisit a site by finding the week and day you last viewed it, clicking the folder for that site and clicking the page you want to see again. You can choose how long Explorer should store details of visited pages by clicking your way to **View | Internet Options | General**.

Are you a furtive surfer?

BY THE WAY

Explorer's History list can be many things – useful, interesting, nostalgic, to name but a few. It can also be a dead giveaway. Although there's no foolproof way to cover your tracks, clearing the History list is a sensible move if you'd prefer to keep your Web-surfing habits private. You can clear the list by clicking the **Clear History** button on the **View | Internet Options | General** page. Of course, you wouldn't dream of surfing questionable sites during business time anyway, would you?!

The Address Bar & URLs

Every page on the World Wide Web has its own unique **URL**. URL stands for Uniform Resource Locator, but it's just a convoluted way of saying 'address'. It's the equivalent of a postcode when using 'snail mail'. You've seen a few URLs already – if you skip back to the beginning of this chapter you'll see the URLs of each Web site screenshot.

You'll also notice URLs at work as you move from page to page in Explorer, provided you can see the address bar (if you can't, go to **View | Toolbars | Address Bar** to switch it on). Every time you open a new page, its URL appears in this text-bar. You can also type a URL into the address bar yourself – just click once on the address bar to highlight the address currently shown, type the URL of the page you want to open, and press Enter.

For example, if you want to look at the Jaguar site mentioned earlier, type: **http://www.jaguar.co.uk/uk/** into the address bar.

Accuracy is everything!

BY THE WAY

URLs can still sometimes be case-sensitive, so make sure you observe any capital letters. Also, in contrast with the directory paths used in Windows computers, URLs use forward slashes rather than backslashes. Actually these don't matter too much – if you forget and use the wrong type, Explorer will know what you mean, though other browsers might complain!

Understanding URLs

You'll come into contact with a lot of URLs on your travels around the Internet, so it's worth knowing what they mean. As a specimen to examine, let's take the URL for the Radio 4 Web site at the BBC and break it up into its component pieces. The URL is:

http://www.bbc.co.uk/radio4/index.html	
http://	This is one of the Internet's many protocols, and it stands for HyperText Transfer Protocol. It's the system used to send Web pages around the Internet, so all Web page URLs have the http:// prefix. In Explorer you can normally leave off this part of the URL as it is accepted as a default.
www.bbc.co.uk/	This is the name of the computer on which the required file is stored (often referred to as the 'host' computer). Computers that store Web pages are called Web servers and their names usually begin with www.
Radio4/	This is the directory path to the page you want to open. Just as on your own computer, the path may consist of several directories separated by slashes.
index.html	This is the name of the file you want. The .html (or sometimes just .htm) indicates that it's a Web page, but your browser can handle any number of different file types, as you'll see in Chapter 12.

GOOD QUESTION

Why do some URLs contain no filename?

Some URLs finish with a directory name (such as **http://www.bbc.co.uk/radio4/**) rather than a filename. When your browser sends this type of URL to a Web server, the server will look in the directory for a default file, often called **index.htm** or **default.htm**. If a file exists with one of these names it will be sent back to your browser; if not, you may receive a rather plain-looking hypertext list of all the files in that directory. The index file is usually a 'Welcome' page introducing a Web site and containing links to other areas of the site.

A little while ago we said your browser was the most powerful tool in your Internet software armoury. In later chapters we'll be looking at other Internet services you can use, and we'll point you towards some of the best software to help you use them. But your browser is a multi-talented chap: some of these services can be accessed directly within the browser itself without the need for any other software, and for those that can't your browser still makes a great jumping-off point.

We've just seen that the World Wide Web service uses a protocol called HTTP, so all your Web page URLs will start **http://**. Here are some of the other prefixes your browser will handle and the results of using them:

Prefix	Result
ftp://	The URL of a library of files on an FTP server. Your browser will display directory and filenames, and allow you to download files. Try typing **ftp://sunsite.doc.ic.ac.uk/ computing/systems/ibmpc** into your address bar to visit one of the best software libraries in the UK. For more on FTP, turn to Chapter 11.
mailto:	Mailto: links crop up a lot on Web pages. You can also type them into your address bar to open a blank e-mail form with the e-mail address already inserted. For example, to send us a message, type: **mailto:info@ topspin-group.com**. (Notice that this prefix and the **news:** prefix below have no // after the colon.) To find out more about sending and receiving e-mail, turn to Chapter 8.
news:	This will be a link to a particular newsgroup for which your browser will start your newsreader software (unless it has its own built-in newsreader) to display the messages in the group. You'll learn about newsgroups in Chapter 9, but for now try entering **news:news.groups** to see a newsgroup for newcomers to the Internet.
file:///	Using this prefix you can open a **local** Web document, that is a file on your own hard-disk that has the .htm or .html extension. Browsers can also open many other types of file (such as images with the .gif or .jpg extension). In Explorer, unlike most other browsers, you can actually leave out this prefix and just type an ordinary file path like **c:\mydirectory\myfile.htm**. In older browsers, you'll have to use this prefix (note the three forward slashes), and replace the colon in the drive-name with a pipe symbol, such as **file:///c\mydirectory\myfile.htm**.
gopher://	Gopher was the forerunner of the Web and is now largely ignored, but your browser will still happily access Gopher sites.

A little less typing

As we mentioned above, when you type the URL of a Web page into your address bar you can leave out the **http://**. Most browsers will assume you're looking for a Web page and add that part themselves. Similarly, if you type an address that starts with 'ftp' (such as **ftp.download.com**) you don't need to type the **ftp://** prefixes either – your browser will know they're not Web sites and will use the correct protocol automatically.

Sometimes Things Go Wrong...

Things don't always go smoothly when you're trying to open a Web page. To begin with, the server might not be running and you'll eventually see a message telling you that the operation 'timed out' – in other words, your browser has waited a minute or so for a response from the server but doesn't think anything is going to happen. If the server is running it might be busy. In this case you might get a similar result, or you might get a part of the page and then everything seems to stop dead. You may be able to get things moving by clicking the **Refresh** button on the browser's toolbar, forcing your browser to request the document again, but be prepared to give up, visit a different Web site, and try this one again later.

And then there's the Mysterious Vanishing Page syndrome. Although all Web pages contain links, sometimes the pages those links refer to no longer exist and you'll see an error message instead. The reason is simple: on the perpetually changing landscape of the World Wide Web, pages (and even entire sites) move elsewhere, are renamed, or just disappear. In fact, the average lifespan of a site is a mere 90 days (but these are usually personal vanity sites rather than planned business ventures). Anyone putting links to these sites in their own pages has no way of knowing when this happens other than by regularly clicking all the links themselves to check them. By the same token, some of the URLs we've included in this book may be defunct by the time you try them. The endless arrivals and departures are a fact of Web life, but also a part of its magic.

What Next?

There's much more to the World Wide Web than we've covered in this chapter, but you've seen enough to know what it is and how to move around it. In the next chapter you'll go a stage further, learning how to use other features of Internet Explorer to make your Web-surfing faster, easier and more efficient.

But just one final parting shot. Although it is a *World* Wide Web, you'll find that the language of the Internet is overridingly English. Even sites prepared in German, French or Japanese invariably have an English element to them.

6

MASTERING YOUR WEB BROWSER

In This Chapter...

▶ **Tricks for easier, faster browsing**

▶ **Discover the power of the mouse's right paw**

▶ **Download and save what you find on the Web**

▶ **Learn how to tweak up the cache and make the most of shortcuts**

In Chapter 5 you learnt the basic moves that let you view Web pages, store the location of a useful page so that you can revisit it later, and use your browser to access a few of the other Internet services. But there's a lot more to the Web than we could reasonably fit into a single chapter. In fact, there's more to it than we can fit into *two* chapters! To give you a good head start on the Web, we're going to linger here a little longer and show you some of the ways in which your browser can power-up your surfing.

Customising Your Browser

Let's start with some browser tips to help you fine-tune your surfing:

▶ **Customise your home page.** If you're content to let your browser download a page every time you run it, you can choose what that page should contain, perhaps to have the latest news stories displayed automatically. You can use any page on the Web as your home page. Click your way to **View | Internet Options |** and either type a URL into the **Address** box at the top of the page, or click the **Use Current** button to set the page you're currently viewing as your Home page.

▶ **Use A blank home page.** Another (and faster) option is to use a blank page. Go to **View | Internet Options | General**, click the **Use Blank** button, then click **OK**.

▶ **Browse faster without images.** The actual text on a Web page downloads very quickly; it's the images that you're often left waiting for, and most pages have at least one image. To skip around the Web faster, you can turn off the display of images, and have them replaced by empty boxes or small 'placeholder' icons on the page. To do this in Explorer, go to **View | Internet Options | Advanced**, scroll down to the **Multimedia** section and remove the checkmark from **Show pictures**. (You can also prevent sounds, animations and videos playing from other checkboxes in this section.) If you want to view an image on a particular page, click it with the right mouse-button and choose **Show Picture**.

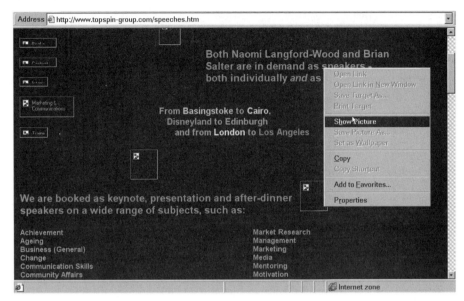

Address 🔲 http://www.topspin-group.com/speeches.htm

◄ With the automatic display of images turned off, you can right-click the placeholder and choose **Show Picture** to reveal the missing image.

► **Rearrange your toolbars.** The toolbar, menu bar and the Address and Links bars have a 'raised' vertical strip to their left. By grabbing the strip with the mouse-pointer you can drag the toolbars around. You can even hide them completely, or remove the text labels from their icons using the options on the **View | Toolbars** submenu. To keep everything visible but make it a bit smaller, go to **View | Internet Options | Advanced**, and check the box beside **Small Icons** in the Toolbar section.

Double Glazing – Opening A New Window

Like most recent applications, Web browsers let you open a second window (and a third, and a fourth, as long as your computer has the memory to cope) so that you can run several Web sessions at the same time. There are several reasons why you might find this useful. If you're searching for a particularly elusive piece of information, you can follow two different paths in the two windows and (perhaps) track it down a little sooner. Or you can view a page in one window while waiting for another page to finish downloading. And one of the most useful reasons: if you find a page full of links to sites you want to visit one by one, open each link in a new window, and then close that window when you've finished – the original window is still waiting patiently for you to try the next link on the list. (It really is a lot quicker than using the Back button or the Favorites menu!) You can close one of these windows without it affecting any of the others – as long as Internet Explorer has at least one window open, it'll keep running.

GOOD QUESTION

Will several windows really turbo-charge my Web-surfing?

Yes and no. If you're downloading a Web page in each window, you're ultimately downloading exactly the same amount of data as you would if you used one window and opened the pages one at a time – only a faster modem will make this happen any quicker. However, if you can organise things so that one window is always downloading a page while you're reading the page in the other window, you can stop some of that waiting around.

To open a new window in Internet Explorer, you can use any of these methods:

▶ Click on **File | New | Window** or press Ctrl+N. The new window will start by showing the same page as your original window.

▶ Click any link with the right mouse-button and choose **Open in New Window** from the context menu.

▶ Type a URL into the address box, and then press Shift+Enter.

▶ If you're still not up to speed with using a mouse, you can press the Tab key repeatedly until the link you want to follow is highlighted, and press Shift+Enter. However, for serious business use we'd suggest you start getting to *love* that little rodent!

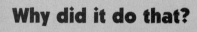

BY THE WAY

Why did it do that?

You may sometimes be innocently clicking links when suddenly a new window opens for a particular page. Web page authors occasionally add an extra piece of code to make a link open in a new window so that you can still find their original page easily. They can also add code forcing your browser not to show toolbars or the status-bar in the new window to give a larger viewing area.

Right-Click For Easy Surfing

We've already mentioned the use of the right mouse-button a couple of times in this chapter – you can open a link in a new window or display an image represented by a placeholder by right-clicking and then selecting the appropriate option from the pop-up context menu. The contents of the menu vary according to the type of item you clicked, but always contain a feast of goodies you won't find elsewhere, so don't forget to use this.

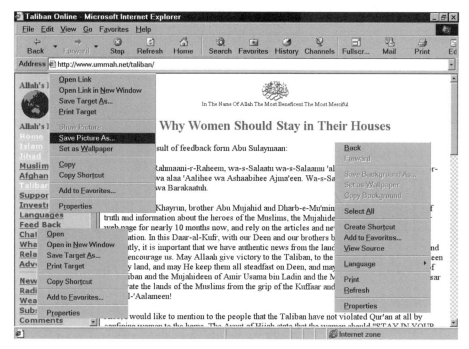

◀ Okay, we've cheated here! This composite screenshot shows the context menus that appear after right-clicking a link (*bottom left*), an image (*top left*) or the page background (*right*) in Explorer.

Let's have a look at what some of these options do:

Clicking This	Does This
Copy Shortcut	Places the link's URL on the clipboard ready for you to paste into another application.
Add to Favorites...	Places a shortcut to this page on your Favorites menu. If you clicked the page background, the URL of the current page will be saved; if you clicked a link, the URL referred to by the link will be saved.
Set as Wallpaper	Replaces the wallpaper on your desktop with the Web page's background. This will remain on your wallpaper list as Internet **Explorer Wallpaper** for you to choose in future, but each wallpaper you save in this way will replace the last.
Create Shortcut	Places a shortcut to the current page on the desktop. See Using Internet Shortcuts later in this chapter to find out more about these.
Save Target As...	Downloads the file to which the link points and saves it onto your disk, but doesn't display it in the browser window. You'll be prompted to choose a location in which to save the file.
Save Picture As...	Stores the image you clicked to a directory on your hard disk. You can also drag the image off the page and onto your desktop to save it.

The last two items lead us neatly into a major area of Internet life, and a likely reason you wanted to become a part of it: there's lots of 'stuff' on the Web, and most of that stuff you can grab for your own use. So how do you do it?

Saving Files From The Web

There are two groups of files you can grab from the World Wide Web – those that are a part of the Web page itself (such as an image), and those that aren't. The second group is huge, covering applications, sound files, videos, spreadsheets, ZIP files, and a whole lot more. Although the methods of saving *any* file are straightforward enough, that second group is going to lead us into a few complications, so let's begin with the first.

Saving Page Elements

▶ **Saving the Web page's text.** To save the text from the entire page, open the **File** menu and choose **Save As....** Select **Text File** from the **Save as type** list and choose a name and location for the file. Alternatively, if you need only a portion of the text on the page, you can highlight it using the mouse, copy it to the clipboard by pressing Ctrl+C, and then paste it into another application.

▶ **Saving the Web page's source.** The source of a Web page is the text you see in your browser plus all the codes added by the page's author that make the page display properly. These codes belong to a language called HTML (HyperText Markup Language) which you'll learn about in Chapter 22. To save the HTML source document, follow the same routine as above, but choose **HTML File** from the **Save as type** list. (If you just want to have a peep at the source, right-click the Web page's background and choose **View Source** from the context menu.)

Why would I want to save the HTML source?

As languages go, HTML is a very easy one. It might look a bit daunting on first sight, but the millions of people who've added their own pages to the Web can attest to its simplicity. Most of these people learnt the language by saving the source files of other Web-pages and then having a look at them in a text-editor such as Windows' Notepad.

▶ **Saving images from the page.** As you learnt above, it just takes a right-click on any image to save it to disk (or a drag, if you prefer). You can also save the background, an image file that the browser tiles to fill the entire viewing area.

Are you cluttering up your disk with unnecessary images?

It's very easy to get carried away saving masses of images that 'could be useful one day' and then find that your disk gets filled up to the detriment of your computer's performance. We would suggest that if you have a tendency to be an 'image junkie' a good filing system and a regular 'spring clean' will not go amiss.

▶ In addition to the **Set as Wallpaper** option mentioned above, you can right-click the background and choose **Save Background As…** to save the image file to the directory of your choice. You can also copy images or the background to the clipboard with a right-click, ready to paste into another application.

Is that *your* image, Sir?

BY THE WAY

Although you can easily copy text and images from someone else's page and use them yourself, remember that copyright laws apply to information on the Internet just as they do to information you find anywhere else.

Saving Other Types Of Files

Although most of the links you find on Web pages will open another page, some will be links to files that you can download (don't worry – it should be obvious, and if it isn't, just hit the Cancel button as soon as you get the chance). As we mentioned earlier, this is where things get a bit more complicated. Come what may, the file must be downloaded to your own computer before you can do anything with it, but how you choose to handle the download will depend upon what you want to do with the file itself. The browser may be multi-talented, but it can't display every type of file that exists!

What it can do, however, is to launch an **external viewer** to display the file. An external viewer is just a slightly technical way of saying 'another program on your computer'. Two vital elements are required for your browser to be able to do this:

▶ You must have a program on your disk that can open the type of file you're about to download.

▶ The browser needs to know which program to use for a particular type of file, and where to find it on your disk.

After you click the link, Internet Explorer will start to download the file it refers to and then show the dialog below. It wants to know what to do with the file when it's finished downloading: do you want to save the file and carry on surfing, or open it immediately using an external viewer?

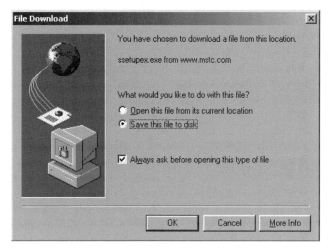

◀ Explorer wants
to know whether
it should open
this file after
downloading, or
save it to your
hard disk.

▶ **Save this file to disk.** If you choose this option, Explorer will present a
Save As dialog box so that you can choose a directory to save the file
into, followed by a smaller dialog box that will keep you posted on the
progress of the download and how much longer it should take. While the
file is downloading you can wait, or continue surfing the Web, and
there's a handy **Cancel** button you can use if you change your mind
halfway through, or if the download seems to be taking too long. The
Save this file to disk option is the best (and safest) option to use.

▶ **Open this file from its current location.** For a file that you want to view
or play straight away, you can select the **Open** option. If Explorer hasn't
previously been told how to handle files of this type it will then prompt
you to choose the program you want to use to view or display the file
once it's been downloaded, so click the **Browse** button in the next dialog
box to locate and double-click a suitable program on your hard disk, and
then click **OK**. Explorer will download the file and then launch that
program to display the file.

There's also a checkbox labelled **Always ask before opening this type of
file**. If you remove the checkmark from this box, Explorer will use the
option you select this time whenever you download the same type of file in
future. So if you choose to **Open this file from its current location**, and
select a program to use, that same program will automatically be used on
all future occasions.

You can view and edit the settings for different types of file by opening **My
Computer** and selecting **View | Folder Options | File Types**. Click a file

type in the list, and click the **Edit** button. If the box beside **Confirm open after download** isn't checked, this type of file will always be opened – you can check this box if you'd like the chance to save this type of file in future or use a different program to open it. To find out which program will open this type of file, click on either **Play** or **Open** in the **Actions** box, then click the **Edit...** button.

BY THE WAY

Virus alert!

Always run a virus-checker before running any program you've downloaded. Although some people might sound a bit too hysterical about it, a business simply cannot afford to take chances as there's a small risk that a program might contain a virus. It only takes a few seconds to do and might just save a lot of hassle later. We'll return to the subject of virus-checkers in Chapter 13.

Configuring Your Browser – Automatic Or Manual?

In the routine above, we've assumed that you do actually have a program on your own system that can play or display the type of file you're downloading. Of course, that won't always be the case. Remember that you can opt to save any file so that you know you've got it safe and sound on your disk, and then go hunting for a suitable player or viewer program afterwards. You can then install the new program in the usual way and use it to open this file.

If you do that, you have three possible options for the future:

▶ Every time you come across a file of this type on the Web you can opt to save it, and open it yourself later on in the same way.

▶ You can wait until you find another file of this type on the Web, click on **Open this file from its current location**, remove the tick from the checkbox below and then direct Explorer to the external viewer that you now possess. If you choose this method, your browser will configure itself automatically to use this viewer for this type of file in future.

▶ You can configure Internet Explorer yourself as soon as you've installed the new program so that it knows exactly what to do next time you choose to open this type of file.

We strongly suggest you go for one of the first two options. If you save the file and view it later, you won't be wasting expensive online time looking at something that'll still be there when you disconnect. And if you wait until the next time you find this kind of file, you'll just have to spend a few seconds pointing Explorer to the correct viewer. However, in business terms it also matters how much time is of the essence in your online search, so you will have to use your judgement first on whether to download first or view online.

If you really do want to configure Explorer yourself, you'll need to know something about file types, extensions, and the way in which particular file types are associated with a certain program. However, that's the sort of technical stuff we're not going to venture into here, and it's rarely necessary to configure these settings yourself when your browser makes such a good job of it. Ask your resident computer boffin or IT department if you're unsure how to do this yourself.

Using Internet Shortcuts

We've looked at a few ways that you can go to a particular page on the Web – you can click a link on a page, type a URL into the address bar and press Enter, or select the site from your history list or Favorites. Another method is the Internet **Shortcut**.

An Internet Shortcut is a tiny file that just contains a Web page's URL. You can keep these little files on your desktop (or indeed anywhere on your computer's hard disk) and double-click them to go to the page they point at. In effect, they work in exactly the same way as the links you find on a Web page.

BY THE WAY

Internet Shortcuts are my Favorites

If you're using Internet Explorer, you'll find a directory called Favorites inside your Windows directory. When you open it, you'll see all the items on your **Favorites** menu. These are all Internet Shortcuts - you can create new shortcuts here, and add subdirectories, all of which will appear on your **Favorites** menu.

The easiest way to create an Internet Shortcut is to click on any link in a Web page and (before releasing the mouse-button) drag it to your desktop. You can also create your own shortcuts by hand. Open a text editor such as Windows' Notepad and type the following:

[Internet Shortcut]
URL = *type the URL here*

After the equals sign, type the URL you want this shortcut to point at, such as **http://www.the-times.co.uk**. Save the file wherever you like with an appropriate name. For instance, you might call this example **Shortcut to The Times**. You can create Internet Shortcuts that use the other protocols mentioned on page 58, such as a link to a newsgroup, an FTP site, or the e-mail address of someone you contact frequently.

To use an Internet Shortcut, just double-click it. Your browser will start and open the page. If your browser is already running, you can drag and drop a shortcut into its window. You can also copy these shortcuts onto a floppy disk or attach them to an e-mail message so that someone else can use them.

Browse Faster Using The Cache

If you've spent some time surfing the Web and skipping backwards and forwards between pages, here's a phenomenon you might have noticed: when you return to a page you've seen before (perhaps by clicking the **Back** button) you don't have to wait – the page appears almost instantly. This is the **disk cache** at work. Every page you view, along with its constituent images, is saved to a directory on your own computer's disk. Most browsers simply call this directory **Cache**, but Internet Explorer uses its own, reasonably intuitive name, **Temporary Internet Files**. For brevity we're just going to refer to it as the cache directory.

Every Web page that Explorer downloads and displays is also saved in the cache directory, along with images and other items on the page. The cache directory will gradually enlarge until it reaches its maximum allowed size, and then the oldest files will be removed to make way for more recent ones.

Whenever you click a link or type a URL into the address bar, the browser looks in the cache first to see if it can grab the files it needs from there instead of downloading them from the Web. Not only does this speed things up for you, it also takes some of the strain off the poor old Internet.

Tweaking The Cache Settings

This isn't a 'must do', but it certainly is a 'might want to do'. Explorer will be set up to use the cache by default, so you're already reaping the rewards.

Click your way to **View | Internet Options | General**. On the part of the page labelled **Temporary Internet Files** you'll see two buttons, **Delete Files...** and **Settings....** The first of these empties the cache directory letting you regain space, but the real action all takes place on a dialog box that appears when you click **Settings** (shown in the screenshot on page 74). Here's a quick description of the controls and what they're for:

▶ **Check for newer versions of stored pages.** Choose when Explorer should look in the cache for a page and when it should download it. If you choose **Every visit to the page**, Explorer will never search the cache, even if you only looked at this page two minutes ago. **Every time you start Internet Explorer** means that if you haven't visited this URL in this Web session Explorer should download the page; if you have, it will retrieve it from the cache. **Never** means that Explorer will never try to download the page if there's a page in the cache with the same URL, regardless of its age.

▶ **Amount of disk space to use.** When it's first installed, Explorer will pick what it reckons to be a sensible percentage of your hard disk to hold cached files. Drag this slider to the left or right to reduce or increase this figure if you think you know better.

▶ **Move Folder** lets you move the **Temporary Internet Files** directory elsewhere. This might be useful if you have another drive with more free space.

▶ **View Files** lets you look at all the cached files. This can be every bit as informative as the History list, giving the names of the files, their original URL, the date you last viewed them, and more. **View Objects** gives a similar view of a directory named **Downloaded Program Files**, which contains ActiveX controls that were installed on your PC by Web pages you've visited (more about ActiveX controls in Chapter 14).

▶ Alter Explorer's
use of the disk
cache and take a
look at the files in
the cache folder.

BY THE WAY

Your files are downloading anyway!

Because Explorer uses the files' original names and locations in the cache
directory, you can open it any time you want to and copy files from it for your
own use. So instead of saving text, source and images from a page as you surf, you could just
come back to the Settings dialog after disconnecting and click **View Files** to locate them.

Which Option Should We Use?

So which of the three **Check for newer versions** options is the best? It really
depends upon the types of Web site you visit most often, and whether you
visit the same ones regularly. Sites specialising in news, weather and stock
quotes often change by the minute or hour, so you'd want to choose **Every
visit to the page** to always see the latest version. However, if you tend to
visit and revisit sites that rarely change, you can speed things up a lot by
selecting **Never** and loading the page from the cache every time.

We chose 'Never'. How can we see if the page has changed?

You don't need to go back and change the cache settings. Just click the **Refresh** button on the toolbar (or press F5). This forces Explorer to download and display the current version of the page from the server, and store it in the cache to replace your old copy.

If in doubt, the safe 'middle option' is **Every time you start Internet Explorer**. This way you'll always see the latest version of the page when you first visit that site in a Web session, but if you return to it later in that session it will be opened from the cache.

7

FINDING YOUR WAY ON THE WEB

In This Chapter...

▶ **Finding Web sites using search engines and directories**

▶ **Tips for getting the best results from your search**

▶ **Locate companies and services using White Pages and Yellow Pages**

▶ **Power searching with Internet Explorer**

▶ **Check out the best (and worst!) that the Web has to offer**

Armed with the information we've covered in the last two chapters you're ready to venture out onto the Web and start surfing. And almost immediately you'll hit a predicament: how on earth can you find what you're looking for? As you probably guessed, the Internet is one jump ahead of you on that score. Whatever you're looking for, there's no shortage of tools to help you find it. Choosing the best tool to use will depend largely on the type of information you want to find, but don't panic: these search tools are easy to use, and you'll probably use several of them regularly. And, yet again, all you need is your trusty browser.

Finding A Search Site

Almost anything you can find on the World Wide Web you can find a link to at one of the Web's search sites. Although finding a search site on the Web is easy (especially as we're about to tell you where the most popular ones are!), picking the one that's going to give the best results is never an exact science. Essentially there are two types of site available: **search engines** and **directories**.

▶ **Search engines** are indexes of World Wide Web sites, usually built automatically by a program called a spider, a robot, a worm, or something equally appetising (the AltaVista search engine uses a program it endearingly calls Scooter). These programs scour the Web constantly, and return with information about a page's location, title and contents, which is then added to an index. To search for a certain type of information, just type in keywords and the search engine will display a list of sites containing those words.

▶ **Directories** are hand-built lists of pages sorted into categories. Although you can search directories using a keyword search, it's often as easy to click on a category, and then click your way through the ever-more-specific sub-categories until you find the subject you're interested in.

Search engines have the benefit of being about as up-to-date in their indexes as it's possible to be, as a result of their automation. The downside is that if you search for **pancake recipe** in a search engine, the resulting list of pages won't all necessarily contain recipes for pancakes – some might just be pages in which the words 'pancake' and 'recipe' coincidentally both happen to appear. Most search engines give you the option of specifying pancake AND recipe, pancake OR recipe, the specific phrase 'pancake recipe' and so on. However, the robot programs used by the search engines all vary in the ways they gather their information, so you'll quite likely get results using one engine that you didn't get using another.

Directories don't have this problem because they list the subject of a page rather than the words it contains, but you won't always find the newest sites this way – sites tend to be listed in directories some three months after their authors have submitted them for inclusion.

Here's a short list of popular search engines and directories to get you started. When you arrive at one of these that you like, it's worth adding it to Internet Explorer's **Favorites** menu so that you can get back again whenever you need to without a lot of typing.

Search Site	URL
AltaVista	http://www.altavista.digital.com
Dogpile	http://www.dogpile.com
Excite	http://www.excite.com
HotBot	http://www.hotbot.com
Infoseek	http://www.infoseek.com
Lycos UK	http://www.lycos.co.uk
UK Plus	http://www.ukplus.co.uk
Yahoo! UK & Ireland	http://www.yahoo.co.uk

You notice above that some of these directories had **.com** endings, whilst others had **.co.uk**. In fact many of the world-wide directories such as Lycos and Excite also have UK-specific directories which may be a better starting point for your search. So, whether you use **www.excite.com** or **www.excite.co.uk** will very much depend on what your objectives are. After all, although we are UK-based, we are working within a global medium and need to change our attitude toward potential customers and information bases accordingly. But if you *know* that the information you require will be found in a UK site, then the **.co.uk** version should be faster at finding the information.

Using A Search Engine

For this example we'll pick **HotBot**, but most search engines work in very similar ways. Indeed, directories such as **Yahoo** and **Infoseek** can be used like this if you like the simplicity of keyword searches.

When you arrive at HotBot you'll see a page like the one shown in the screenshot below. For the simplest sort of search, type a single word into the text box, and click on **Search**. If you want to search for something that can't be encapsulated in a single word, HotBot allows you to specify whether you want occurrences of every word, or the exact phrase – but there are a few tricks you can use that most search engines will understand (and those that don't will generally just ignore them).

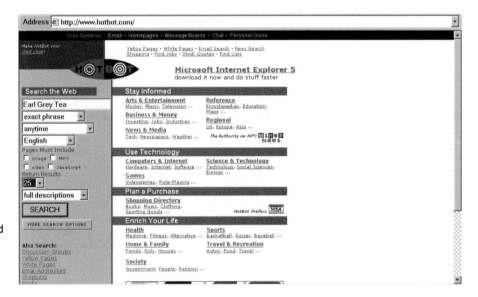

▶ Type a keyword into the search engine's text box and click **Search**.

▶ If you enter several keywords, type them in descending order of importance. For example, if you wanted to find pictures of aircraft, type **aircraft pictures**. The list will then present good links to aircraft sites before the rather more general links to sites just containing pictures.

▶ Use capital letters only if you expect to *find* capital letters. Searching for **PARIS** may find very little, but searching for **Paris** should find a lot. If you don't mind whether the word is found capitalised or not, use lower case only (**paris**).

▶ To find a particular phrase, enclose it in 'quote marks'. For example, a search for '**plaster of paris**' would find only pages containing this phrase and ignore pages that just contained one word or the other.

▶ Prefix a word with a + sign if it must be included, and with a – sign if it must be excluded. For example, if you're an economist searching for banking information, you might enter **bank –river** to ensure that you didn't find documents about river banks. Similarly you could enter **+printer inkjet –laser** if you wanted to find pages about printers, preferably including inkjet printers, but definitely not mentioning laser printers.

After entering the text you want to search for and clicking the **Search** button, your browser will send the information off to the engine, and within a few seconds you should see a new page like the one pictured below listing the sites that matched your search criteria. We used the keywords **Earl Grey Tea**, and HotBot has found 120 different pages. It's worth remembering that when some search engines say they've found pages *about Earl Grey Tea*, they've really found pages that contain the words 'Earl Grey Tea' somewhere within the page's text. Many of these pages may be *about* something entirely different.

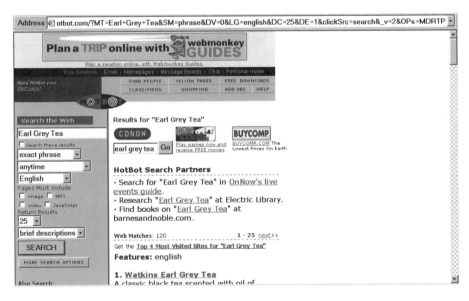

◄ A search for 'Earl Grey Tea' finds more than enough results to keep us going until dinner time.

Of course, you won't find all 120 pages listed here. Instead you'll see links to the 25 most relevant pages, with a few words quoted from the beginning of each. At the bottom of the page you'll find a button that will lead you to the next 25 on the list, and so on. In true Web style, these are all hypertext links – click the link to open any page that sounds promising. If the page fails to live up to that promise, use your browser's **Back** button to return to the search results and try a different one.

Save your search for later

When the search results appear, you can add this page to Internet Explorer's **Favorites** menu. Not only is the URL of the search site stored, but also the keywords you entered for the search. It's a handy option to remember if you don't have time to visit all the pages found in the search straight away.

Most search engines give the pages a score for relevancy, and these are worth keeping an eye on. In many cases, a page scoring below about 60 per cent is unlikely to give much information. If you can't find what you want using one search engine, always try another – because their methods are different, their results can vary dramatically.

Some search engines such as Dogpile and Microsoft's All in One are amalgams of a number of different search engines, so if you want to find every possible mention of your favourite subject you could try using one of these.

It's a 404!

Sometimes you'll click a link on a search results page, only to see a dull grey screen and a **Not Found** message. This is due to the constant rise and fall of Web sites that we mentioned on page 59. Some search engines are more reliable than others in this department, and some seem to offer almost nothing but out-of-date links. (The '404', incidentally, comes from a similar message for a page that couldn't be found: **HTTP Error 404**. In popular Net jargon, almost anything that can't be found is said to be 404'd rather than lost.)

Searching The Web Directories

Yahoo was the site that invented the whole Web-searching concept, and it's still a well-loved and widely-used workhorse. It has many country-specific sites including a 'UK & Ireland' site at **http://www.yahoo.co.uk**. When you first arrive at the Yahoo site, you'll see a search engine style text box into which you can type keywords if you prefer to search that way. However, you'll also see a collection of hypertext links below that, and these are the key to the directory system. Starting from a choice of broad categories on this page, you can dig more deeply into the system to find links to more specific information.

To take an example, click on the **Computers and Internet** link. On the next page, you'll see the list of sub-categories, which includes **Graphics, Hardware, Multimedia, Training**, and many more computer- or Internet-related subjects. Click on the **Multimedia** link, and you'll see another list of multimedia-related categories, shown in the screenshot below. Below this list of categories, you'll see another list: these are links to multimedia-related sites rather than more Yahoo categories. To find out more about multimedia generally, you might click one of these to visit that site; to find out more about a specific area of multimedia such as sound, video or virtual reality, you'd click that category in the upper list.

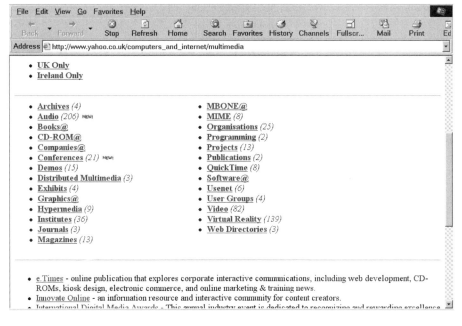

◀ Choose a more specific Yahoo category from the upper list, or a direct link to a Web site from the lower.

The layout is pretty easy to follow when you've browsed around for a few minutes, but Yahoo has simplified it further by using bold and plain text to help you identify where you're going. Bold text means that this is a link to another Yahoo category; plain text indicates that it's a link to a page elsewhere on the Web that contains the sort of information you've been searching for. Beside most of the bold category-links, you'll also see a number in brackets, such as **Pictures (448)**. This number tells you how many links you'll find in that category.

GOOD QUESTION

Why do some of the categories finish with an '@' symbol?

The '@' symbol indicates a cross-reference to a different main category. For example, click on **Companies@** and you'll be moving from the **Computers and Internet** heading to the **Business and Economy** heading. You'll find links to multimedia companies here, but other categories will be related more to business matters than to computing.

Yellow Pages – Searching For Businesses

So far we've been looking at fairly general searches – you want a particular type of information and you don't mind where it is or who put it there, and consequently the results can be hit-and-miss. Searching for a specific business or service is different; either you find it or you don't. But businesses want to be found, to the extent that they'll pay to be listed in specialised 'yellow pages' directories, so these searches will almost always yield results. Two of the most useful for finding UK businesses are Yell (the Yellow Pages we all 'know and love', in its online incarnation), and Scoot.

Yell, at **http://www.yell.co.uk**, is an ideal place to begin a search for a UK company. Click one of the icons on the left to look for a company's Web site by category or in an alphabetical list. There's also a search engine dedicated to finding UK Web sites of all types. The links on the right take you to an automated search of the Electronic Yellow Pages: enter a company's location, and either a Business Type or Company Name, to start the search. The results mirror those you'd expect to find in the paper version.

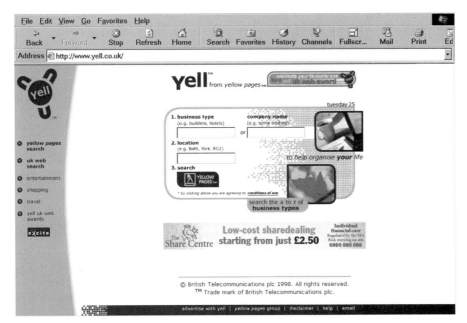

◀ The Yellow Pages online – an ideal place to find the Web sites and contact details of UK companies.

Guesswork is good

BY THE WAY

If you can't trace the URL of a company's Web site, try typing a few guesses into your browser's address bar. Most companies use their own name as their domain name, so if you're looking for a company called Dodgy Goods plc, try **www.dodgygoods.com**, **www.dodgygoods.co.uk**, **www.dodgy-good.co.uk**, or even **www.dodgy_goods.co.uk**. If you look at the company URLs given throughout this book, you'll see how likely this is to get a result.

The Scoot site, located at **http://www.freepages.co.uk**, is dedicated to finding companies' addresses and phone numbers, and works in a slightly different way from Yell. Begin by entering a town or city in which the company is based. On the next page, confirm the county listed is correct. Finally, on the third page, choose a category of business to search for from the drop-down list box. The search will return a list of all the businesses of that type in your chosen area. This is a great way to search if, for example, you need a courier service and you're in too great a hurry to care which courier it is.

If you haven't found the company yet, it's either American or it doesn't want to be found! To search for US companies, head off to Excite at **http://www.excite.com** and click the **Yellow Pages** button. Enter a company name and category description, together with location details if known, and click the **Search** button. If the category you chose doesn't match an Excite category, you'll be given a list of similar categories to choose from. You can also try **http://www.companiesonline.com**, a new addition to the Lycos search engine family. If you're looking for financial or performance-related information about a company, visit Infoseek and select **Company Profiles** from the drop-down list to search through almost 50 000 US companies. Finally, of course, there's the good old workhorse, Yahoo. Visit **http://www.yahoo.co.uk/Business_and_Economy/Companies** and you'll be presented with a list of over 100 categories. The sites you'll find in Yahoo's categories cover the UK and Ireland as well as America and elsewhere.

Easy Web Searching With Internet Explorer

To reach a search site quickly in Internet Explorer, click the **Search** button on the toolbar (a globe icon with a magnifying glass). A frame will appear at the left of Explorer's window, similar to the Favorites and History list panels, displaying a mini version of a search engine. Explorer chooses the search engine for you, but you can choose a different one from the **Select provider** list. Type in your query, click the obvious button and the results will appear in the same frame with the usual **Next 10** button at the bottom.

Instant searching

BY THE WAY

Instead of clicking the **Search** button and waiting for the search page to load, Explorer offers a quicker method. In the address bar, type a question mark, followed by two keywords you want to search for, such as **?motor racing** and press Enter. You'll be taken immediately to the search results page. If you want to search for only one keyword, you'll need to enter it twice (e.g. **?squirrels squirrels**).

The great benefit of this method of searching is that you can click any entry in the list to open it in the main part of the window without losing track of the search results.

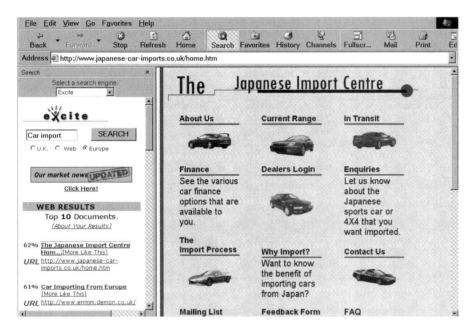

◀ Internet Explorer's search panel keeps your results visible as you work your way through the most promising links.

Surf's Up! Now Where Shall We Go?

All dressed up and nowhere to surf? The sheer unpredictability of the World Wide Web will almost certainly tempt you at times, even if there's nothing in particular you need to do or find. You may think that surfing is a waste of time, certainly as far as your business is concerned. But if you don't surf you won't know what's out there, who's doing what, how they're presenting it and what's good and bad about the sites you visit. For your business to have a successful Web presence you need to know what works and what doesn't on the Web. So indulge yourself a little and use the time as market research to see what your competitors are up to. Here's a brief list of sites that gives you somewhere to start. (The official term for these, sad to relate, is 'cool sites'. On the Web, you have to aspire to being 'cool'.)

▶ **Cool Site Of The Day.** A single cool site every day. And every day the entire universe goes to visit the lucky recipient of the title. You'll also find

The Still Cool Archive, The Cool-O-Meter, and Cool Site Of The Year. Bucketloads of cool, and you'll find it all at **http://cool.infi.net**.

▶ **PC Magazine's Top 100 Web Sites.** Top sites chosen by the magazine's editors, and sorted into categories: Commerce, Computing, News, and Reference. Go to **http://www.zdnet.com/~pcmag/special/web100** for this one.

▶ **Top 50 UK Web Sites.** A simple list of sites numbered 1–50 according to how many visitors (or 'hits') each site has had in the last week. You'll find a huge variety of stuff here, but they must all be good, mustn't they? Skip off to **http://www.top50.co.uk**.

▶ **The Weekly Hot 100.** Links sorted into 60 categories from the obvious (Sport, Music, Travel) to the not-so-obvious (Auctions, Wine, Jobs). The sites are sorted by how many visits they get. Head for **http://www.100hot.com**.

▶ **Jacob Richman's Hot Sites.** 32 categories of useful links sniffed out and sorted by Jacob himself, including Humour, Education, Law and Music. Although he has no greater claim to fame than any other Web-surfer, Jacob has a keen eye for good sites and a well-organised collection of links. Find this at **http://www.jr.co.il/hotsites/hotsites.htm**.

The World Wide Web is an art form and, like any form of art, some people can do it and some people can't. Depending on your viewpoint, bad art can be far more entertaining than good art: there are countless Web sites out there which, far from being 'cool', have been caught with their trousers round their ankles. If you've overdosed on cool, try the following as an antidote and a very good way of seeing what *not* to do:

▶ **The Worst Of The Web.** Click on the large image to take a trip through the current 'worst sites', accompanied with comments from your three cartoon hosts. Alternatively, follow the links below the image to see previous award-winners in this category. Visit **http://www. worstoftheweb.com** for this 'bland bombshell'.

Portals

A phenomenon that is a late arrival to the Internet has also made a dramatic impact. Portals offer news, reviews, weather, e-shopping, games, business events – in fact anything that can be guaranteed to attract visitors to come back for more. They make an ideal model for those new to the web, in a hurry, or frustrated by not being able to find what they want.

Portals are now found everywhere. Many of the search engines and directories have become portals:

▶ Excite　　　　**http://www.excite.com**

▶ Yahoo　　　　**http://www.my.yahoo.com**

▶ Lineone　　　 **http://www.lineone.net**

▶ Freeserve　　 **http://www.freeserve.co.uk**

as have many of the Online Service Providers:

▶ AOL　　　　　**http://www.aol.co.uk**

▶ MSN　　　　　**http://www.msn.com**

▶ Virgin Net　　 **http://www.virgin.net**

It is predicted that in the next few years the Internet will be dominated by about five portals. AOL, for instance, boasts more visitors to its portal than any other. Microsoft's MSN is also in the running in the popularity stakes, but this is hardly surprising as it is the default address on Explorer when it first starts. The BBC's own portal at **http://www.bbc.co.uk** has a huge readership made up of visitors who have been directed there from its broadcast stations.

If you are serious about setting up your own business site and attracting visitors, it may well be worth your while getting it listed on one or many of these portals. But we'll be looking at Web site promotion in a later chapter. For now, then, let's move on to the most popular use of the Internet. Turn the page to find out more!

8

EXCHANGING MESSAGES BY E-MAIL

In This Chapter...

▶ What's so great about e-mail anyway?

▶ Choose and set up your e-mail software

▶ Send and receive your first e-mail message

▶ Take the mystery out of sending files by e-mail

▶ Learn the secret language of the Internet – emoticons and acronyms

E-mail is the old man of the Internet, one of the reasons the Network took off in the first place. It's one of the easiest areas of Net life to use, and the most used – for many people, sending and receiving e-mail is their only reason for going online. By the end of this chapter you'll be able to send e-mail messages and computer files to thousands of people all over the world in practically less time than it takes to stick a stamp on an envelope.

Why Should We Use E-mail?

First, it's incredibly cheap. A single first class stamp costs 26p and will get a letter to a single, local (in global terms) address. But for a local phone call costing a few pence you can deliver dozens of e-mail messages to all corners of the world. Second, it's amazingly fast. In some cases, your e-mail might be received within just seconds of your sending it. (It isn't always quite as fast as that, however: on occasions, when the Net conspires against you, it might take several hours.) Third, it's easy to keep copies of the e-mail you send and receive, and to sort and locate individual messages quickly.

JARGON BUSTER

Snail mail

A popular term for ordinary mail, whose speed is closer to that of a certain mollusc than e-mail.

There's a possible fourth reason, but it should be regarded with some caution. If you agonise for hours over ordinary letter-writing, e-mail should make life easier for you. An inherent feature of e-mail is its informality: spelling, grammar and punctuation are often tossed to the wind in favour of speed and brevity – but as you will see, you have to consider whether this is a good idea in a business environment.

Everybody's First Question

Whenever the subject of e-mail comes up with Internet beginners, the same question is guaranteed to arise within the first minute. So that you can concentrate on the rest of the chapter, we'll put your mind at ease by answering it straight away. The question is: *What happens if e-mail arrives for me and I'm not online to receive it?*

The answer: e-mail arrives at your access provider's computer (their **mail server**) and waits for you to collect it. In fact it will wait there a long time if it has to: most mail servers will delete messages that remain uncollected for several months, but if you take a week's holiday you can collect the week's e-mail when you return.

Newbie

JARGON BUSTER You're a newbie! This just means that you're new to the Internet. You wouldn't be proud to describe yourself as a newbie, but you might want to do so when appealing for help in a newsgroup, for example, to keep responses as simple as possible.

Understanding E-mail Addresses

There are two easy ways to spot an Internet 'newbie'. The first is that their messages begin 'Dear…' and end 'Yours sincerely'. The second is that they tell you their 'e-mail number'. Don't fall into either trap! We'll show you how to avoid the first pitfall later in the chapter; in the second case, you definitely have an e-mail *address*!

E-mail addresses consist of three elements: a username, an '@' symbol, and a domain name. Your username will usually be the name in which your account was set up, and the name that you log on with when you connect. The domain name is the address of your business, IAP or online service. For example, our company is called Topspin Group; our domain name is **topspin-group.com** and we can be contacted at **info@topspin-group.com**.

Quoting Your E-mail Address

BY THE WAY

If you have to say your e-mail address out loud, replace the dots with the word 'dot' and the @ symbol with the word 'at'. Our e-mail address is pronounced 'info at topspin hyphen group dot com'.

E-mail Addresses & Online Services

The e-mail address of someone using an online service is structured in a similar way, although CompuServe calls the username a 'User ID' and AOL calls it a 'Screen Name'. If you have an account with an IAP, and you want to send e-mail to an AOL member, use the address *ScreenName*@**aol.com**. To send to a member of MSN, *use **username*@msn.com**, and for CompuServe members use *UserID*@**compuserve.com**.

Members of online services can also send e-mail out onto the Internet to someone with an IAP account. In fact, for members of AOL and MSN they can use the e-mail address without making any changes to it. If you're a CompuServe member, though, you'll have to insert the word 'Internet:' (including the colon) before the address. To send Brian a message, for example, a CompuServe member would use the address **Internet:brian@topspin-group.com**. The word 'Internet' isn't case-sensitive, and it doesn't matter if you leave a space after the colon.

If you're a member of an online service, and you want to e-mail another member of the same service, all you need to enter is the username (or User ID, or Screen Name) of the person you want to e-mail.

What Do We Need?

If you have an account with an online service such as CompuServe or AOL, you don't need anything more – the software you use to connect to and navigate the service has built-in e-mail capability. If you have an IAP account, you'll need an e-mail client (jargon for 'a program that works with e-mail'). There are many of these to choose between, and your IAP might have provided one when you signed up. There are three major factors to consider when choosing an e-mail program:

▶ It's compatible with the protocols used by your e-mail account (we'll come to that in a moment).

▶ It will let you work offline.

▶ It will let you organise incoming and outgoing messages into separate 'folders'.

offline

Software that lets you work *offline* allows you to read and write your messages without being connected to your IAP or online service and clocking up charges. You need to go *online* only to send your messages and receive any new e-mail. In the 'old days' e-mail had to be written online, which is why speed mattered more than spelling.

There are a number of protocols used to move e-mail around, the most common of which are **SMTP** (Simple Mail Transfer Protocol) and **POP3** (Post Office Protocol, which is currently in its third version). SMTP is the protocol used to send e-mail messages to the server. Although SMTP can also handle the delivery of messages if it has to, POP3 is the protocol of choice for the job. What you need to know is whether you have a POP3 e-mail account, and your IAP should have made that quite clear. There are several technical reasons why a POP3 account is better than an SMTP-only account, but the reason you care about right now is that you'll have a far wider range of e-mail software available to choose from.

If you do have a POP3 account, the most popular e-mail clients on the Internet are:

▶ **Outlook Express, Outlook 97 and Outlook 98.** These Microsoft packages give you both e-mail and newsgroup programs which integrate themselves with Internet Explorer very neatly. In fact, when Explorer (or Windows 98) was installed on your system, these should have been installed along with it. You can check for newer versions at **http://www. microsoft.com/ie/download**.

▶ **Pegasus Mail.** An excellent free program that you can download from **http://www.let.rug.nl/pegasus/ftp.html**.

▶ **Eudora Light.** This is 'postcard-ware' (it's basically free, but the author would like a picture-postcard of your home town as payment). You can download it from **http://www.eudora.com**.

GOOD QUESTION

What about Microsoft Exchange?

Exchange (also known as Windows Messaging) is included in earlier versions of Windows 95, but we wouldn't recommend using it: it's slow, and unfriendly. However, if you have Microsoft Outlook (also included in the Microsoft Office suite) we suggest you try that and see how you get on. It's the big brother to Outlook Express and offers a range of extra features well suited to busy offices such as a contacts manager and appointments scheduler. A word of warning: if your machine is low on memory and/or disk space we wouldn't recommend you install Outlook in its full version. Some dub it bloat-ware, whilst others are not so complimentary for the same reason! See how you get on with Outlook Express instead.

If you use the Netscape Navigator browser, you are likely to have an e-mail program already. Navigator is part of an integrated suite of programs named Netscape Communicator, and this suite includes Netscape's own e-mail program. You can find Communicator on Netscape's site at **http://www.netscape.com** but, just as with Internet Explorer, if you prefer to use an unrelated e-mail program, the choice is entirely yours.

Setting Up Your E-mail Program

Before you can start to send and receive e-mail, your software needs to know a bit about you and your e-mail account. This simply involves filling in the blanks on a set-up page using some of the information given to you by your access provider (see page 20). The first time you start the program it should prompt you to enter this information, but it's worth knowing where to find it in case you ever need to change it in the future.

▶ In **Outlook Express**, choose **Tools | Accounts** and click the **Mail** tab.

▶ In **Eudora**, go to **Tools | Options**. Click the icons in the left pane to open the various option pages. The settings you're concerned with at this point are scattered over the first five pages. On The **Sending Mail** page, remove the checkmark from the **Immediate Send** box.

▶ In **Pegasus**, click **Tools | Options**. Click on **General Settings** and
Network Configuration in turn to fill in the details.

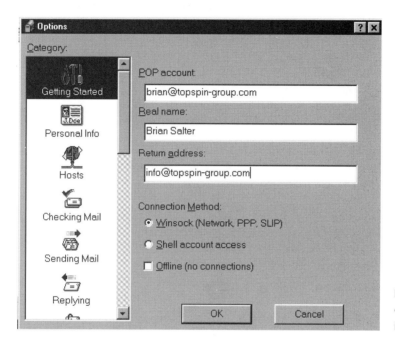

◀ Entering
personal e-mail
account details
into Eudora Light.

In all these programs you'll find a bewildering array of checkboxes and
options. Ignore them! Just fill in personal details about your e-mail address,
POP3 account name and password, SMTP and POP3 mail server addresses,
and so on. We'll look at some of the other options later in this chapter. For
now, though, they're set at sensible defaults, so leave them this way until
you're sure you want to change something.

Sending An E-mail Message

You probably feel an overwhelming temptation to e-mail everyone you
know and tell them you've 'joined the club', but hold that thought for a
moment. Start by sending a message to yourself instead – that way you can
check that everything's working, and learn what to do when you receive a
message as well.

Fire up your e-mail program or your online service's software and click the button that opens a message window. In Eudora and Pegasus, the button shows a pen and paper; in Outlook, click the **Compose Message** button.

▶ Outlook Express's mail message window.

Although all of these e-mail programs look a little different, the important features are the same:

To: Type the e-mail address of the person to whom you want to send the message. In Outlook, as you type the first few letters, the program may try to match the name with an entry in your Address Book (see page 106).

CC: Carbon copy (or more recently adopted as *Courtesy Copy*). If you want to send the message to several people, type one address in the **To** field and the rest in the **CC** field. Using this method, all recipients will know who else received a copy of the message.

BCC: Blind Carbon Copy. If you want to send the same message to several people but you don't want any of them to know who else is getting a copy, place their addresses in this field instead of the CC field.

From: You'll rarely see this in the message window, and the e-mail software will enter your e-mail address automatically from the information you entered when you set up the program. This tells the recipient who the message was from.

Subject: Enter a short description of your message. In some e-mail programs you can send a message with a blank subject line, but avoid doing this. Although most people will open any e-mail they receive (even if the subject is blank), this entry really comes into its own when the recipient is looking for this message again in six months time.

Attached: Lists the names of any computer files you want to send to the recipient along with the message. You'll learn about attaching files later in this chapter.

Below these fields is the area in which you type the message itself. Because you're going to send this message to yourself, type your own e-mail address into the **To** field, and anything you like in the **Subject** field (just to get into the habit!), and then write yourself a welcoming message.

Now you need to send the message. Once again, the programs differ here, but look for a button marked **Send**. Some programs will send e-mail immediately, and try to log on to your service to do so; others add mail to a 'queue' of messages to be sent all together when you're ready to do so. You may even have two Send buttons with a choice of Send Now or Send Later. Pegasus and Outlook score highly for ease of use in this department: messages you write are automatically queued, and you can click a single button in the main window that will send all mail in the queue and retrieve any incoming mail in a single operation. If you have to make a choice on an Options page about how the program should send mail, always choose to queue/send later.

If you're not sure how your program handles all this, just take a deep breath and click the Send button. (You'll have to go online first, but your e-mail program may start your connection automatically when you click Send.) If the message really is being sent, something on the screen should tell you so. If nothing seems to be happening, look for a button or menu option that says something like **Send Mail Now** or **Send Queued Mail**.

Don't hold your breath!

BY THE WAY

If your program sends and receives mail in a single operation, the e-mail you're posting to yourself may come back to you instantly. On the other hand, it may not. E-mail messages usually take a few minutes to get to where they're going, and can take hours (or even days in the very worst cases.)

We've Got New Mail!

You really feel you've arrived on the Internet when you receive your first message, but how do you know there are messages waiting for you? You don't, unfortunately – your e-mail program has to go and look. With an online service account, you'll see an on-screen indication that new mail is waiting after you log on, and you can retrieve it by clicking the obvious button. With an IAP account, if you're using one of the e-mail programs mentioned earlier, you'll have a button labelled something like **Check for new mail**, or you might have the more useful combined **Send & Receive All Mail** button.

▶ When you log on to CompuServe a message at the bottom of the screen informs you of new messages. Click the envelope-button beside it to retrieve them.

Most e-mail programs use an Inbox/Outbox system: e-mail waiting to be sent is placed in the Outbox, and new mail will arrive in the Inbox. When new mail arrives, you'll see a single entry giving the subject line of the message and the name of the sender (although some programs give a wealth of information including dates and times of sending and receiving the message, its size, and the number of attached files). To read the message, double-click this entry.

Something else for your appraisal

BY THE WAY

Each of the programs mentioned here can be set to check for mail automatically at regular intervals (usually entered in minutes) and give an audible or visual prompt when new mail arrives. This is a feature best suited to busy offices.

At this point you can decide what to do with the message. You can delete it if you want to, but until you do it will remain visible in the program's Inbox or main folder. You should also be able to print it onto paper. Good e-mail programs allow you to create named folders to store and organise your messages more efficiently (you will need, for example, to create Business and Personal folders and subfolders within these), and you can move or copy messages from the Inbox to any of these folders. In addition you might be able to save a message as a separate file onto your hard disk or a floppy disk.

Replying & Forwarding

One of the things you're most likely to do with an incoming message is send a reply, and this is even easier than sending a brand new message. With the message open (or highlighted in your Inbox) click on the program's **Reply** or **Reply to Author** button. A new message window will open with the sender's e-mail address already inserted and possibly the entire message copied as well. Copying the original message this way is known as **quoting**, and it's standard practice in e-mail. The program should insert a greater-than sign (>) or something similar at the beginning of each line, and you can delete all or any of the original message that you don't need to include in the reply.

What's the point of quoting in replies?

The main reason is that it helps the recipient to remember what it is you're replying to. In this regard it's more user-friendly than letters or faxes, as you can have the whole discussion contained in one document. For example, if someone sends you a list of questions you can type the answer after each quoted question, saving the recipient the need to refer back to his previous message. Remember that the aim of quoting is not to build up a message containing your entire conversation, though – so it may be best to remove anything being quoted a second time (>>), and cut the rest down to the bare memory-jogging essentials.

The Reply button also inserts the word **Re:** at the beginning of the subject line, indicating to the recipient that it's a response to an earlier message. Although you can change the subject line of a reply, it's often best not to – many e-mail programs have search and sort facilities that can group messages according to subject (among other things) making it easy to track an earlier e-mail 'conversation' you've long since forgotten about.

You can also send a copy of a received message to someone else, and you'll probably have a **Forward** button on the toolbar that does the job. Enter the recipient's e-mail address and any extra message you want to add, then click the Send button. Just as in new messages, you can include **CC** or **BCC** addresses when replying or forwarding. Forwarded messages usually have **Fwd:** inserted at the start of the subject line.

Getting Attached – Sending Files Via E-mail

Basic e-mail messages are plain text (7-bit ASCII) files, and used to have a size limit of 64Kb. While 64Kb is an awful lot of text, it's a pretty small measure in terms of other types of computer file you might want to send with a message. Most other types of file are **binary** (8-bit) files, but nowadays you really don't need to understand the difference.

It may be text to you...

BY THE WAY

Remember that a text file is just that – plain ASCII text. A formatted document created in a modern word processor may look like ordinary text but it needs to be encoded to be sent as an attachment. The acid test is: Will the file look exactly the same if you open it in a text editor such as Windows Notepad? If not, it's a binary file and must be encoded.

However, most modern e-mail programs are much more capable: you choose the file or files you want to attach, your e-mailer converts them to ASCII ready to be sent, and the recipient's e-mailer converts them back again at the other end. In most cases it really should be as simple as that. The only blot on the landscape is that there are several methods used to do it, and both sender and recipient must be using the same method.

▶ **UUencode** The original (rather messy) conversion system for PCs. The file is converted into ASCII and, if necessary, broken up into chunks to get around the e-mail size restriction. It looks like pure gobbledegook until converted back by a **UUdecoder**.

▶ **MIME** A modern successor to UUencoding, and now the main method used on the Web for transferring files. It can identify the type of file you're sending and act appropriately, and the whole system works completely unaided at both ends.

▶ **BinHex** A conversion system used mostly on Macintosh computers, similar to UUencoding.

Which method should we use?

GOOD QUESTION

If at all possible, use MIME. If your e-mail program can't handle MIME, replace it with one that can. If you have a choice of methods on your Options page, set MIME as the default. Only use a different system if your recipient doesn't have a MIME-compatible e-mail program (and refuses to do the sensible thing!). Online services now handle MIME attachments, making it easy to send files to members of the same service, a different service, or an Internet e-mail account.

If you know that your software and that of your recipient both use the same system, attaching files is simple: look for a toolbar button with a paperclip symbol and click it (in Outlook and Pegasus you'll find the button in the New Message window itself). You can then browse your computer's directories to find and double-click any files you want to attach; the software will handle the rest itself.

Attachments in Outlook Express appear as file icons. Right-click the icon to open or save the attached file, or drag it to your desktop or a directory on your hard disk.

Receiving attachments in incoming e-mail should be just as simple, especially if your e-mail program recognises both MIMEd and UUencoded attachments, as many do. Eudora, for example, will decode attachments and put them in a directory called Attach; Outlook Express will show an attached file as an icon at the bottom of the message window.

Fatal attachment

BY THE WAY

Despite the occasional scare stories about so-called 'e-mail viruses', e-mail messages are just plain text and therefore can't harbour computer viruses. But files included as attachments may be executable programs or documents that can contain executable macros such as Microsoft Word files, and these certainly can carry viruses. In the Spring of 1999, a particularly pervasive virus known as Melissa travelled the world attaching itself to the address books within e-mail clients and multiplying itself in a very short time. Melissa was in fact a macro program that was disseminated using Microsoft Word's capabilities. You should always check these attachments with a virus-checker utility before running them, and be especially wary of attachments in messages from someone you don't know – there are some weird people out there!

Attachments That Use A Different Conversion Method

Although you've got the whole attachment business sorted out, and you're happily MIME-ing files to all and sundry, you may still receive a UUencoded file from someone else, or need to UUencode a file for someone who doesn't have MIME. Even if your e-mail software can't handle the conversion for you, there are utilities available that you can use to do the job yourself. Two of the best (both of which handle MIME and UUencode as well as several other methods) are WinZip and ESS-Code. You'll find WinZip on **http://www.winzip.com**; ESS-Code can be downloaded directly at **http://tucows.cableinet.net/files/ecd75w95.zip**.

What Else Should We Know About E-mail?

Like most simple tools, e-mail software has grown to offer a lot more than the basic requirements of writing, sending, receiving and reading. Once you feel comfortable using the program you've chosen, spend a little time reading the manual or Help files to see what else it offers. (Remember that you can keep sending yourself test messages to find out if or how an option works.) Here's a selection of options and issues worth knowing about.

Address Books

An address book is simply a list of names and e-mail addresses. Instead of typing the recipient's address into a new message (risking mistakes and non-delivery), you can click the Address Book button and double-click the name of the intended recipient to have the address inserted for you. You may be able to add new addresses to the book by clicking on a message you've received, or the name of the sender, and selecting an **Add to address book** option. Many programs will allow you to create multiple address books, or to group addresses into different categories for speedy access to the one you want.

GOOD QUESTION

How can we find someone's e-mail address?

Believe it or not, the only truly reliable way is to ask! But there are search facilities on the World Wide Web that can find people rather than places, and you'll learn where to find them and how to use them later in this chapter.

A similar option is the **address group** (known by different names in different programs). You can send the same message to all the addresses listed in a group by simply double-clicking the group's name. This is an option worth investigating if you need to send an identical memo or newsletter to a number of recipients.

Signatures

An e-mail 'signature' is a personal touch to round off an e-mail message. You'll find a **Signature** option on one of your program's menus that provides a blank space for you to enter whatever text you choose, and this will be added automatically at the end of all the messages you write.

A signature commonly gives your name, and might also include the URL of your Web site if you have one, your job description and company if you're sending business mail, and perhaps even a sales message. Try to resist getting carried way with this, though – eight lines should be an absolute maximum for a signature. If you incorporate a business message of any sort into your signature, do remember to change it regularly. There is nothing worse than bombarding people with the same message time after time.

Careless talk...

BY THE WAY

As some businesses have also found to their cost, employees have sometimes got the company into trouble with the contents of their e-mails, and so it might be a wise decision to insist on your staff using a corporate disclaimer along the lines of 'The comments included in this e-mail do not necessarily reflect the views of the company'. We look at the legal implications of this in Chapter 13.

Something that many businesses fail to realise in the use of company e-mail is that regulations concerning communications are just as applicable to e-mail as they are to letters and faxes. Hence, for instance, you should always have your company name and registration number on external e-mails and financial firms should also identify the financial regulator that supervises them. Particularly important in the latter case is that they should understand that e-mail content that constitutes investment advice is controlled tightly by the regulators. Some firms resort to using content-checking software such as MIMEsweeper (details from **http://www.reeseweb.com/mimeswee.htm**). This can be configured to check for certain key words or large program attachments. However, this works only if all e-mails are sent over the network, rather than by individual modems.

Emoticons & Acronyms

Emoticons, otherwise known as 'smilies', are little expressive faces made from standard keyboard characters used to convey feelings or to prevent a comment being misunderstood in e-mail messages, newsgroup postings and text-chat. As an example, you might put <g> (meaning 'grin') at the end of a line to say to the reader 'Don't take that too seriously, I'm just kidding'. Actually, most business users wouldn't bother to use these at all, but you can use them for adding a personal touch. Here's a little bundle of the more useful or amusing emoticons. (If you've haven't come across emoticons before, look at them sideways.)

Symbol	Meaning	Symbol	Meaning
:-)	Happy	:-#)	Has a moustache
:-(	Sad	:-)>	Has a beard
:-))	Very happy	(-)	Needs a haircut
:-((	Very sad	(:-)	Bald
;-)	Wink	:-)X	Wears a bow-tie
>:-)	Evil grin	8-)	Wears glasses
:-D	Laughing	:^)	Has a broken nose/Nose put out of joint
:'-)	Crying	:-w	Speaks with forked tongue
:-O	Surprised	:-?	Smokes a pipe
:-&	Tongue-tied	:-Q	Smokes cigarettes
:-|	Unamused	*-)	Drunk or stoned
:-||	Angry	<:-)	Idiot
X-)	Cross-eyed	=:-)	Punk rocker

Acronyms came about as a result of Internet users having to compose their e-mail while online and clocking up charges. Although messages are now mostly composed offline, these acronyms have become a part of accepted e-mail style, and have been given new life by the emergence of online text-chat which you'll learn about in Chapter 10.

In fact most of these aren't acronyms at all, but they fall under the banner of TLAs (Three Letter Acronyms) even though they don't all consist of three letters!

Acronym	Meaning	Acronym	Meaning
AFAIK	As far as I know	IOW	In other words
BCNU	Be seeing you	KISS	Keep it simple, stupid
BST	But seriously though	L8R	Later (or See you later)
BTW	By the way	LOL	Laughs out loud
FAQ	Frequently asked question(s)	OAO	Over and out
FWIW	For what it's worth	OIC	Oh I see
FYI	For your information	OTOH	On the other hand
GAL	Get a life	OTT	Over the top
IMO	In my opinion	ROFL	Rolls on the floor laughing
IMHO	In my humble opinion	TIA	Thanks in advance
IMNSHO	In my not-so-humble opinion	TNX	Thanks

Another common need in e-mail and newsgroup messages is to emphasise particular words or phrases, since the usual methods (bold or italic text, or underlining) may not be available in some of the older e-mail programs. This is done by surrounding the text with asterisks (*never*) or underscores (_never_).

Undelivered E-mail

If an e-mail message can't be delivered it will normally be 'bounced' straight back to you, along with an automatically generated message telling you what went wrong. If the address you typed doesn't exist, or you made a mistake, the message should come back within seconds or minutes. In some cases a message might be returned to you after several days, which usually indicates that the problem lies in delivering the message at the other end. If this happens, just send the message again. If the problem persists, try altering the address so that it looks like this:

> **[SMTP:***username@domain***]**

(including those square brackets) or send a message addressed to **postmaster@***domain* (using the domain of the person you were trying to contact) asking if there's a problem with e-mail delivery and quoting the e-mail address you were trying to send to.

Other E-mail Bits & Pieces

▶ **Filtering** Modern e-mail programs offer filtering options (sometimes known as 'Rules') that let you decide how to handle certain types of incoming e-mail. You might choose to have all messages from a particular person moved to a special folder as soon as they arrive, for example.

▶ **Formatting** Many e-mail programs allow you to add formatting to your e-mail as if it were a word processed document, choosing fonts, colours, layout styles, and even themed background pictures, creating a result that looks a lot like a Web page and is sent in the same format. The problem is that your recipient must be using an e-mail program that can understand all this formatting or he'll just receive a plain message with all the formatting codes placed in a meaningless attached file. More and more e-mail programs do understand these formats now, however, so the problem crops up a lot less often. It's best not to add background images though – some people receive dozens of messages every day and don't want to wait ten times as long for one of yours to download!

▶ **Delete on receipt** As soon as you collect your e-mail it should be deleted from your access provider's mail server. The reason for this is that your provider won't give you unlimited space for e-mail on the server: when your mailbox is full, mail will just be bounced back to the sender. Your e-mail software may give you an option to delete retrieved messages, but usually it will be switched on by default. (Of course, this means that you can only retrieve a message once, so think carefully before deleting a message from your own system!)

BY THE WAY

Yes, it's electronic mail, but...

It's not supposed to look like a letter. You don't need to put the date or the recipient's postal address at the top, or use any letter-writing formalities. For business, you would want to include your own postal address and phone number – probably in your e-mail signature, so you don't have to keep typing it in – companies need to do this anyway. Companies should also – in theory – show their registered number and address to fit in with company law, although in our experience this is regularly overlooked.

▶ **Writing style** Don't start with 'Dear…' or end with 'Yours sincerely'. You might send a message that starts 'Hi Naomi', or 'Hello Brian' if you really want some sort of salutation, but it's perfectly acceptable just to get straight into the message, and this is not regarded as rudeness. Similarly you might sign off with 'Regards' or 'Best wishes', but there's no need to put anything at all but your name. (You might find it a hard habit to break, but don't think people rude when they do it!)

E-mail Netiquette

The term 'netiquette' is an abbreviation of 'Internet etiquette', a set of unwritten rules about behaviour on the Internet. In simple terms, they boil down to 'Don't waste Internet resources' and 'Don't be rude', but here are a few specific pointers to keep in mind when dealing with e-mail:

▶ Reply promptly. Because e-mail is quick and easy, it's generally expected that a reply will arrive within a day or two, even if it's just to confirm receipt. Try to keep unanswered messages in your Inbox and move answered messages elsewhere so that you can see at a glance what's waiting to be dealt with.

▶ DON'T SHOUT! LEAVING THE CAPS LOCK KEY SWITCHED ON IS REGARDED AS 'SHOUTING', AND CAN PROMPT SOME ANGRY RESPONSES. IT DOESN'T LOOK AT ALL FRIENDLY, DOES IT?

▶ Don't forward someone's private e-mail without their permission.

▶ Don't put anything in an e-mail message that you would mind seeing on the Nine o'clock News! Anyone can forward your e-mail to a national newspaper or your boss, so there may be times when a phone call is preferable.

Finding People On The Net

Finding people on the Internet is a bit of a black art – after all, there are in excess of 40 million users, and few would bother to 'register' their details even if there were an established directory. In addition, of course, if you move your access account to a different online service or IAP, your e-mail address will change too (more on that in Chapter 14). So it's all a bit hit and miss, but let's look at a few possibilities.

Flick Through The White Pages

In the UK, the term Yellow Pages is synonymous with finding businesses. White Pages is a type of directory listing *people* (what we usually just call a phone book), and the Internet has a few 'white pages' directories that may turn up trumps. Some of these rely on people actually submitting their details voluntarily; others take the more crafty approach of searching the newsgroups and adding the e-mail addresses of anyone posting an article. Searching white pages is just like using any other search engine, usually requiring you to enter the user's first and last names and click on a Search button.

▶ **Bigfoot at http://bigfoot.co.uk.** Don't be fooled by the URL – the search engine itself is in America – but this is the directory most likely to find the e-mail address of a UK Internet user. It's a very useful site which will be mentioned again in later chapters.

111

▶ **Four11 at http://www.four11.com.** The biggest and most popular 'people locator' in the States, which searches the Internet for e-mail addresses and accepts individual submissions. Details found here may include a user's hobbies, postal address and phone number, but most entries are from the USA.

▶ **Infospace at http://www.infospace.com/info/people.htm.** Another American service, again unlikely to produce an e-mail address for anyone living outside the States.

GOOD QUESTION

Are there any other white pages we can search?

On the Internet, there's always more of anything! Head off to **http://www. yahoo. com/reference/white_pages** for links to other white pages. Or you could try Yahoo UK's own people finder at **http://www.yahoo.co.uk/mailsearch/e-mail.html**.

If you're prepared to wait a little while for a result, you could try MIT (Massachusetts Institute of Technology), which regularly scans Usenet archives to extract names and e-mail addresses. Send an e-mail message to **mail-server@rtfm.mit.edu**, with the text **send usenet-addresses/***name* as the body of the message (remembering not to add your e-mail signature on the end). Provided that the person you're trying to trace has posted a message to a newsgroup in the past, you should receive a reply containing the e-mail address.

Back To The Search Engines

Some of the popular search engines mentioned in Chapter 7 have 'people-finder' options too. Lycos has a **People Find** button which leads to their own e-mail search pages. Excite has buttons marked **People Finder** (for addresses and phone numbers) and **E-mail Lookup** (for e-mail addresses). In Infoseek, click the arrow-button on the drop-down list box and choose **E-mail Addresses**, then type someone's name into the text box.

NEWSGROUPS – THE HUMAN ENCYCLOPAEDIA

In This Chapter...

▶ What are newsgroups all about?

▶ Choose a newsreader and download a list of available newsgroups

▶ Start reading (and writing) the news

▶ Send and receive binary files with news articles

▶ Mailing lists – have your news delivered by e-mail

News, as we generally think of it, is a collection of topical and business events, political embarrassments, latest gossip, and so on. All of that, and more, can be found on the Internet, but it's not what the Net calls 'news'. The newsgroups we're talking about here are more formally known as **Usenet discussion groups**; there are over 30000 of them (and counting!) covering everything from accommodation to zebra fish.

Newsgroups are extremely powerful – but often unrecognised – global power bases of concentrated knowledge, interests, mutual help and mentoring. As yet, their power within the global marketplace appears to be underestimated by governments and multinationals.

Newsgroup discussions take place using e-mail messages (known as **articles** or **postings**), but instead of addressing articles to an individual's e-mail address they're addressed to a particular group. Anyone choosing to access this group can read the messages, post replies, start new topics of conversation, or ask questions relating to the subject covered by the group.

How Does It Work?

Your access provider has a computer called a **news server** that holds articles from thousands of newsgroups that form part of the Usenet system. This collection of articles will be regularly updated (perhaps daily, or perhaps as often as every few minutes) to include the latest postings to the groups.

Using a program called a **newsreader**, you can read articles in as many of these groups as you want to, and post your own articles in much the same way that you compose and send e-mail messages. Messages you post will be added to the server's listings almost immediately, and will gradually trickle out to news servers around the world (the speed with which this happens depends upon how often all the other servers update themselves).

Although there are currently more than 30000 groups, you won't find every group available from your access provider. Storage space on any computer is a limited commodity so providers have to compromise. In addition, many providers are now taking a moral stance against groups involving pornography and software piracy (among others) and these are unlikely to be available. But if you really needed access to a group concerned with grape-growing in Argentina (and one existed), most reasonable providers would subscribe to it if you asked nicely. If a suitable group doesn't exist, and you think the world is itching to discuss the Argentine grape with you, you could even talk to your IAP about setting up the newsgroup yourself in the 'alt' hierarchy (more about that below).

GOOD QUESTION

If my IAP doesn't subscribe to it, how can I find out if it exists?

If you're looking for a group dedicated to tortoise farming and your IAP doesn't seem to have one, use your browser to search the lists of newsgroup names at the following Web sites, using the keyword 'tortoise'. If you find a promising group, ask your IAP to subscribe to it.

http://www.nova.edu/inter-links/usenet.html
http://www.magmacom.com/~leisen/master_list.html

Newsgroup Names

Newsgroup names look a lot like the domain names we met in earlier chapters – words separated by dots. Reading the names from left to right, they begin with a **top-level** category name and gradually become more specific. Let's start with a few of these top-level names:

▶ **biz**   The accepted place for commercial postings such as **biz.comp.accounting.**

▶ **comp**   Computer-related groups such as **comp.windows.news**.

▶ **rec**   Recreational/sports groups like **rec.arts.books.tolkien**.

▶ **sci**   Science-related groups such as **sci.bio.paleontology**.

▶ **misc**   Just about anything such as **misc.consumers.frugal-living**.

▶ **soc**   Social issues groups such as **soc.genealogy.nordic**.

▶ **talk**   Discussions about controversial topics such as **talk.atheism** or **talk.politics.guns**.

▶ **uk**   UK-only groups such as **uk.transport.ride-sharing**.

A little moderation

BY THE WAY

Some newsgroups are *moderated*, meaning that the creator of the group (or someone else appointed to run it) reads all the messages and decides which to post. The aim is to keep the topics of discussion on course, but they often tend to weed out deliberately argumentative or abusive messages too.

One of the largest collections of groups comes under a completely different top-level heading, **alt**. The alt groups are not an official part of the Usenet service, but are still available from almost all service providers. Because almost anyone can set up a group in the alt hierarchy they're sometimes regarded as anarchic or somehow 'naughty', but in truth, their sole difference is that their creators chose to bypass all the red tape involved in the Usenet process.

What Do We Need?

You need two things: a program called a **newsreader** and a little bit of patience. We'll come to the second of those in a moment; first let's sort out the newsreader. These come in two flavours. First, there's the **online newsreader** – you don't want one of those! Reading and posting articles all takes place while connected and clocking up charges. Second is the offline newsreader, and that's definitely the type you want, but **offline readers** also vary. Some offline readers automatically download all the unread articles in your chosen group so that you can read them and compose replies offline; the problem is that in a popular group you may have to wait for several hundred articles to download, many of which you won't be interested in. The second (and by far the best) type of offline reader just downloads the **headers** of the articles (the subject line, date, author and size). You can select the articles you want to read, based on this information, and then reconnect to have them downloaded.

If you don't already have a good offline newsreader, here are our recommendations:

▶ **Outlook Express/97/98.** As mentioned in the previous chapter, this integrates nicely with Microsoft's Internet Explorer browser, and gives you an e-mail client too. If you have Windows 98, you should have Outlook already installed.

▶ **Agent or Free Agent.** A popular newsreader available in two versions – one is free, the other you'll have to pay for (guess which is which!). Point your browser at **http://www.forteinc.com** for information about Agent.

Having got your hands on one of these, the setting up is fairly simple. The program should prompt you for the information it needs the first time you run it, which will include your name, e-mail address, and the domain name of your news server (usually **news.*accessprovider.co.uk***). You'll probably see other options and settings, but don't change anything just yet.

Now switch on your patience circuits! Before you can go much further, your newsreader has to connect to the server and download a list of the newsgroups you can access. How long this takes will depend upon the number of groups available, the speed of your modem, and how fast a connection you have. It might take only two or three minutes, or it might take more than 15.

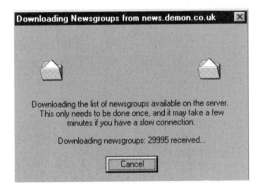

◀ While your newsreader downloads a list of groups, you'll have to sit tight – or better still, go and put the kettle on!

That was the bad news. The good news is that you'll need to download the group list only once, as long as you don't decide later that you want to use a different newsreader. In future, when your newsreader connects to the server to download new articles, it will automatically fetch the names of any new groups that have been created and add them to the list.

Newsgroups & online services

To access newsgroups in AOL, use the keyword **newsgroups**; in CompuServe, use the Go word **usenet**. When you look at the list of groups your online service provides, many may be missing (such as the entire 'alt' hierarchy). In many cases you *can* access these, but you need to 'switch on' access to them yourself. For example, AOL has an Expert Add function for this. Check the Help files for details, or contact the service's support line.

Subscribing To Newsgroups

Before you can start reading and posting articles, you need to subscribe to the groups that interest you. ('Subscribing' is the term for letting your newsreader know which groups to download headers from – there are no subscription fees!) Although you can scroll your way through the thousands of groups in the list, it's easier to search for a word you'd expect to find in the group's name. In Outlook, click the button with the newspaper symbol on the toolbar (or press Ctrl+W), and type a keyword into the box above the list; in Agent, click the toolbar button with the torch symbol and type a word into the dialog box.

To subscribe to a newsgroup in Outlook, click its name, and click the **Subscribe** button. When you've subscribed to all the groups you want, click **OK**. In Agent right-click a newsgroup's name and click **Subscribe**.

Can't get the group you want?

If you want to subscribe to a group that your access provider doesn't (and won't) subscribe to, you may be able to access it through one of the public-access news servers instead. Visit **http://www.jammed.com/~newzbot** for a list of public servers. There are no lists of the groups covered by each server, so you'll have to configure your newsreader to connect to it, download a list of groups, and see if the group you want is there.

▶ If you need to find out whether a newsgroup exists on a particular topic, or you want to search the newsgroups for information, turn to Searching The Newsgroups later in this chapter to find out how to do it.

Reading The News

When you've chosen the groups to which you want to subscribe, you're ready to download the headers from one of the groups. In Outlook, click the name you chose to describe your news server in the Outlook Bar on the left, and then double-click the name of one of your subscribed newsgroups in the upper window. The program will connect to your news server and download the headers from articles in the selected group (shown in the screenshot below). By default, Outlook will download 300 headers at a time (as long as there are that many articles in the group!), but you can change this figure by going to the **Tools** menu, selecting **Options** and changing the figure shown on the **Read** tab.

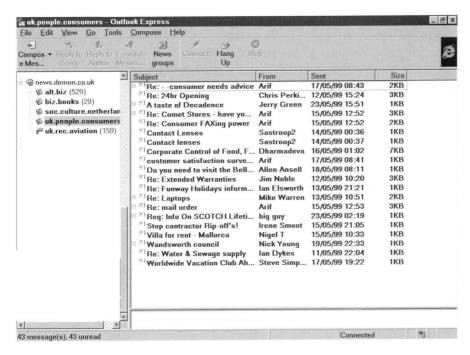

◀ Reading the news in Outlook Express.

In Agent, click on **Group | Show | Subscribed Groups** (or click the large button marked **All Groups** until it says **Subscribed Groups**). You'll see the list of newsgroups you subscribed to, and you can double-click one to download its headers. Agent will present a dialog box asking if you want to collect all the headers, or just a sample of 50. Some popular newsgroups have several thousand articles, so it's best to start with a sample just to get a flavour of the group first. Change the figure if you want to, and then click the button marked **Sample Message Headers**.

To download and read an article immediately in the preview window, click the header once in Outlook, or double-click it in Agent.

Usually you'll want to download articles to read offline, and Outlook makes this easy: just tell it which articles you want. If you want to grab every article in the group, click **Tools | Download All**. If you just want selected articles, either right-click each article separately and choose **Mark Message for Download**, or hold the Ctrl key while clicking all the required articles and then right-click on any of them and choose **Mark Message for Download**. Beside the headers for messages you've marked you'll see a blue arrow indicator so that you can tell what you've chosen at a glance. You can now select another group to download headers for, and mark those in the same way. When you've finished marking the articles you want in all groups, open the **Tools** menu and click the appropriate **Download** button.

GOOD QUESTION

Why can't I download some of the articles listed?

Although the headers are displayed, you might find that some of the articles are no longer available. To make room for new articles, older ones have to be deleted. In the most popular groups, which receive several hundred messages per day, articles might vanish within a matter of days.

Agent (and most other newsreaders) use similar methods. To mark a message for download in Agent, highlight it and press **M**, or right-click it and choose **Mark for Retrieval**. Once you've marked all the articles you want to download, click the toolbar button with the blue arrow and thunderbolt symbol and Agent will fetch them for you and mark them with a little 'page' icon.

Threads – Following A Conversation

Although a newsgroup is dedicated to one *subject*, there may be dozens (or hundreds!) of different conversations going on. Fortunately all newsgroup articles have a subject-line just like e-mail messages, so all messages with the same subject-line will be part of the same conversation, or in newsgroup parlance, the same **thread**. Most newsreaders let you choose how you want to sort the list of articles (by date or by sender, for example), but the best way to view them is by thread so that articles from one conversation are listed together.

Subject ▲	From	Sent	Size
Contact Lenses	Sastroop2	14/05/99 00:36	1KB
Contact lenses	Sastroop2	14/05/99 00:37	1KB
Corporate Control of Food, F...	Dharmadeva	16/05/99 01:02	7KB
customer satisfaction surve...	Arif	17/05/99 08:41	1KB
Do you need to visit the Bell...	Allen Ansell	18/05/99 08:11	1KB
Re: Extended Warranties	Jim Noble	12/05/99 10:20	3KB
Re: Funway Holidays inform...	Ian Elsworth	13/05/99 21:21	1KB
⊟ Re: Laptops	Mike Warren	13/05/99 10:51	2KB
⊟ Re: Laptops	Tony	13/05/99 23:37	2KB
⊟ Re: Laptops	David Jenn...	14/05/99 10:49	2KB
⊟ Re: Laptops	Mike Sutton	19/05/99 14:55	2KB
Re: Laptops	Sniper	20/05/99 09:38	2KB
⊟ Re: Laptops	Paul Picke...	23/05/99 13:05	1KB
Re: Laptops	Nickma	23/05/99 17:58	2KB
Re: Laptops	Tony Bryer	23/05/99 23:30	1KB
Re: Laptops	Steve	24/05/99 01:00	1KB
Re: Laptops	Nick	24/05/99 07:05	1KB
⊞ Re: mail order	Arif	15/05/99 12:53	3KB
⊞ Req: Info On SCOTCH Lifeti...	big guy	23/05/99 02:19	1KB
Stop contractor Rip-off's!	Irene Smoot	15/05/99 21:05	1KB
Villa for rent - Mallorca	Nigel T	15/05/99 10:33	1KB
⊞ Wandsworth council	Nick Young	19/05/99 22:33	1KB
Re: Water & Sewage supply	Ian Dykes	11/05/99 22:04	1KB
Worldwide Vacation Club Ah...	Steve Simp...	17/05/99 19:22	1KB

◀ Click the '+' icon to reveal the rest of the thread, or the '–' icon to hide it.

So how do threads work? When you post a brand new message to a newsgroup, you're starting a new thread. If someone posts a reply, their newsreader will insert the word **Re:** in the subject-line (just as in e-mail replies). Your newsreader gathers together the original message and all replies (including replies to replies) and sorts them by date. The original message will have a little '+' icon beside it indicating that it's the beginning of a thread and you can click this to reveal the other articles in the thread.

GOOD QUESTION

Why does this message have nothing to do with the subject line?

Some threads go on and on for months and may eventually have nothing to do with the article that started it all, despite the subject line. All it takes is for someone to raise a slightly different point in a reply, and someone else to pick up on it in their reply, for the entire thread to veer onto a whole new course.

Marking Messages

In most newsreaders, as soon as you open an article to read it, the article will be marked as **Read**. (In Outlook the read articles turn from bold type to normal; in Agent they turn from red to black.) You can also mark a message as Read even if you haven't read it, or mark an entire thread as Read (perhaps you read the first couple of articles and decided everyone was talking rubbish). In modern newsreaders this just acts as a useful way to remember what you've read and what you haven't – you might just as easily delete messages you've read if you won't want to read them again.

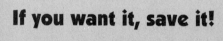

BY THE WAY

If you want it, save it!

Modern newsreaders automatically store the list of downloaded headers, and all downloaded articles, but they'll eventually delete them before they swallow up too much of your hard disk. If there are particular articles you want to keep for future reference, you can usually save them to a special folder, or to any directory on your hard disk. You should also be able to print an article, or copy it to the clipboard to be pasted into another application.

Older newsreaders don't store the headers: they download them, display them, and then forget them again when you move to a different newsgroup or log off. All they know is which messages are marked as Read. Next time you open this newsgroup, the unread headers will be downloaded, so it makes sense to mark as Read any headers that you're definitely not interested in so that they're not continually being downloaded. (You can even mark every message in the group as Read so that you'll only see any newer messages that appear.)

Posting Articles To Newsgroups

It's a funny old language really. Newsgroup messages work just like e-mail: the only difference is that the address you use is the name of a newsgroup, not an e-mail address. But even though you *send* an e-mail *message*, you *post* a newsgroup *article*. Don't ask why, just accept it! Don't forget that you're not just sending a complaint to a company's customer care centre, but you're publishing it for all to see. So be careful with the laws of libel and slander.

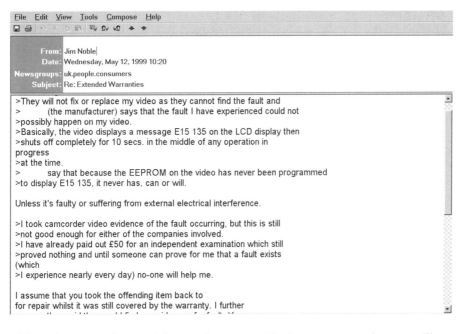

◀ If your company is perceived to have given bad service, don't be surprised if the world is told about it.

Although just reading articles can be very addictive, sooner or later you'll want to get involved. There are various ways to post articles, and they're common to just about every newsreader you'll come across. In the following list we'll take Microsoft's Outlook Express as an example, but if you're using something different you'll still have all the same options (although their precise names may vary).

Test the water first

BY THE WAY

Before posting an article to a 'proper' newsgroup where everyone can see it, you probably want to send a test message first as you did with your e-mail program in the previous chapter. You can send a message to **alt.test**, but it's worth checking to see if your access provider has its own 'test' group. You might even get a reply from another newcomer. Allow at least a few minutes before checking the group to see if your message is listed.

▶ To reply to a message you're reading, click the **Reply to Group** button, or right-click the header and choose **Reply to Newsgroup**. (In many newsreaders, a reply is called a **Follow-up**). A new message window will open with the name of the group already entered, and the same subject-line as the message you were reading. Type your message and click the **Post** button (or press Alt+S).

▶ To reply to the author of the article privately by e-mail, click the **Reply to Author** button and follow the routine above. In this case the article won't be posted to the newsgroup.

▶ To reply to the newsgroup and send a copy of your reply to the author by e-mail at the same time, go to **Compose | Reply to Newsgroup and Author**. Once again the routine is the same as above.

▶ To create a new message (and start a new thread), click the **Compose Message** button (or press Ctrl+N). A new message window will open with the currently-selected newsgroup shown. To send to a different newsgroup, or to more than one group, click the newspaper icon beside the name to add and remove groups from the list. Enter a title for the article on the **Subject** line, and then write your message. Click **Post** to send.

In keeping with e-mail, any replies to newsgroup articles automatically **quote** the original article. Make sure you delete any of the original article that doesn't need to be included. Remember that newsreaders list earlier messages in the thread in a well-organised fashion, so most people will have already read the message you're replying to.

Don't change the subject!

BY THE WAY

When replying to an existing thread, don't change the subject line at all! If just one character is different, newsreaders will regard it as the start of a new thread and won't group it with the other articles in the thread.

Attachments & Newsgroup Articles

At the risk of being boring, let's just say again: newsgroup articles and e-mail messages are so similar even their mother couldn't tell them apart. A case in point is that you can send and receive computer files as part of a newsgroup article just as you can with e-mail. So we're going to assume that you've read the section on attachments in the previous chapter, beginning on page 102.

In most newsreaders, attaching a binary file to an article is a simple case of clicking a button marked **Attach File** (often marked with a paperclip icon), browsing your directories for the file you want to send, and double-clicking it – your newsreader should do the rest. Most modern newsreaders, including those mentioned earlier in this chapter, will also decode any attachments in an article you open, with no need for intervention on your part: these may be automatically saved to a directory on your computer, or you may have to click a button on the toolbar (as in Agent) to view them. Outlook Express displays news attachments as an icon at the bottom of the window in the same way as it handles e-mail attachments (see page 104).

How can I tell if an article has an attachment by looking at the header?

Newsreaders show the number of lines in an article as part of the header information in the list. Even a long text-only article shouldn't run to more than about 60. An attached picture or sound file will usually range from about 200 up into the thousands. Only newsgroups that have the word 'binaries' somewhere in their name should have articles that include attachments, so you'll probably be expecting to find a few if you're in one of these groups. Outlook Express helpfully lists the size in kilobytes rather than the number of lines.

On occasion, an attached file might be split into several messages due to its size (known as a **multi-part attachment**) and the subject lines for each message will include additions like [1/3], [2/3] and [3/3] to number the parts of a three-part file. If you try to open any one of these, many newsreaders will realise that the file isn't complete and automatically download the other two as well and piece them together. In some programs, however, you'll have to select all three parts in advance.

If you have any problem with attachments, it'll be that you open an article with an attached file that uses a format your newsreader can't handle (not all newsreaders can decode both UUencode and MIME files). In this case you'll see line upon line of textual gibberish in the article. These characters will be in an endless stream, and will often use more symbols than letters and numbers. In this case you'll need to decode the attachment yourself by saving the message onto your own disk, and using one of the programs mentioned on page 101.

Newsgroup Netiquette & Jargon

Newsgroups are pretty hot on Netiquette, the 'rules' you should follow when using them, and Usenet has invented its own brand of weird language to go with some of these.

▶ It's good practice to lurk awhile when you visit a new group (especially as a newcomer to the whole idea of newsgroups). So what's 'lurking'?

Reading newsgroups articles without posting any yourself. Getting an idea of the tone of the group, the reactions of its participants to beginners' questions, and the types of topic they cover.

▶ Before diving in and asking a question in the group, read the FAQ. This stands for Frequently Asked Question(s), and it's an article that tells you more about the group, its topics, and other related groups. Many groups post a FAQ every few weeks, but if you don't see an article with 'FAQ' in its header, send a short message asking if someone could post it.

▶ Don't post 'test' articles to any newsgroup that doesn't have the word 'test' in its name.

▶ Don't post articles containing attachments to any newsgroup that doesn't have the word 'binaries' in its name. This is out of respect for people whose newsreaders give them no choice but to download every article and who don't expect to spend five minutes downloading an attachment they don't want.

▶ Don't spam! 'Spamming' is a lovely term for sending the same article to dozens of different newsgroups, regardless of whether it's relevant. These messages are usually advertising mailshots, get-rich-quick schemes, and similar stuff that no-one finds remotely interesting. The risk is greater than just being ignored though; you might get mail-bombed – many people will take great delight in sending you thousands of e-mail messages to teach you a lesson! So, why 'spamming'? Monty Python fans might remember a sketch about a certain brand of tinned meat… try asking for a copy of the script in **alt.fan.monty-python**!

▶ When replying to an article requesting information, or an answer to a question, it's good practice also to send the author a copy by e-mail, in case your newsgroup reply doesn't get noticed. By the same token, if someone asks for answers by e-mail, post your answer to the group as well – it may be of interest to others.

▶ Don't rise to flame bait! Some people delight in starting arguments, and deliberately post provocative articles. Personal attacks in newsgroups are known as 'flames', and on occasions these can get so out of hand that the whole group descends into a 'flame war', with little else going on but personal abuse.

Be aware!

Posting your name to a newsgroup could result in your getting lots of unwanted e-mail. Many spammers regularly surf the newsgroups 'harvesting' e-mail addresses to target these people for advertising. Following an EU ruling in May 1999, as with other kinds of unsolicited mail the onus is now on the consumer to notify the e-mail equivalent of the mailing preference service that they do not wish to receive unsolicited e-mails. In the same way as with surface mail, this can take six to nine months to implement.

BY THE WAY

Searching The Newsgroups

There's more value to searching Usenet newsgroups than there first appears. For example, with so many thousands of groups to choose from, a quick search for the keywords that sum up your favourite topic might help you determine the most suitable newsgroup to subscribe to. Or perhaps you need an answer to a technical question quickly – it's almost certainly been answered in a newsgroup article.

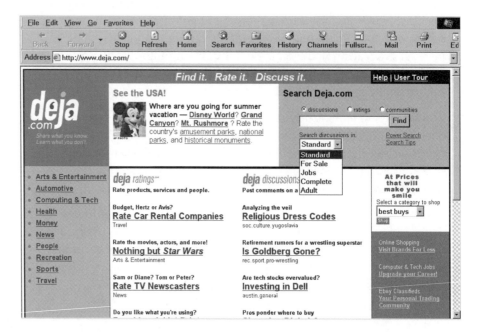

▶ Deja.com – the first place to look for Usenet postings.

One of the best places to search for newsgroups and articles is Deja.Com (previously known as Deja News) on the Web at **http://www.deja.com. Deja.Com** looks just like any other search engine you've come across on your travels except that you search for *newsgroups* rather than web pages. The search results list 20 articles at a time (with the usual button at the end of the page to fetch the next 20), and include authors' details and the names of the newsgroups in which the articles were found. Click on one of the articles to read it and you'll find a handy button-bar added to the page that lets you view the topic's thread, read the next or the previous article, and post replies to the newsgroup or to the article's author by e-mail.

BY THE WAY

Stick to what you know

If you search Deja.Com for newsgroups, you can click any newsgroup you find on the results list to read its articles. But, although it's possible, it's not the easiest way to navigate a newsgroup – you'll find it simpler to run your newsreader program and read the articles from the chosen group with that instead.

The great value of Deja.Com is that articles are available here long after they were first posted to Usenet. The only possible fly in the ointment is that the group you want may not be covered. If it isn't, head for Infoseek's search engine and choose **Usenet** from the drop-down list.

Mailing Lists – More Discussions

You may feel that a choice of over 30 000 discussion groups is enough, and we wouldn't disagree. But let's round off this chapter with a look at a different system that can add another few thousand to that total – **mailing lists**.

A mailing list is like a newsgroup that arrives by e-mail: once you've subscribed, all the messages from the group are delivered automatically to your mailbox for you to download when you like. In most cases, you can opt to receive a *digest* version which gives a single, large, daily or weekly message rather than a constant stream of separate ones. Many web sites have tailored subscription lists (many of which are free) and which update you with key points about your identified areas of interest. To subscribe to a mailing list takes a single e-mail message, as does unsubscribing.

Mailbox mayhem

BY THE WAY

Be very wary of mailing lists – if you like the general idea, start by subscribing to one list and see how things go. Popular lists generate a huge amount of e-mail, and it's not a good idea to be subscribed to half a dozen of those while you're still finding your feet!

Mailing lists come in many shapes and forms, but the two primary systems are **Listserv** and **MajorDomo**. Like most mailing list systems, these are automatic, run by a program on a computer which reads the e-mail you send to subscribe and adds your e-mail address to its list. For automatic lists, your e-mail message must be constructed in a certain way.

Listserv Mailing Lists

Listserv is one of the major automated systems, and requests for information and subscriptions are made by sending an e-mail message to one of the computers on the Listserv system. All Listserv computers are linked together, so it doesn't matter which one you use for requests; if you don't know of any other, send your messages to **listserv@listserv.net**. The request message you send needs nothing in the **Subject** line, although if your e-mail program insists you enter something, just type a dot. The message itself must contain nothing but the request (so make sure you turn off your e-mail program's Signature option!).

To do this	Type this request in your e-mail message
Subscribe to a list	**SUB** *listname your name*
Unsubscribe to a list	**SIGNOFF** *listname*
Get information about a list	**INFO** *listname*
Receive the digest version of a list	**SET** *listname* **DIGEST**
Get a list of request commands	**HELP**
Find all the lists on this system	**LIST**
Find all LISTSERV lists in existence	**LISTS GLOBAL**

Be a bit wary of that last option – the message you'll receive containing a list of all the mailing lists available will be about half a megabyte in size! Most LISTSERV lists can also be read using your newsreader – you'll find them in the **bit.listserv** hierarchy.

To send messages to a list you've subscribed to, you'll need to know which computer runs that list (the **sitename**, which should be in the details that are returned to you). You can then take part in the discussion by sending messages to *listname@sitename*. Make sure you don't get these two addresses confused. The first address opposite is only for making requests and queries about lists, and this second address is only for messages that you intend every subscriber to read. If you send your requests to the second address, a copy will be sent to everyone on the list, but the request itself won't be processed!

MajorDomo Mailing Lists

The MajorDomo system is similar to LISTSERV, but each computer on the system is independent so you need to know which computer handles the list you're interested in (the **sitename**). Armed with this information, send an e-mail message to **majordomo@*sitename*** containing one of the following requests:

To do this	Type this request in your e-mail message
Subscribe to a list	**subscribe** *listname*
Unsubscribe to a list	**unsubscribe** *listname*
Find all lists on that computer	**list**

More mailbox mayhem

If you're going on holiday for a while and won't be able to download your e-mail, consider unsubscribing from your mailing lists while you're away. Otherwise you might be faced with a barrage of e-mail when you next log on!

There May Be An Easier Way...

We mentioned a moment ago that you can get a flavour of some of the Listserv lists before subscribing by using your newsreader. Many mailing lists also have their own page on the World Wide Web giving information about the list, and a simple form you can fill in online if you want to subscribe. To find lists of mailing lists on the Web, use your browser to go to **http://www.liszt.com** (where you can search for a mailing list by typing in a keyword) or **http://www.neosoft.com/Internet/paml/bysubj.html** (where you can choose a subject from a list of hundreds, as shown in the screenshot above).

▶ Pick one of hundreds of subjects from thousands of lists.

CHAT & TALK WITHOUT MOVING YOUR LIPS

In This Chapter...

▶ **Chat, Talk and VON – What's it all about?**

▶ **Using online services' chat rooms**

▶ **Take part in IRC chat sessions on the Internet**

▶ **Comic Chat – does it have a role in business?**

▶ **Cut your phone bill using Talk and Voice on the Net**

Chat *and* talk? In Internet-speak, chatting and talking are two different things, but what they have in common is their immediacy: you can hold conversations with people from all over the world at a speed almost comparable with talking on the phone. In most cases, you won't know who these people are, and you may never 'meet' them again.

Reactions to this area of cyberspace vary considerably. Many find it inane, frustrating or offensive and totally inappropriate for business. However, because the use of Internet technologies is revolutionising the way we do business, we are describing the whole of Chat & Talk so that the background knowledge is there for you to dip into if and when its use becomes appropriate for your business.

Quite simply, these services bring Internet users into the closest possible contact with one another, and are used by many to meet members of the opposite sex. However unsatisfying you might imagine cybersex to be, it's very real, and all potential 'chatters' should be aware of its existence before taking part. Because of its very nature, business use of discussion rooms has not really developed except within the confines of an internal company 'Intranet', where its implementation can be very useful, especially in reducing the need to travel in order to meet face to face.

JARGON BUSTER

Intranet

An Intranet is a network based on TCP/IP protocols belonging to an organisation, usually a corporation, accessible only by the organisation's members, employees, or others with authorisation. An Intranet's Web site looks just like any other Web site, but the firewall surrounding an Intranet fends off unauthorised access. Like the Internet itself, Intranets are used to share information. Secure Intranets are now the fastest-growing segment of the Internet because they are much less expensive to build and manage than a private network based on proprietary protocols. We'll be returning to Intranets in Chapter 21.

What Are Chatting & Talking?

Chatting means holding live conversations with others by typing on your keyboard. You type a line or two of text into a small window and press Enter, and the text is visible to everyone else taking part almost instantly. They can then respond by typing their own messages, and you'll see their responses on your own screen almost instantaneously. Chatting usually takes place in a **chat room**; the room may contain just two or three people, or as many as 50.

Doesn't everyone talk at once in a chat room?

GOOD QUESTION

Sometimes, yes. Sometimes no-one seems to talk at all. Sometimes there are two or three conversations going on between little groups of people, with all the messages appearing in the same window, and things can get a bit confusing. But although there may be 35 people in a room, many are just 'listening' rather than joining in.

Talk is a little different. Although the method of sending messages to and fro is the same, 'talk' usually takes place between just two people, and in a more structured way. Using a talk program, you'd usually enter the e-mail address of the person you want to talk to, and if that person is online (and willing to talk to you!) the conversation begins. To cloud the issue a bit, *chat* programs also allow two people to enter a private room and 'talk', and many *talk* programs will allow more people to join in with your conversation if you permit them to enter (usually referred to as a **conference** facility).

As you can tell, the boundary between chat and talk is a bit smudged. Making things even more complicated is **Voice on the Net** (VON), by which people can really talk to each other using microphones. Most talk programs support VON, and it's being added to chat as well. Actually this isn't all as confusing as it sounds. Let's take them one at a time to see how each works.

Chat & The Online Services

One of the major reasons for the early popularity of online services was their built-in, easy-to-use chat systems. The major online services put a lot of effort into improving their chat facilities, and also now offer parental controls that can bar access from certain chat areas. As a measure of how seriously they regard these facilities, online services regularly enlist celebrity guest speakers to host chat sessions and answer questions. (Even the Prime Minister has found the time to host a chat session.) The simplicity of these chat areas makes them a good introduction to the workings of chat, even if you have an IAP account, so we'll look at the online services' offerings first.

Both AOL and CompuServe have a large button on their desktops marked **Chat** that will take you to the chat rooms, or you can use the Go or Key word 'chat'. In CompuServe this will lead to a short menu from which you can choose the General or the Adult chat forum. Click the forum of your choice and you can use the buttons on the left to switch between chat, file and message areas. The list of chat rooms shows how many people are in each room, and the Who's Here tab behind it gives a list of CompuServe members currently chatting and the rooms they're in. To enter a chat room, click its name and then choose **Participate** or **Observe** (depending upon how adventurous you're feeling!).

Make CompuServe chat your Favourite

BY THE WAY

Like many areas of CompuServe, the chat forums take about five minutes to load the first time you access them. Make sure you add the forum to your list of Favourite Places when you arrive and this should shave a few minutes off subsequent visits.

In AOL you'll see a menu allowing you to choose between UK and US chat. Choose either, and you'll be launched into a chat room called the New Members Lobby. You'll also see a list of the other chat rooms you can enter. To enter a room, double-click its name in the list. In both AOL and CompuServe you can leave a chat room by closing its window.

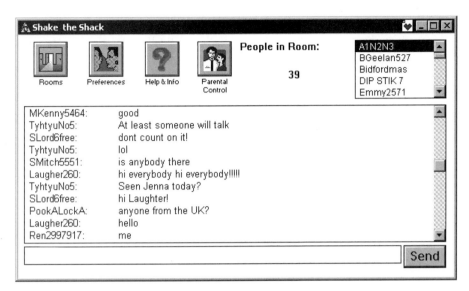

◀ Chatting in AOL's Shake the Shack room.

Once inside a chat room you can watch the conversations unfold in the upper portion of the window, or participate by typing text into the space at the bottom and pressing Enter. (Don't type your username before each line – the chat program displays that automatically.) AOL shows a list of the people in the room in the top right corner; in CompuServe, click on the **Who's Here** button for a similar list. Some members fill in a Member Profile giving details such as age, location and interests which can shed some light on the people you're chatting to. In AOL double-click the name in the **People In Room** list and click the **Get Info** button; in CompuServe, click **Who's Here**, click on a name, then select **Member Profile**.

You can also invite someone to 'talk' privately. In AOL, double-click the name of the person you want to talk to in the **People In Room** list, click the Message button and type a short message (such as 'Do you want to talk?'). If the person accepts, a small window will open in which you can type messages back and forth. In CompuServe, click the **Private Chat** button.

Chatting On The Internet

The Internet has its own chat system called Internet Relay Chat, or **IRC**. Like all the other Internet services, you'll need to grab another piece of software to use it. One of the best, and the easiest to use, is **mIRC** from

http://www.mirc.co.uk. The first time you run mIRC, you'll see the dialog box shown in the screenshot below into which you can enter the few details needed by the program.

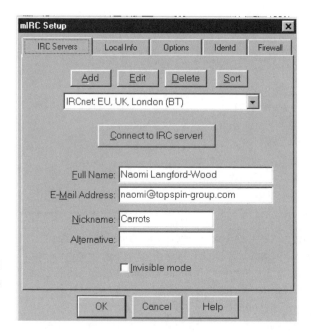

▶ Here Naomi (aka Carrots) filled in the three boxes and was up and running.

Enter your name and e-mail address in the appropriate spaces, and choose a nickname (or *handle*) by which you'll be known in chat sessions. A nickname can be anything you choose: it may give an indication of your hobby or job, or a clue to your (adopted?) personality, or it may just be meaningless gibberish, but it can't be more than nine characters in length. Finally choose a UK server from the list and click **OK**.

Channels

In the weird world of IRC, which bases its jargon heavily on CB radio, a channel is the term for a chat room.

Now you're ready to connect and start chatting. Make sure you're connected to your service provider first (mIRC won't start the connection for you), and then click the thunderbolt-button at the extreme left of the toolbar. As soon as you're connected, you'll see a small dialog box listing a collection of channels that mIRC's author thinks you might like to try. You could double-click one of those to enter that channel, but now is a good time to use one of the many IRC commands. Close the little list of channels, type **/list** in the box at the bottom of the main window, and then press Enter. A second window will open to display all the channels available on the server you chose (see the screenshot on page 140). There could be several hundred channels, so this might take a few seconds. Beside each channel's name you'll see a figure indicating how many people are on that channel at the moment, and a brief description of the channel's current subject of discussion. Choose a channel, and double-click its list-entry to enter.

You don't even need an IRC program

BY THE WAY

A number of web sites are now set up to allow you to enter chat rooms within the confines of that particular site, just by typing into your web browser. Some of the search engines, for example, include chat rooms. Try **http://www.excite.com** or even **http://www.bbc.co.uk**.

Some long-time IRC users can be a bit scathing towards newcomers, so it's best to choose a beginners' channel while you take your first faltering steps. Good channels to start with are **#beginners**, **#mirc** (for mIRC users), **#irchelp** or **#ircnewbies**. You may see some more channel names that refer to help, beginners or newbies – try to pick a channel that has at least half a dozen people in it already so that you won't feel too conspicuous!

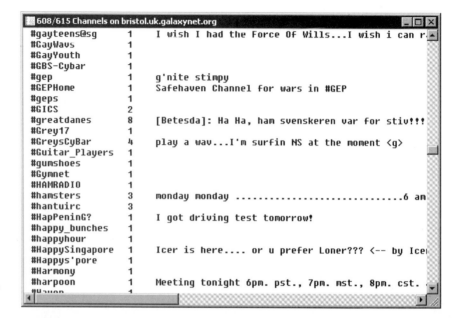

```
 608/615 Channels on bristol.uk.galaxynet.org                    _ □ ✕
#gayteens@sg        1      I wish I had the Force Of Wills...I wish i can r.▲
#GayWavs            1
#GayYouth           1
#GBS-Cybar          1
#gep                1      g'nite stimpy
#GEPHome            1      Safehaven Channel for wars in #GEP
#geps               1
#GICS               2
#greatdanes         8      [Betesda]: Ha Ha, ham svenskeren var for stiv!!!
#Grey17             1
#GreysCyBar         4      play a wav...I'm surfin NS at the moment <g>
#Guitar_Players     1
#gumshoes           1
#Gymnet             1
#HAMRADIO           1
#hamsters           3      monday monday ............................6 am
#hantuirc           3
#HapPeninG?         1      I got driving test tomorrow!
#happy_bunches      1
#happyhour          1
#HappySingapore     1      Icer is here.... or u prefer Loner??? <-- by Ice
#Happys'pore        1
#Harmony            1
#harpoon            1      Meeting tonight 6pm. pst., 7pm. mst., 8pm. cst.
#Haven              1
```

▶ The complete channel listing from GalaxyNet's Bristol server. Choose any channel from 615 possibles!

When a channel window opens, you'll see your nickname listed among the channel's other occupants on the right, with the conversation taking place on the left. As soon as you enter the channel, your arrival will be broadcast to everyone else (you'll see this happen when others arrive and leave) and you may receive an automated Welcome message, or someone might even say Hello. To join in with the chat, just start typing into the text box at the bottom and press Enter to send. If you want to leave a channel, type the command /**leave** and press Enter.

GOOD QUESTION

How can I start chatting without 'butting in'?

Whenever you arrive in a channel there's likely to be a conversation going on. If no-one brings you into the chat, it's a good idea to 'lurk' for a few moments to see what it's all about, but it's quite acceptable to type something like **Hi everyone, how's it going?** and you'll usually get a friendly response from someone. If you don't, follow the conversation and try to interject with something useful.

IRC Commands – Chat Like A Pro

The IRC system has a huge number of commands that you can learn and put to good use if you're really keen, and mIRC includes a general IRC help-file explaining how they work. You certainly don't need to know all of them (and mIRC has toolbar buttons that replace a few), but once you feel comfortable with the system you can experiment with new ones. Here are a few of the most useful to get you started.

Type this	To do this
/help	Get general help on IRC.
/list	List all the channels available on the server you connected to.
/list –min n	List all the channels with at least n people in them (replace n with a figure).
/join #channel	Enter a channel. Replace channel with the name of your chosen channel.
/leave #channel	Leave the specified channel (or the channel in the current window if no channel is specified).
/quit message	Finish your IRC session and display a message to the channel if you enter one (see below).
/away message	Tell other occupants you're temporarily away from your computer, giving a message.
/away	With no message, means that you're no longer away.
/whois nickname	Get information about the specified nickname in the main window.

So what are those 'messages'? When you quit, you might want to explain why you're leaving, by entering a command like **/quit Got to go shopping. See you later!** Similarly, if you suddenly have to leave your keyboard, you might type **/away Call of nature. BRB** to indicate that you'll be back in a minute if anyone tries to speak to you. (BRB is a common shorthand for 'Be right back'). When you return, just type /**away** to turn off this message again.

An easy way to make a fool of yourself

BY THE WAY

All commands start with a forward slash. If you type the command without the slash it will be displayed to all the participants in your channel, and give everyone a good giggle at your expense.

You can also 'talk' privately to any of the participants in a channel. If you want to start a private talk with someone called Zebedee, type the command **/query Zebedee Can I talk to you in private?** (of course, the message you tag on the end is up to you). Zebedee will have the opportunity to accept or decline the talk: if he/she accepts, a separate private window will open in which the two of you can exchange messages.

BY THE WAY

Easy window management

You can keep windows open in mIRC as long as you want to. The program places each new window on a taskbar so that you can switch between open channels and lists to your heart's content. Many people even keep several 'chats' going at once in this way!

Starting Your Own IRC Channel

If you always connect to the same server, and always use the /**list** command to get a list of channels you might notice that the number of channels varies. Channels are dynamic – anyone can create a new one, and when the last person leaves that channel it ceases to exist. Here's how to create your own channel.

1 Pick a channel name that doesn't already exist and enter it. To create a channel called Euro, type **/join #Euro**.

2 To put yourself in charge of this channel you have to promote yourself to 'channel operator' status. Do this by typing **/op** *nickname* (entering your own nickname). As operator, your nickname will be displayed with an '@' prefix to indicate your status to anyone who enters your channel.

3 Now set a topic that will displayed in the channel list and (with luck!) attract some passers-by. Type **/topic** followed by a description of what your channel would be discussing if there was someone else to discuss it with. As people join your channel and the discussion moves to different areas, use the **/topic** command to update the description.

As channel operator you are all-powerful: you can invite people into your channel using **/invite** followed by their nickname and the name of your channel (for example, **/invite Zebedee #Euro**), and you can kick someone out if their conduct is offensive or disruptive using **/kick #Euro Zebedee**. You can also use the **/op** command to promote other visitors to channel operator status if you wish to.

Chatting Can Be Comical!

Simple though it is, chatting can be very addictive. But it's still plain text, and in Internet-land that just won't do. Graphical chat software allows you choose a cartoon character called an **avatar** (pronounced Aviator) to represent you. These programs offer you a list of avatars to choose from, and some even let you create your own if you're handy with a graphics program. The following screenshot shows one of the most popular graphical chat programs, **Microsoft Chat** (which also supports ordinary textual chat if those avatars get on your nerves!) You can download **Microsoft Chat** from **http://www.microsoft.com/ie/chat**. As you can see from the screen shot, the business uses of Comic Chat are likely to be extremely limited.

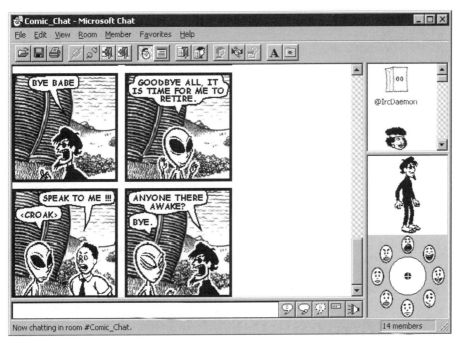

◀ Microsoft's visual Chat program lets you choose an avatar, and select different emotions to match your text.

143

Whilst in business terms we can currently see little or nothing to commend Comic Chat, the forum is there that could be used to great effect in brainstorming, where inhibitions can be broken down by the use of humour and a change of environment.

Finally on the subject of chat, a word about personal security: never give out personal details other than your name, age, sex and e-mail address. After chatting with someone for a while, it's easy to forget that you really know nothing about them but what they've told you (and that may not be true!).

Voice On The Net – Talk Really *Is* Cheap!

The sort of chat we've looked at so far is 'unplanned' – you arrive in a channel or chat room and chat to whoever happens to be there. If you get on well enough, you might invite someone else to have a private chat (a 'talk') in a separate window. But what if there's someone in particular you want to talk to? Until recently, your options were limited: you could agree to meet in a chat room at a certain time and take it from there, or you could pick up the phone.

But why not try **VON** (Voice on the Net), which is the Internet equivalent of a telephone: you start the program, choose an e-mail address to 'dial', and start talking. But in this case, talking is really talking. You can hold live conversations with anyone in the world by speaking into a microphone and hear their responses through your speakers or a headset.

Will they be online?

You can only talk to someone else if they're online and have their VON software running. Many American users have access to free local phone calls and can stay online all day, but if you want to contact another UK user you might still have to arrange to be online at a pre-specified time.

So how does VON differ from an ordinary telephone conversation? First and foremost, the price – because you're only dialling in to your local access provider, you're only paying for a local phone call although you may be speaking to someone in Australia. But it's the extra goodies that VON programs offer that make them valuable. Depending on the program you use, you can send computer files back and forth, hold conferences, use a whiteboard to draw sketches and diagrams, and you can even take control of programs on the other party's computer (if they're happy to let you do that).

How practical is this for business use?

BY THE WAY

Because of the way you have to set up each conversation this is not going to be the answer to reducing your overheads whilst maintaining your image. Whereas the actual telecoms costs can be reduced if you make the connection at predefined times, the time it takes to set this up, combined with the somewhat 'Heath-Robinson' image is likely to cost you more and do your business damage. The only business benefit is likely to be if one of your staff needs to call in from abroad.

Even the fabled 'video phone' is now a reality; however, because of the bandwidth required for the extra video information, the transmission delays can be considerable, and the pictures are small and jerky (even with a fast modem) and a bit blurred, but you can finally see and be seen while you talk! In tests we carried out using two computers 'talking' to each other within the same room, and both connected through the same IAP, the delay on the pictures was in the order of seven seconds, whilst the delay on the audio feed was around two seconds.

If you want to try it out, you'll need a digital video camera (a so-called 'webcam') and software, but these can be bought for less than £100.

There are also programs such as Net2Phone (from **http://www. net2phone.com**) that allow you to dial someone's phone number rather than e-mail address, making it possible to make these cheap international calls to someone who doesn't even have an Internet account!

What Do We Need?

Unlike the other services you use on the Net, VON programs have some definite hardware requirements. To begin with, you'll need a soundcard. It doesn't need to be a flashy, expensive card since the quality of these voice calls isn't high, but look out for a **full-duplex** card. And you'll need a microphone and speakers plugged into your soundcard; the quality of these doesn't matter too much and any computer peripherals store can supply them very cheaply.

Full duplex

JARGON BUSTER

There are two types of soundcard: full duplex and half duplex (sometimes known as Simplex). A full duplex card can record your voice while playing the incoming voice so that you can both talk at the same time if you want to (ideal for arguments, for example!). With a half duplex card you can either talk or listen, but not both – you'd normally switch off your microphone after speaking as an indication you'd finished (rather like saying 'Over' on a walkie-talkie).

Next there's your Internet connection and modem to consider. A 28.8Kbps modem is really the minimum speed to consider, but you'll get much smoother results from a 56Kbps model, with almost all access providers now supporting this speed. Finally, of course, you need the software. There are many different programs to choose from, some of which are aimed more at business rather than personal use, but here's a brief selection:.

▶ **PowWow.** A very friendly, free program from Tribal Voice which we'll look at in a moment. Details from **http://www.tribal.com/powwow**

▶ **NetMeeting.** Microsoft's free VON program aimed largely at business users, but (seemingly) used more by personal talkaholics. NetMeeting supports video, voice, and multi-user conferences, and you can use programs on the other person's computer by remote control.

▶ **Web Phone.** A multi-talented, and very stylish, VON program based on a mobile phone design with features such as video, text-chat and answerphone, as well as four separate voice lines. You'll need to 'activate' the evaluation copy (an unusual way of saying 'pay for') to unlock some of its smartest features by visiting **http://www.itelco.com**. Although inexpensive, Web Phone is targeted more at the business user than is NetMeeting or (particularly) PowWow.

▶ **Internet Phone.** A true VON program, in that it has no 'text talk' or whiteboard facilities so it'll be no good to you without soundcard, microphone and speakers. Until you pay for your copy, your talk time will be limited. You can get details by pointing your browser at **http://www.vocaltec.com**.

BY THE WAY

BT's Internet bundle of services now includes the ability for businesses to link their voice branch exchanges via PCs to the Internet. Using Microsoft's NetMeeting software embedded in Explorer 5, the service is being targeted at home workers to stay in touch with their main offices more cheaply. However, it is also ideal for making long distance calls – perhaps one reason why BT has not been specifically targeting businesses with this package.

Start Talking

As usual, most VON programs have similar features, although their names and toolbar-buttons vary. It's probably an inescapable fact of life that the most popular VON programs are the free ones, so let's take a look at Tribal Voice's **PowWow** as a representative example.

When you first run PowWow you'll be prompted to enter your name, e-mail address and a choice of password. The program will then dial up and register these in the main PowWow database and you're ready to start. Click the **Connect** button at the left of the toolbar and type in the e-mail address of the PowWow user you want to contact. To save their details to the Address Book for future use, fill in their name or nickname and click **Add**. Make sure you're connected to your IAP and click the **Connect** button. If the other person is online and running PowWow (and willing to speak to you, of course) the main window will split into two and you'll see their reply. Just as in any Chat program, you simply type your side of the conversation and press Enter.

How can I tell who's online and available for chat?

It depends on the program. In some programs you can't – you have to send a request and see if you get a response. In other programs, such as NetMeeting and Internet Phone, as soon as you connect you'll see a list of users currently online, so take your courage in both hands and double-click one!

To speak to someone using your microphone, click the **Voice** button. Although PowWow lets you text-chat with up to seven people, you'll only be able to have a voice conversation with one at a time. Here's a brief run-down of features you'll find in PowWow (and most other VON programs):

▶ Transfer files by clicking the **Send File** button and choosing a file to send. You can continue to talk while the file is being transferred.

▶ Set up an Answering Machine message that will be sent to anyone trying to contact you when you're unavailable. Some programs (such as Web Phone) can also record messages left by anyone trying to contact you.

▶ Send a picture of yourself to the other user by entering its location in PowWow's setup page. Most programs can send images to be displayed on the other user's screen without interrupting the conversation.

▶ Click the **Whiteboard** button to collaborate in drawing pictures using a similar set of tools to those found in Windows Paint. This aspect has been developed with businesses in mind and is one of the more popular business uses of chat.

▶ Host a conference with up to 50 people taking part in text chat. This is particularly useful on company-wide Intranets where the participants can all make their contributions without having to leave their own offices.

10

CHAT & TALK WITHOUT MOVING YOUR LIPS

In This Chapter...

▶ Chat, Talk and VON – What's it all about?

▶ Using online services' chat rooms

▶ Take part in IRC chat sessions on the Internet

▶ Comic Chat – does it have a role in business?

▶ Cut your phone bill using Talk and Voice on the Net

Imagine you've been left alone in a room full of computers with huge hard disks. You can root around as much as you like, grab any files you want, and take them home with you. If that sounds like a little slice of happiness, you'll like FTP – that's what it's for. FTP stands for File Transfer Protocol, and it works a lot like Windows Explorer or File Manager. You can open directories by clicking them, browse around, and click on any file to copy it to somewhere else. There's just one difference: on your own computer you might copy a file from one directory to another, or to a floppy disk, but FTP copies the file to or from a different computer – your own.

We've already looked at links to files on the World Wide Web in Chapter 6. What you may not have realised is that you were already using FTP just by clicking these links and letting the file download. Some of the files are stored on a Web server, others are stored on an FTP server, but you don't need to know what the main job of the computer is: you click the link, the file is sent, end of story. (If you're interested, move your mouse pointer onto the link and look at your browser's status bar to see where the link points. If the address starts with **ftp://** you'll know it's an FTP site. It might be worth knowing, as you'll learn in a moment.)

GOOD QUESTION

I couldn't connect to the site. What went wrong?

It might be closed, or it might be very busy. Some FTP sites put a limit on the number of people that can visit at once, and others don't allow anonymous logins during business hours, so try again later. Of course, you might just have typed the address wrongly – always the first thing to check!

Using Your Browser For FTP

FTP addresses look a lot like Web addresses: they begin with the name of the computer, and continue with the directory path to the file you want. To use your browser to visit an FTP site, you'll usually need to prefix the whole thing with **ftp://** (the only exception is when the name of the computer starts with 'ftp', but you can still use the prefix in these cases if you prefer to). To get acquainted with FTP using the browser, let's visit an FTP site. Start up your browser, type the following address into the address bar, and press Enter.

ftp://sunsite.doc.ic.ac.uk

Addresses, names & numbers

Sometimes you'll see an FTP site address given as a bundle of numbers and dots (an IP address) instead of a name. Instead of **sunsite.doc.ic.ac.uk** you might see **193.63.255.1**. Don't worry about it – they work the same way. You could type **ftp://193.63.255.1** to get to this site.

Once you're connected to the site, you'll see a plain background with a plain welcoming message. (This is how the whole World Wide Web looked until a few years ago!) Scroll downwards in the window and a list of blue hypertext links will come into view. In true Web style, the blue text is clickable and will lead somewhere else. To the left of each hypertext entry you'll see either **Directory** or a set of figures. The word Directory indicates that this is a link to another directory (like clicking a folder icon in Windows); the figures show that the entry links to a file and give its size. Further to the left you'll see the date and time that the file was placed on the computer. On some FTP sites, you might see friendly icons next to the hypertext links – a folder icon for a directory, and a page icon for a file.

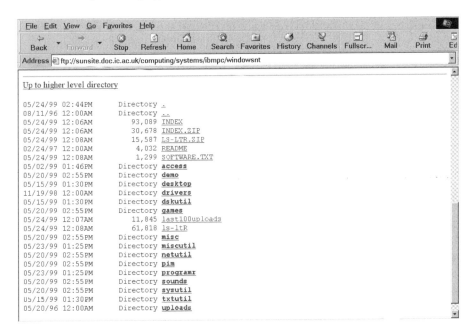

◄ One-click browsing through an FTP site using Internet Explorer.

To get to the directory shown in the screenshot, click on the directory entry **computing**. Explorer will display the contents of the **computing** directory and you can then click on the **systems** directory, followed by **ibmpc**, and then **windowsnt**. From here, you could click on another directory to open it, or click on one of the files to start downloading it. To go back to the **ibmpc** directory you just left, click the text at the top of the list that reads **Up to higher level directory**, or click the second entry in the list that consists of just two dots.

Avoiding the scenic route

BY THE WAY

If you know exactly where you need to go, don't waste time clicking your way through all the directories. For example, to get to the 'windowsnt' directory in the example, type **ftp://sunsite.doc.ic.ac.uk/computing/systems/ibmpc/windowsnt** into the address bar. Better still, if you know the name of the file you want to download from this directory, add **/filename** on the end. Explorer will connect and start downloading the file, but won't waste time showing you the FTP directory.

Keep a look out for files called **Index**. These will tell you something about the site you're visiting, and give a list of all the files on the site or in the current directory (depending on the individual site – some give more detail than others). As you can see in the screenshot, there are two Index files. One is a text file that you could read in any word processor or in your browser's window; the other is a *compressed* version of the same file (indicated by its **.zip** extension and much smaller size) and needs a program like WinZip to decompress it, which you'll learn about in Chapter 12. It's well worth grabbing Index files to read offline: they usually include a brief description of each file to supplement the rather cryptic filenames you see listed on the screen.

Private Sites & Anonymous Sites

To gain access to any FTP site you have to log in, just as you do when you connect to your IAP or online service. Some of these sites are *private*, and you'll need a username and password to get access. For example, another business might allow you access to their site in order to upload information or files rather than sending them by e-mail. If you create your own Web site and upload the files by FTP, you'll have a username and password to prevent anyone else having access to your directory and tampering with your Web pages.

Heading straight for the pub

Many anonymous sites will give free access only to certain areas; some directories will be 'roped off' and you won't be allowed into them. Keep a look out for a directory called **pub**, which will contain all the files and subdirectories available to anonymous visitors.

Many other sites are accessible to the public, and anyone can log on and delve in. These are known as *anonymous* sites, because the system doesn't need to find out who you are before letting you in. To access these sites, you'll log in with the username **anonymous** and give your e-mail address as the password. Using your browser, this is handled automatically and you won't be prompted to enter anything. Using an FTP program, as you'll learn in a moment, you just click a box labelled **Anonymous** to have the details entered for you.

Why would I want to upload files?

If you've logged in anonymously you won't be able to upload any files. The main time you'll want to do this is when you or your company's Webmaster create your own Web site, and have to copy the files to your access provider's Web server. You'll learn more about doing that in Chapter 24.

Using A 'Real' FTP Program

So if the browser can cope with FTP, why would you want to use anything different? Quite simply, a 'real' FTP program is custom-built for the job. With a few minutes' practice, it's actually easier and friendlier to use, and it can usually connect to an FTP site faster than your browser can, speeding up the transfer of files that you download. It also gives you more information about the progress of downloads from FTP sites than your browser does. Finally, it will let you upload files as well as download them which, at the moment, browsers can't do.

First you'll need to grab a copy of an FTP program, and three of the best are listed below. For the rest of this chapter we're going to assume you're using FTP Explorer, but don't worry if you're not: all three programs have very similar features.

▶ **FTP Explorer.** A neat program for Windows 95 and later, shown in the next screenshot and found at **http://www.ftpx.com**.

▶ **CuteFTP.** No more cuddly than the others, but every bit as good. If you choose to use this program for longer than 30 days, head for **http://www.cuteftp.com** to register it.

▶ **WS_FTP Professional.** One of the most popular programs, despite the dull name. You can download an evaluation copy from **http://www.ipswitch.com**.

Setting up FTP Explorer couldn't be easier: when you first start it up, you'll be asked to enter your e-mail address, and that's it. A dialog box will appear to ask if you'd like some 'sample profiles' to be created, and it's worth clicking the **Yes** button: this puts a list of useful FTP sites just a couple of clicks away, and you'll see this list in the next window that opens, the **Connect** dialog box.

If there's a particular site you want to visit and you know you'll only want to visit it once, you can cancel this dialog, and use the Quick Connect option instead. Click the toolbar button with the lightning flash, type the URL of the site and click **OK**, and FTP Explorer will try to connect you.

GOOD QUESTION

Can't I use the FTP program in my Windows directory?

Well you could, yes. But it's like nailing jelly to the ceiling. It's an MS-DOS program with an unfriendly set of commands, and takes a lot of very precise typing. We'd give it a miss.

The more practical way of working is to create a new 'profile' for the site. This can be saved so that you can use it again in the future (rather like Internet Explorer's **Favorites** menu). As an example, let's set up a profile for the SunSite FTP site we visited earlier using the browser. In the **Connect** dialog box, click the **Add** button and follow these steps.

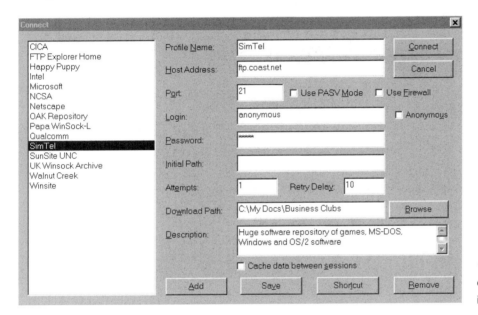

◄ Creating a new connection profile in FTP Explorer.

1 In the **Profile Name** box, type any name that will help you recognise the connection to this FTP site in future.

2 Type the address of the computer you want to connect to in the **Host Name/Address** box

3 If you're visiting a private site, type your logon name in the **Login** box and your password in the **Password** box.

4 In the **Initial Path** box, you can type the path to the directory you want to see after connecting. If you leave this blank, you'll arrive at the root directory.

5 In the box marked **Download Path**, you can type the path to a directory on your own computer that you want any files to be downloaded into. This directory will be selected for downloads every time you connect to this site.

6   Click **Save** to add this new profile to the list on the left. In future you can click the **Connect** button on the toolbar to see this dialog box again and click Connect to visit it. For now, as the dialog box is already in front of you, click Connect and FTP Explorer will dial up (if necessary) and try to connect to the site.

FTP and the online services

BY THE WAY

The major online services will also let you transfer files by **FTP**. In AOL, use the keyword **ftp**; in CompuServe, use the Go word **ftp**. In either program you can click on the big **Internet** button on the main desktop and choose FTP from the next menu.

Exploring the contents of the FTP computer is as easy as exploring your own hard disk: use the tree structure in the left pane to select directories and open directories, and view their contents in the right pane. Select the file or files you want to download and click the Download button on the toolbar to copy it to the directory you entered into the **Download Path** box. A small dialog box will keep you posted on the transfer progress. You can also drag and drop files from FTP Explorer's main window to your desktop or elsewhere to download them. If you find an Index or text file that you'd like to read immediately rather than store, right-click it and choose the **Quick View** option.

Which mode should I use?

GOOD QUESTION

Most FTP programs give you a choice of two modes, **ASCII** and **Binary** (FTP Explorer has buttons marked A and B on its toolbar for this). ASCII mode can only be used to download plain text files and will do so faster than Binary mode. But since text files tend to be small anyway, the time difference is negligible. It's simplest to stick to Binary mode for everything, unless you come across an FTP server that insists on using ASCII mode for its text files.

Uploading files is just as easy as downloading them. You can click the Upload button on the toolbar and choose one or more files from a standard file dialog, or simply drag them from one of your own directories and drop them into FTP Explorer's main window. You can also drag folders into this window and the folder will be uploaded along with its contents. To create a new directory on the server, right-click on a blank area in the main window, choose **New** and **Folder**, and type a name. You can then just double-click this new folder to open it and start copying files into it.

Finding The Stuff You Want

The big trick with FTP is actually to locate what you're looking for. There may be dozens of directories, all containing more directories, and the structure may not always be as intuitive as the way you structure your own hard disk. Let's look at several things you might want to do, and come up with some solutions.

▶ If you know the name and location of the file you want, type it into your browser's address bar, or type the path into FTP Explorer's **Initial Path** box and look for the file when the directory's contents are shown.

▶ If you know the location of the file you want, but not its name, visit that directory and either 'Quick View' or download one of the Index files which should give a short description of each file in that directory.

▶ If you don't know the location of the file (or the location you were given is wrong), but you know its name, there are several options. One is to see if it's listed in an Index file, another is to use your browser to visit FTP Search at **http://ftpsearch.ntnu.no/ftpsearch**. Type the name of the file into the **Search for** box and click the **Search** button. (If FTP Search doesn't do the trick, a similar search at **http://www.snoopie.com** may yield different results.)

▶ Directory names tend to become more specific as you dig deeper. For example, if you were looking for e-mail programs, start in the pub directory, and from there you might find a 'computing' directory, which would lead you to 'software', then 'Internet', then 'e-mail'. If the pub directory has an Index or Readme file, grab that first – it may contain a listing of all its subdirectories and an explanation of what each contains.

3

USING THE INTERNET

In This Part...

SHAKING THE SOFTWARE TREE

In This Chapter...

▶ **Unravel the mysteries of shareware, nagware, and postcard-ware**

▶ **Explore the top software collections on the Web**

▶ **Organise your directories and simplify your life**

▶ **Compressed archives and software installation**

▶ **Viruses, file types, and the Top 5 file viewers**

The Internet is knee-deep in software, and much of it is free. You can find just about any type of file you want, from word processors to personal organisers. And with just a single click, you can download them and start using them immediately.

The Internet is reckoned to be the software supply-line of the future. Within a few years, we'll be purchasing and downloading all our software over the Internet, and programs will update themselves automatically when newer versions and improvements become available. In fact, Windows 98 is one of several major products to provide this 'self-updating' facility via the Web already. One bonus of this is that software should become much cheaper and more readily accessible by removing the middleman and the need for flashy packaging.

Shareware, Freeware, Everyware

Every piece of software you find on the Internet is something-ware, and the two terms you'll come across the most are **freeware** and **shareware**. Freeware is easily explained – it's free! If you like it, you keep it, no questions asked. However, there are usually a few limitations: the author will usually retain copyright, and you won't be allowed to sell copies to anyone.

GOOD QUESTION

Why is 'freeware' free? Doesn't it work?

Freeware is often as good as an equivalent product you'd pay for. For many programmers, the reward comes in knowing that their creation is being used and appreciated. On a more fundamental level, perhaps, the administration involved in collecting money from all over the world takes up a lot of time that could be more enjoyably spent programming something else!

Shareware is an economical method of selling software that bypasses packaging, advertising and distribution costs, resulting in a much cheaper product for us and a much easier life for its author. In fact it is the most successful type of e-commerce on the Net. The most important benefit of the shareware concept is that you get the opportunity to try out the software before you buy it, but the understanding is that you should pay for it if you continue to use it beyond the specified trial period (known as **registering** the software). In return for registering, you'll normally receive the latest version, and you might be entitled to free upgrades as they become available. Apart from shareware and freeware, there are a few more terms you'll come across in reference to software.

Term	Meaning
Postcard-ware	Instead of paying for the software, you send the author a picture-postcard of your home town.
Nagware	A type of shareware program that nags you to register it by regularly displaying a little 'Buy Me' dialog box that has to be clicked to make it go away. Only money can stop it doing that.
Crippleware	The software is crippled in some way that prevents you making full use of it until you pay, usually by removing the options to save or print anything you create with it. Sometimes more formally referred to as save-disabled.
Time-limited	You have full use of the program for a set period (usually 30 days) after which the software won't run until you enter a valid registration number.
Alpha versions	These are very early versions of a program which may (or may not) be unreliable, but are released to anyone willing to try them. The author hopes that you'll report any problems you find so that they can be fixed. Unless you're a very experienced computer-user, avoid any software labelled as an alpha.
Beta versions	Later, and usually more stable, versions of a program than alphas, but still not regarded as a saleable product. You might prefer to wait a little longer for the finished article.

Most of the software you download will include several text files that you can read in a text editor such as Windows Notepad or any word processor. Keep a lookout for a file called **Readme.txt** or **Register.txt** that will tell you about any limitations of use, provide installation details, and explain where and how to register the software.

Software can take a while to download from the Internet: typically 10 minutes for a 1Mb file using a 56k modem. However, if you compare the length of time taken in tying up the machine plus the cost of your phone bill with the time costs of travelling to and waiting in a shop or ordering by telephone, the business advantages and immediacy speak for themselves.

Where Can We Find Software?

The best places to find software are all on the World Wide Web. Most of the software sites use a directory layout from which you select the type of software you're looking for, browse through a list of software titles and descriptions, and click a link to start downloading the file you want. Within your business you're probably already using one of the popular office suites such as MS Office or Lotus Smartsuite; but for non-mainstream applications you could do a lot worse than look up one of the many software sites to see if they have just the piece of software you need. Here's a quickfire list of some of them.

JARGON BUSTER

Mirror site

The most popular Web sites are those that give something away, and software are sites are top of that list. If everyone had to visit the same site, that server would slow to a crawl and no-one would be able to download anything. So exactly the same collection of files is placed on other servers around the world to spread the load, and these are called *mirrors*. When you get a choice of sites to download from, you'll usually get the quickest results by choosing the site geographically closest to you.

▶ **Tucows.** The definitive site when you want to find Internet applications for Windows. Tucows has mirror sites all over the world, but visit **http://tucows.cableinet.net** for a good, responsive connection in the UK.

▶ **Download.com.** One of the best sites for software of all types, located at **http://www.download.com**. This has a keyword search facility to help you track down a particular program by name, or find a type of program.

▶ **WinFiles.com.** An excellent site providing all kinds of software for Windows 95 and later, found at **http://www.winfiles.com**.

◀ Navigate the WinFiles.com site by clicking icons instead of dull hypertext links.

Apart from directories of software, there are a number of other avenues worth exploring. If you visit **http://www.yahoo.com/Computers_and_Internet/Software/Shareware** you'll find a long list of links to shareware pages, most accompanied by useful descriptions. Or go to one of the search engines mentioned in Chapter 7 and use the keyword **software** or **shareware**. If there's a particular type of program you're looking for, such as an appointments calendar, try searching for **freeware shareware +calendar**.

BY THE WAY

Shareware news by e-mail

If you want to keep up with the latest shareware releases, hop over to **http://www.shareware.com/SW/Subscribe/?swd**, type your e-mail address into the box, and click the **Subscribe** button. Every week you'll receive an e-mail message listing the most popular downloads at Shareware.com and details of the latest arrivals.

Downloading – Set Up Your File System

If you plan to download a lot of software, it helps to create a few directories first to keep things organised. When you click a file to download and choose to save it to disk, the browser will ask you to choose a directory to save into. In the same way that you save your word processed documents in a particular folder – usually a subdirectory of 'My Documents', you should create a special area for Net downloads on your hard disk. That way you won't have extraneous files dotted around wherever they happen to end up.

Many of the programs you download will be compressed (see below) and if you create a folder especially for these compressed programs they will be easier to find and delete once you have installed the contents.

As with all the other work on your computer system, a key element for any business is in being organised and this applies to your hard disk as much as to your filing cabinet.

What Are Compressed Archives?

If you wanted to send several small packages to someone through the post, you'd probably put them all in a box and send that for simplicity. An archive works in a similar way – it's a type of file that contains other files, making them easy to move around on the Internet. Most of the software you download will consist of several files, including the program itself, a Help file, text files that tell you how to register, and so on. Downloading a single archive that contains the whole package is far simpler than downloading a dozen separate files one at a time. Before you can use the files in the archive they have to be extracted from it.

Most archives are also *compressed* (just as when microfiche was introduced to replace rooms full of filing cabinets). Files can be squeezed into these archives so that they take up much less space – sometimes only a few per cent of their original size – which means that downloading an archive will be a vastly quicker job than downloading its constituent files individually. When you extract the files from the archive, they'll be automatically uncompressed at the same time.

There are a few different types of archive, but all are easy to handle, and you'll be able to recognise them by their icons, shown in the following screenshot.

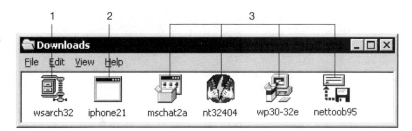

◀ Archive files are easy to recognise by their icons.

1 A ZIP archive – these files have the file extension **.zip**. You'll come across a lot of these, and they may contain just one file or many. You'll need a special program to extract the files from a ZIP archive, and the best of the lot is called WinZip (shown in the next screenshot). You can download it yourself from **http://www.winzip.com**. It's very easy to use, and includes good Help files. (If you have the Plus! 98 add-on to Windows 98, these archives will appear as Compressed Folders – a folder icon with a zipper down one side. You can simply double-click these to open them, just like any ordinary directory, rather than using a separate program.)

2 This is an MS-DOS self-extracting archive with the extension **.exe**. Copy this file into a directory, double-click it, and its contents will be extracted automatically and placed in the same directory.

3 These are all types of self-extracting archive, also with the **.exe** extension, but they're even easier to use than 2. Double-click the file's icon, and everything should happen automatically. The files will be extracted, the setup program will run to install the software, and the program should then delete the extracted files to clean up any mess it made.

GOOD QUESTION

What is a 'file extension'?

A group of three (or sometimes more) characters at the end of a filename, preceded by a dot. For the file **readme.txt** the extension is **.txt**. The extension tells you and your computer what type of file it is, which determines what type of program is needed to open that file.

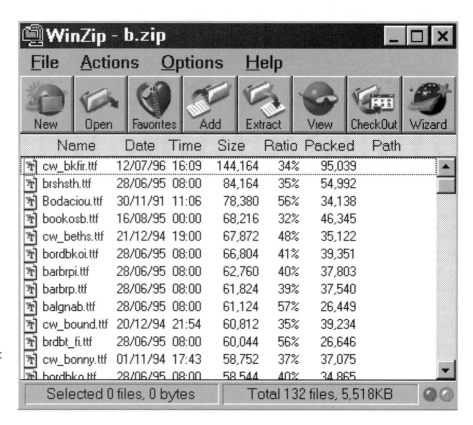

▶ View and extract the contents of an archive using WinZip.

There are several other types of archive, and they'll get a mention later in the chapter, but almost every piece of software you download will either be a **.zip** or an **.exe** archive. Archive files don't just contain programs, though – you might find a collection of pictures or icons gathered into an archive, or word processor documents, or sound and video clips. Their portability and smaller size makes them the favourite way to transfer all types of file over the Internet.

Installing Your New Program

Before you start to install any software you've downloaded, your first job should be to check it for viruses. The last thing you want – especially in a business environment – is for your precious data to be corrupted by someone's idea of 'fun'.

The risk from viruses on the Internet is far less significant than some of the hysterical chatter would have you believe. And if you are unfortunate enough to get a virus on your computer, it won't necessarily be harmful – some viruses are jokey little things that do no more than make your computer go beep once a year. But there are others that can make a nasty mess of your system by trashing your files, swallowing your disk space, and filling your memory, and these are definitely best avoided in any business. They're also *easily* avoided.

What is a virus?

GOOD QUESTION
A virus is a small piece of code maliciously inserted into an ordinary program or 'macro', such as within a word processed document. When the program is run, the virus starts running too, and begins to do whatever it was programmed to do. Most viruses can replicate themselves and often invade other programs.

There are two widely used virus-checking programs, and both can be downloaded from the Internet. One is McAfee VirusScan, available from **http://www.mcafee.com**, and the other is Norton AntiVirus from **http://www.symantec.com/avcenter/index.html**. There are many others available, some of which you will find on the cover-mounted discs of popular computer magazines. Which of these you choose doesn't really matter, but what does matter is that you update it every couple of weeks to make sure you're protected from the latest viruses.

So, what sort of files should you scan for viruses? Any file with an **.exe** extension, including self-extracting archives. After extracting files from a ZIP archive, always virus-check any .exe files it contained before you run them. You should also check any documents containing little 'macro' programs such as files created by Microsoft Word or Excel. Files that are simply displayed by a program (such as a picture, video, or plain text file) are usually safe. Virus checking software will tell you if a file contains a virus, and can usually 'kill' any it finds at the click of a button. If you're unsure whether a particular file constitutes a risk, virus-check it – it only takes a few seconds.

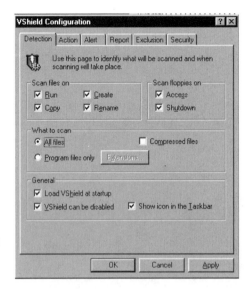

▶ McAfee
VirusScan, a simple
but effective virus
checker.

What you do next depends upon the type of file you downloaded. If it's a
ZIP file, use WinZip to extract its contents to a directory; if it's an MS-DOS
self-extracting file, copy or move it to a directory and double-click it. Next,
have a look in that directory for a file called **install.exe** or **setup.exe**. If you
see one of these, double-click it and follow any onscreen instructions to
install the software. If you can't see one of these files, the software may not
have an automatic setup program. Create a new directory somewhere,
move the files into it, and create a shortcut to the program on your Start
Menu or in Program Manager for easy access. With the new program
installed, you can delete all those extracted files in the original directory.

Close your programs first

BY THE WAY

Before you install any new software, it's a good idea to close any programs
you're running (some setup programs remind you to do this). Sometimes the
setup program needs to alter existing files on your computer while installing the software, and
if another program is running it might not be able to do so.

The other types of self-extracting archive just need a double-click. Usually their setup program will run automatically and you can just follow the instructions to complete the installation. Occasionally, though, you might find one of these that just extracts all the files and leaves you the job of finding the **install** or **setup** file, and of deleting the extracted files afterwards.

What if you don't like the software and want to uninstall it? If the software had its own setup program that installed it for you, the same program can usually uninstall it too – look in its directory for a file called **uninstall.exe** and double-click it. If there's isn't one, run the **install** or **setup** program again to see if there's a button marked Uninstall (if there isn't, click **Cancel** to escape). Failing that, Windows may be able to uninstall it for you. Open **Control Panel**, double-click **Add/Remove Programs** and see if this program is on the list; if it is, select it and click the **Add/Remove** button to uninstall it. If you simply created a new directory and copied the program files into it, you can delete the directory and its contents, and remove any shortcuts you added.

What Are All Those File Types?

So far we've only looked at downloading programs from the Net, but you'll find many different types of file there – documents, sounds, videos, images, and a lot more. Clicking a link to any file will download it regardless of what type of file it is, and your browser will ask you whether you want to open it immediately or save it to disk to look at later (as we discussed in Chapter 6). But first you'll need to be able to recognise these different types of file by their extension and make sure you've got a program that can display them.

The list of computer file extensions is almost endless, but here's a brief description of the file extensions you're most likely to find on the Net. Some of these can be displayed or played by your browser itself, and many are compatible with programs included with Windows.

You'll notice that some of these files have slightly different extensions (such as **.htm** and **.html,** or **.jpg** and **.jpeg**). This is simply because MS-DOS and Windows 3.11 can't work with four-character extensions, so shorter versions are used instead. The file types are exactly the same, so don't worry if some of the files you download have a **.jpg** extension and others have **.jpeg**.

File extension	Description of file type
.arc, .arj	Two older types of compressed archive, similar to ZIP files.
.au, .aif, .aiff, .snd, .aifc	Types of sound file used by Apple Mac computers. Internet Explorer will play these files itself.
.avi	A Video For Windows file. Windows Media Player will play these once they're downloaded.
.bmp, .pcx	Bitmap files. View these in Windows Paint or Paintbrush.
.doc	A Microsoft Word document. If you don't have Word you can use Windows 95's WordPad (although you may lose some of the document's formatting) or search **www.microsoft.com** for a viewer called WordView.
.flc, .fli, .aas	Animation files. Once downloaded, Windows Media Player should handle these.
.gif, .jpg, .jpeg, .jpe, .jfif, .jif	Image files often used on Web pages, and displayed by your browser.
.gz, .gzip	Another less common type of compressed archive.
.htm, .html, .asp	World Wide Web documents (better known as 'pages').
.mid, .rmi	MIDI files, a type of compact sound file. Windows Media Player can play these after you've downloaded them.
.mov, .qt	A QuickTime movie file.
.mpg, .mpeg, .mpe	An MPEG video.
.mp2	An MPEG audio file.
.pdf	Portable Document Format, a hypertext document similar to web pages that can be read only by Adobe Acrobat.
.ra, .ram	A RealAudio sound file.
.rtf	A Rich Text document that can be read by almost any Windows word processor.
.tar	Yet another type of compressed archive.
.txt, .text	A plain text file. Your browser should display these, or you can read them in Windows Notepad or any word processor.
.uue	A UUencoded file (see page 103).
.wav	A Windows wave audio sound. Your browser should play these automatically, or you can use Media Player or Sound Recorder.
.wri	A Windows Write document. Most Windows word processors will display these if you don't have a copy of Write.
.wrl	A VRML (virtual reality) 3D object. (We'll look at virtual reality in Chapter 14.)

The Gang Of Four – The Most Used Aids To Successful Web Use

A few of the file types listed in the table above can't be viewed or played by any program included with Windows – you'll need to find a separate program if you download files of these types. Without further ado, here are our Top 4 recommended accessories and viewers which, between them, will leave you ready for almost anything the Internet can throw at you.

▶ **WinZip** from **http://www.winzip.com**. Apart from handling ZIP files, WinZip will extract files from almost any type of compressed archive, and can also decode UUencode or MIME attachments sometimes included in e-mail messages and newsgroup articles. Don't even stop to think about it – you need this program as soon as you hit the Net!

▶ **Paint Shop Pro from http://www.jasc.com.** A popular image processor that supports all the popular file formats, as well as some of the not-so-popular ones.

▶ **Acrobat Reader from http://www.adobe.com.** PDF is a popular format for documents such as magazines and research literature. Documents can include embedded images and fonts, together with hyperlinks to help you navigate long documents easily. The free Acrobat Reader is designed for viewing these documents only; to create them you'll need Adobe Acrobat, a retail product.

▶ **Real Audio from http://www.realaudio.com.** RealAudio is a streaming audio format. Many Web sites now have RealAudio sound, and some radio stations use it to transmit live over the Internet. This type of program is known as a **plug-in** because it automatically 'plugs itself into' your browser and waits invisibly in the background until it's needed. If you have Windows 98 installed you will almost certainly have Real Audio as part of the suite.

JARGON BUSTER

Streaming

You'll come across the terms 'streaming audio' and 'streaming video'. *Streaming* means that the file will start to play almost as soon as you click the link to it; you can watch or listen to it while it downloads instead of having to wait until the download has finished.

SAFETY ON THE INTERNET

Safety, or the lack of it, is a much-hyped area of Internet life. According to many press articles, as soon as you go online you're going to be faced with a barrage of pornography, your credit card number will be stolen, your personal e-mail messages will be published far and wide, and your children will be at the mercy of paedophile rings.

Of course, articles like these make good news stories; much more interesting than 'Child surfs Internet, sees no pornography', for example. In this chapter we'll sort out what the risks actually are, and what you can do to minimise them.

The Internet has its fair share of sex and smut, just as it has business, motoring, cookery, sports, films, and so on. We're not going to pretend that your staff and kids can't come into contact with explicit images and language, but there are two important points to note. First, you're no more likely to stumble upon pornography while looking for a sports site than you are to stumble upon film reviews or recipes. If you want to find that sort of content, you have to go looking for it. Second, most of the sexually explicit sites on the World Wide Web are private – to get inside you need a credit card. Nevertheless, there are dangers on the Net and, given unrestricted freedom, you could come into contact with unsuitable material. If you're worried about young people accessing unsuitable material there are many software programs around that can identify the actual content of sites to be viewed, such as:

▶ **Net Nanny** from **http://www.netnanny.com**

▶ **CYBERsitter** from **http://www.solidoak.com/cysitter.htm**

▶ **SurfWatch** from **http://www.surfwatch.com**

▶ **Cyber Patrol** from **http://www.cyberpatrol.com**

Is It Safe To Use My Credit Card On The Internet?

It is now possible to buy a wide range of products and services, for business and personal use, over the Internet using credit cards. However, a popular myth about the Internet which will almost certainly be raised by some of your customers is that credit card transactions are risky because your card number can be stolen. To put this in perspective, consider how you use your credit or debit card in the 'real world'. How many people get to see your card number during a normal week? How much time does your card spend out of your view when you use it? The truth is, card numbers are *easy* to steal. It takes a lot more effort and technical know-how to steal numbers on the Internet, and a single card number isn't valuable enough to warrant the exertion.

Making the computer hacker's job more difficult in this department, modern browsers now encrypt the data they send, and most of the Web sites at which you can use your credit card run on **secure servers** that have their own built-in encryption. So when you visit one of these secure sites, enter your card number, and click the button to send it, your number will appear as meaningless gibberish to anyone managing to hack into the system. In fact, credit card companies actually regard online transactions as being the safest kind.

We will be looking at some of the practical considerations of accepting credit cards and other forms of payment on your business Web site in Chapter 19.

How can I tell when I visit a secure Web site?

JARGON BUSTER In Internet Explorer, look for a little padlock symbol in the lower right corner of the browser. In Netscape's lower left corner you'll see a similar padlock which will be 'locked' at secure sites and 'unlocked' at the rest. You'll also notice that the **http://** prefix in the address bar changes to **https://**. More and more shopping sites are becoming secure all the time, and those that aren't usually offer alternative payment methods.

Protection From (Over) Active Web Pages

Another piece of jargon has recently been added to the language of the World Wide Web: **active content**. This is a term covering various types of small program that can be included in Web pages to provide interactivity and animation. The result of active content is that the Web is better able to function as a productivity tool.

There are several programming languages used to create this active content, with names such as Java, JavaScript and Dynamic HTML. The language we're interested in right now is called **ActiveX**. This is an extremely powerful and capable language, but its capability means that it can be used to write programs that get into mischief when they run on your computer. At present, ActiveX programs can only run in Internet Explorer, and Explorer also gives you all the options you need to be able to control what's going on.

JARGON BUSTER

Controls

ActiveX programs are usually referred to as *controls by* Internet Explorer, or sometimes, more vaguely, just *objects.*

Explorer's default settings are going to be fine for most users, but we'll quickly tell you where they are and what they mean. Start Internet Explorer, click on **View | Internet Options** followed by the **Security** tab and you'll see the dialog shown in the screenshot below which lets you choose a security level. If you choose **High**, Explorer will not run any controls it doesn't recognise. The **Medium** setting will give you the choice of viewing or ignoring any unrecognised control. Don't even consider selecting **Low** – however minimal a risk may be, there should never be a time when your business doesn't want protection from it!

▶ Click an option to choose how Internet Explorer handles active content in Web pages.

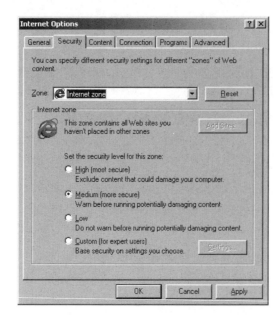

If you choose **Custom** the **Settings** button comes alive and you can choose your own security settings for a variety of active content types. As the caption says, this is an option for experts. Unless you're worried about the possible effects of active content (and you really have no reason to be) it's best to stick with the Medium option.

So how does Explorer know when a control is 'safe'? It uses a system of **publisher certificates**. These certificates are granted to companies by particular authorities, and are automatically installed on your computer when you visit a certified site. When Explorer finds a control on a Web page, it searches for an accompanying electronic 'certificate' that says the control is from a trustworthy company. If it doesn't find one, it will either not run the control, or it will notify you and ask whether or not you want to run it anyway (depending whether you selected **High** or **Medium** security). You can view details of the certificates you've accepted by going to **View** | **Internet Options** | **Content** and clicking the **Publishers...** button.

Code-signing and Authenticode

Code-signing is a term for the technology that makes this whole certification business work, allowing software writers to put a recognised 'signature' into their controls. Authenticode is a trademark for the same technology.

Cookies – Are They Safe To Eat?

They sound cute and harmless, but what are they? Well, they're not particularly cute, but cookies are small text files that are stored on your computer's hard disk when you visit certain Web sites. To take a look at them, open your Windows directory, and then open the Cookies directory you find inside – you can double-click any of these cookies to read its contents in Notepad.

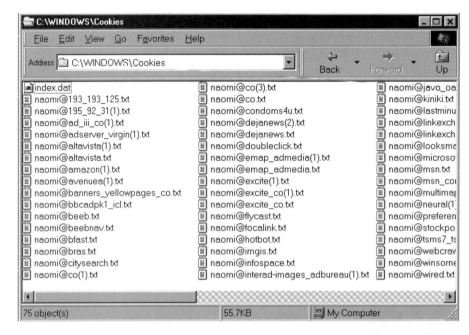

▶ As you can imagine, Naomi cooked up a storm when we started researching this book!

Cookies can serve several uses. They might contain a unique code that identifies you, saving the need to enter a name and password when you visit, and perhaps allowing you to access restricted areas of a site. They're also often used by online shopping sites as a sort of 'supermarket trolley' that keeps track of the purchases you select until you're ready to pay and leave. Sites that rely heavily on displaying banner advertisements for their income might track 'click-throughs', keeping a log of the path you follow through the site and the pages you decide to visit. Knowing a bit about your interests in this way helps enable the site to target you with the type of adverts most likely to get your attention.

Do all cookies have practical uses?

No. You may visit a personal site that asks you to enter your name which it then stores in a cookie. On every future visit, you'll see a message like *Hello Brian; you've visited this page 4 times*. It's pointless, but it's still harmless.

So, are they safe? Yes, they are. Cookies are often misunderstood – they can't be used to read any other data from your hard disk, to find out what software you've got installed, or to pass on personal information. When you visit a Web site, the page doesn't 'search' your hard disk for a cookie; instead, your browser sends the cookie containing the URL of the site as soon as you type in the address or click the link.

The wider question is whether you want anyone using your hard disk as a type of mini-database in this way – it's a point of principle rather than safety. If you want to join the anti-cookie ranks, Internet Explorer can help. Click on **View | Internet Options | Advanced** and scroll down to the section headed **Cookies** near the bottom of the window. Here you can choose **Prompt before accepting cookies** to be given the choice of accepting or rejecting a cookie when a site tries to store one, or **Disable all cookie use** if you want to take a tougher stand against them. Be warned though – some sites just won't let you in if you won't eat the cookie! A more practical method is just to delete the entire contents of your Cookies directory as soon as you've finished surfing for the day.

How Private Is My Company E-mail?

Although e-mail has opened up a whole new avenue for improving communications both within and without the corporate environment, it has by its very nature opened up new dangers that all businessmen should be aware of.

The words 'e-mail' and 'private' don't go together well. E-mail can get you into trouble (and people have got into very hot water from using e-mail where a phone call or a quiet chat would have been wiser). If you're concerned about who could read it, don't write it.

The most obvious problem is that your 'private' messages can be easily forwarded or redirected, or the recipient might simply fail to delete an incriminating message after reading it. But apart from existing on your computer and the recipient's computer, however briefly, the message also spends time on your access provider's mail server and that of the recipient's access provider. Will the message really be deleted from both? And what if the administrator of one of these systems decides to run a backup while your message is waiting to be delivered?

The fact is that you have to reckon on the fact that e-mail leaves a permanent trail behind it, even if you think you have deleted all traces of it.. One company that found this out to its cost is the Norwich Union Insurance Company which, in what has become a notorious case, was ordered to pay £450 000 damages plus legal costs to its competitor Western Provident Association after libellous and defamatory messages were circulated internally on e-mail at Norwich Union. The case – the first time that a company has received damages for being libelled by e-mail – illustrates graphically the fact that e-mailing must be treated with the same degree of caution that relates to the publishing of a story in a newspaper or magazine.

After this particular case, a statement issued by both sides read: 'In the middle of 1995, rumours circulated... that Western Provident was insolvent, in financial difficulty and under investigation by the Department of Trade and Industry. These rumours were disseminated by some of Norwich Union's staff via its e-mail systems with the result that they could be used to the detriment of Western Provident in order to obtain new business.'

WPA's Chief Executive was quoted after the hearing as saying 'People regard electronic mail as a transient medium in that the message disappears into the ether. The reality is that everything you type and send is recorded almost for all time and is available to be reassembled at a later date by the written or spoken word.'

We can all identify only too well with the wish to gain market share and the occasional Friday afternoon banter involving the death of the competition but in this case they went too far.

The moral is clear. You should ensure that your staff do not use e-mail to discuss competitors, potential acquisitions or mergers, or to give information about another firm. In the same way, you should never provide references by e-mail. It is just asking for trouble.

If you really must use e-mail to exchange sensitive messages, you might want to consider using **encryption** to scramble them. Messages are encrypted and decrypted using two codes called **keys** that you type into the encryption software. One is your private key, the other is a public key that you'd hand out to anyone who needed to use it, or perhaps post on the Internet. If someone wanted to send you an encrypted message, they'd use your freely available public key to encrypt it, and then send it off as usual. The message can only be decoded using your private key, and only you have access to that key. Likewise, if you wanted to send someone else a private message, you'd use his public key to encrypt it.

Need more encryption information?

BY THE WAY

The most popular encryption program is called PGP (Pretty Good Privacy). Although unbreakable, it isn't easy to use and you might want an extra program that sits on top and puts a 'friendlier face' on it. Go to **http://home.earthlink.net/~rjswan/pgp** to learn more about the system and the software available.

Moral Dangers

It is an unfortunate fact of Internet life that an increasing area of concern focuses on aggressive e-mails. Within a corporate environment business bullying is now recognised by industrial tribunals as a form of illegal behaviour. Sexual harassment and stalking over e-mail are also growing and you should ensure that your company has a policy made known to every employee that such behaviour will not be tolerated and could even lead to dismissal. In 1995 the oil company Chevron agreed to an out-of-court settlement of $2.2m after four female employees sued the company following a company-wide posting of an e-mail entitled '25 reasons why beer is better than women'. The US may be currently more litigious than the UK, but the principle is the same. If your staff are made aware that every e-mail will be held on a server long after they have been sent, this will, in itself, discourage many people from such behaviour.

FAQS – INTERNET QUESTIONS & ANSWERS

In This Chapter...

▶ **Having trouble connecting to a Web site?**

▶ **How you can keep your e-mail address for life**

▶ **Combat Spam – junk e-mail, the bane for business**

Shifting once again into 'quickfire' mode, this chapter contains a collection of answers to recurring questions, problem fixes, and pointers to more sites offering useful information.

Why Do We Sometimes Have To Start Our Connections Manually?

This is a question that sometimes crops up for users of Windows 95 and later. Windows uses a system called Dial-Up Networking (DUN) to handle your Internet connection, and, in theory, whenever you start an Internet program and try to access a Web site, send e-mail, or whatever, the DUN connection will kick in and connect you automatically.

The trouble is, this works only with 32-bit programs. When you try to do the same with a 16-bit Internet program, it has a look at your system and simply gives up when it can't find an active Internet connection, rather than making one. In some cases you might be able to find a more recent, 32-bit version of the program (or even swap to a completely different 32-bit program if you find this really annoying), but a few programs are still available only in 16-bit form. For these programs you'll have to start your Dial-Up Networking connection manually.

JARGON BUSTER

32-bit and 16-bit programs

This is technical stuff that we don't really need to go into in detail. Suffice it to say that 32-bit programs are newer and built to run on Windows 95 and later, while 16-bit programs were designed for Windows 3.1. Many programs are available in both 16-bit and 32-bit versions so that you can choose the one that will run on your system.

Can we, though, reiterate *once again* that any business that is still using Windows 3.x as its operating system really needs to think very carefully whether the time is not now right to upgrade to a 32-bit system.

Why Is The Web So Slow Today?

There could be several answers to this one. To start with, it may be to do with the time you connect. The Internet is at its quietest (and therefore its speediest) while America is sleeping, and at varying degrees of 'busy' at all other times. You'll normally get a faster response by going online in the morning than the evening. If you're having trouble with just one particular site, you can sometimes get things moving by clicking the link again or, if the page started to download and then stopped, clicking the **Stop** button on the toolbar followed by the **Refresh** button. But if absolutely everything seems unusually slow, try logging off and then dialling up again – this sometimes results in a faster connection.

Why Can't We Open This URL?

When you click a link to a Web page, type in a URL, or even select an entry on your Favorites list, you may not be able to open the page. Either you'll see a plain grey page with the stark heading 'Not Found', a friendlier-looking page that says essentially the same thing, or a dialog box from Internet Explorer like the one shown in the next screenshot. So what went wrong?

◀ This dialog box usually indicates a problem with the domain name in the URL.

Let's take an imaginary URL as an example:

http://someplace.co.uk/food/fruit/peaches/Stones.htm. If you see one of those 'Not Found' pages, the first thing to do is to try exchanging that capital 'S' in 'Stones' for a small 's' and pressing **Enter** (web URLs don't often use capital letters, so it's worth a shot although this is usually more of a problem for users of the Unix operating system than for those logging on in Windows). Failing that, try changing that **.htm** extension to **.html**. Web designers who author their sites using the Apple Macintosh system use

.html extensions rather than Windows' cut-down .htm. If that doesn't work either, it suggests that the document no longer exists. Try deleting **Stones.htm** from the address bar and pressing Enter again, and gradually work your way back, deleting **peaches**/next, and then **fruit**/ until you do find a document on that site – it may contain a link to the (now retitled) page you were looking for.

If you see a dialog box similar to that shown above instead, it suggests that the domain name (the bit following **http://**) is wrong, which is likely to be a typing mistake. In the screenshot, for example, there should be a dot after **bang**. Check the spelling in the address bar, or try altering any part of the domain that you think looks wrong, and pressing **Enter** to try it again.

Of course, it could just be a failure of the server which is hosting the site, in which case there is nothing you can do until such time as it becomes operational again!

GOOD QUESTION

I clicked a link, so the URL isn't in the address bar.

If Internet Explorer can't find the domain and shows this dialog, it won't place the URL of the link you clicked into the address bar. You can get around this by right-clicking the link, selecting **Copy Shortcut**, and then pasting it into the address bar to edit.

Our Connection Crashed During A Download – Have We Lost The File?

The answer to this is a definite 'maybe'! As a mark of how Internet software is always improving, later versions of Internet Explorer will sometimes pick up the download from where they left off. If yours doesn't, or the 'Downloading File' dialog is no longer on your screen, click the same link to the file as if you were starting the download again from scratch. Internet Explorer should find the matching incomplete file in its cache directory and just grab the missing portion.

If We Leave Our Service Provider, Will We Lose Our E-mail Address?

This depends on whether you have registered a company domain name or whether you only have an e-mail address through an IAP (or OSP) itself. Simply speaking, with a registered name (such as **naomi@topspin-group.com**) the IAP will redirect your e-mails to the registered address such that the process itself is transparent to the users. If, however, you are using the IAP's own address as part of your e-mail address – such as **naomi@topspin.demon.co.uk** (Demon Internet being the IAP) – then, of course, you will lose this address if you leave the IAP.

I Suppose Our Web Site URL Will Change Too?

If you took advantage of your service provider's allocation of free Web space to create your own organisation site, you'll find that this generosity comes to a sudden halt if you cancel your account with them. You should have all the files that make up your site on your own hard disk, of course, so you can recreate this site quickly and easily by uploading them to your new IAP's computer. The problem is that your site's URL will change and your regular visitors won't know where to find it.

How Can We Stop All This Junk E-mail Arriving?

Junk e-mail – or Spam mail – got its name from the TV classic *Monty Python's Flying Circus* in which a café had only Spam on its menu. What it consists of is the posting of multiple copies of the same message to different people or the sending of unwanted, unsolicited e-mail. It has become a scourge of the Internet as almost everyone with an e-mail account receives Spam at one time or another.

Some people see it as a legitimate form of mass advertising and others see that the sheer volume of junk mail could bring the Internet to its knees.

The main problems with Spam are that the cost is borne by the recipient who pays for the download time (not a problem in America where Spam originated because of 'free' local calls); the content may not be appropriate for you at all as Spammers are essentially lazy people who have not done their market research appropriately, if at all; and the messages are quite often extremely long, which again adds to the cost.

Whereas this might be thought of as just annoying on a personal basis, within a business time has a cost too. There are, however, some things you can do to minimise the impact of Spam on your business:

▶ **The use of filters to block messages from certain addresses.** When you get a Spam mail, if you enter the originator into your filter (known as Inbox Assistant in MS Outlook), it will delete the original file without downloading it and you should receive no more Spam from that source.

▶ **Send an e-mail to the company's access provider explaining what happened and request that it enforces the small print in its contract with the company that prohibits this abuse of the e-mail system.** To find the source IAP in MS Outlook, open the offending message and go to **File | Properties | Details | Message Source**. AOL forced one of its clients – Cyber Promotions – to pay a 'fine' of $60 000 for breaking the terms of its agreement and the same company was blacklisted by other IAPs.

Could Someone Be Forging Our E-mail?

Yes, they could. It doesn't happen often, but it does happen. It's easy to do, too. Every time you send an e-mail message, your name and e-mail address are attached to its header. When the recipient retrieves his e-mail, these details are displayed so that he can see who the message is from. But how does your e-mail program know what details to enter? When your company e-mail was installed, someone filled in those little boxes on its options page! So, of course, if you go back to that options page and enter something different, those are the details that will go out with your e-mail.

So it's entirely possible that someone could attach your name and e-mail address to a message they send from their computer, and it would be more difficult (but certainly not impossible) to trace it back to them.

Which Of These Sites Should We Download From?

A major conundrum when you're about to download a large file is that some Web sites are just too helpful! You arrive at the download page, and they offer you a dozen different links to the same file. Which one should you choose? Here's a couple of rules worth following. First, discount any links pointing to FTP sites if you can – your browser often takes longer to connect to them, and downloads tend to be slower and less reliable. Second, choose the HTTP link that's geographically closest to you, ideally marked as a UK or European site.

Of course, there's no guarantee that you've found the best link using this method. And even if you have got a fast link, you'll still be sitting there wondering if a different one may have been quicker still! For times like this, there's a nifty little utility called Dipstick, from **http://www.klever.net/ kin/dipstick.html** that's worth keeping handy. Drag the links into Dipstick's window and it will test the speed of each, and then automatically begin downloading from the site that gave the fastest response.

Do We Need A Better Computer For Multimedia?

Multimedia is a sort of ex-buzzword. In 1996, a 'multimedia computer' had all the trimmings, cost a lot more, and was everyone's dream machine. In 2000, however, the word is rarely attached to computers – almost all new computers have a soundcard, CD-ROM or DVD-ROM drive and a capable graphics card, which are the essentials of multimedia. But here's a quick hardware rundown for *good* multimedia:

▶ If your graphics card has 2Mb or more of memory fitted, letting you display more than 256 colours, visual elements like videos and virtual reality worlds will be clearer, smoother, and generally more appealing.

▶ Some of the larger virtual worlds take their toll on both processor and memory: ideally, you should have at least a Pentium 200MHz processor and a minimum of 32Mb RAM, but with the price of computers having dropped dramatically in the past year, this is considered as way below entry level anyway.

▶ The modem matters most. If you are buying a new system it would be madness to consider anything less than 56Kbps.

Do We Need A Lot Of Extra Software?

There are literally hundreds of plug-ins and viewers out there for different types of multimedia file, and you certainly don't want them all! Some, of course, cover the same types of file as others and you can simply choose the one you like best. Others are proprietary programs that let you view a type of file created by one particular company – if this format isn't in wide use on the Web you might prefer not to bother installing the software for it.

GOOD QUESTION

What's the difference between a plug-in and a viewer?

A plug-in is a program that displays a file in your browser's own window by adding capabilities to your browser that it doesn't have already. A viewer is an entirely separate program that opens its own window to display or play a file you've downloaded.

May we make two suggestions to simplify things: first, start with the software that is included on the free CD-ROM that accompanies this book – not only are these some of the best programs of their kind, but you don't have to download them either! Second, go and buy an uninstall utility such as Quarterdeck's CleanSweep: these utilities monitor every change and addition made to your system when a new program is installed so that you can remove all trace of it later if you decide you don't like it.

Explore Virtual 3D Worlds

Virtual Reality is something that's going to get used more and more widely as computers get ever more powerful. Using on-screen controls (often combined with right mouse-button menus), you can select angles from which to view the scene, walk or fly through it, zoom in and out, and interact with objects you find. True VRML files have the extension **.wrl** (although they're often accompanied by a collection of GIF images that form various elements of the world), and you'll need to install a plug-in before you can start exploring. These can be brilliant for businesses like estate agencies where virtual viewing of the plan of a house could save a tremendous amount of time for architects, builders and stage designers who wish to illustrate a development or design concept.

VRML

An abbreviation of Virtual Reality Modelling Language, the programming language used to build these graphical 'worlds'.

In fact, there are many companies also producing proprietary plug-ins for their own brands of 3D world, but most plug-ins are pretty big programs, and the worlds themselves can be slow to download and slow-moving once you start to explore – you'll definitely benefit from a fast Internet connection and a fast processor! That being said, VRML is a whole new experience you've got to try at least once, so grab one of these **.wrl** plug-ins:

▶ **Superscape Viscape** from **http://www.superscape.com.** You'll find a world full of more virtual worlds hosted by Superscape at **http://www.com**.

▶ **WIRL** from **http://www.platinum.com.** A large plug-in which adds a few extra facilities to ordinary VRML. These come into their own when you start exploring the unusually fast and interactive worlds you'll find at the same site.

▶ **Cosmo Player** from **http://cosmosoftware.com**, which also has links to more sites that make great use of VRML.

▶ A virtual flight through Tokyo.

GOOD QUESTION

Where can I find other plug-ins?

You'll find the best selection at Tucows, a great site for Internet-related software. Head for **http://tucows.cableinet.net/window95.html** and click the **Plug-ins** heading.

Meet The Multilingual Web

After visiting some of the sites we mention in this book, you might have realised that there's something funny going on – Web pages are getting pretty clever! A Web page is just plain text with a few extra little codes added to set colours, fonts and layouts, insert pictures, and other simple stuff. But there are now several different computer languages that can be used to write programs that will run on (or from) a Web page – any program that you can run on your computer's own operating system can now be inserted into a page. Here's a brief introduction to the three that are used the most:

▶ **JavaScript.** The simplest of the three to learn and use, constructed specifically for use on the Web. This is a *scripting* language – it's written in plain text (although it looks very technical), and slots straight into the page with no extra files needed. This way, the script can run as soon as the page arrives at your browser, making it an ideal language for flashy effects (one of its main uses). To see some JavaScript pages in action, head for **http://home.netscape.com/people/jamie/jwd_javascript_qs.html** and follow the links you find there. Or see Javascript in action on our own business Web site **http://www.topspin-group.com**.

▶ **Java.** This is related to JavaScript, but Java programs can run on any computer and aren't restricted to the Web. Java can be used to write full-blown applications such as word processors and databases, though one of its main uses is still in creating interesting ornaments for Web pages – referred to as **applets**. Java programs have to download to your computer before they can run, which they do automatically when you arrive at the page. The program files have the extension **.class**. Check out some of the applets created by Sun, the designers of Java, at **http://www.javasoft.com/applets/js-applets.html**.

Strange, but true

BY THE WAY

Java? Strange name. The basics of this programming language were thrashed out during many long sessions in a coffee house in Silicon Valley, so the language was christened with the American slang for coffee.

▶ **ActiveX.** This is a Microsoft language known, until recently, as OLE. ActiveX programs are known as **controls**, and are normally downloaded to your system when you visit pages that contain them. Once there, they remain in place so that any other pages you visit containing the same control can be viewed instantly without waiting for the same components to be installed again. To see some of these controls in action, visit Microsoft's ActiveX Gallery at **http://www.microsoft.com/activex/gallery**.

THE WEB – YOUR GUIDE TO ONLINE INFORMATION

In This Chapter...

▶ Keep up to date with the *latest* news

▶ Let the Net push information to your staff

▶ Probe the pertinence of online politics

▶ Move in to the morass of money markets

▶ Trust the Net for transport and travel

▶ Ease the search for corporate entertainment

▶ Use electronic TV and radio guides

It's a paper world. It doesn't matter what you want to do, nine times out of ten you have to consult a piece of paper before you can do it. Want to keep up-to-date with the news, check availability of flights, check out trade events, select shows for corporate entertaining? If you do any of those things, you've probably got a mountain of guides, catalogues, brochures and local newspapers, and many of them are probably out of date! Alternatively someone has to spend hours on the phone in one of those interminable queuing systems. So let's go paperless…

Read Your Newspaper On The Web

Everybody in the world wants news of one sort or another. And, of course, there's plenty of it – it's being made all the time! But where traditional newspapers can print no more than two or three editions per day, Internet news services can be updated hour-by-hour, or even minute-by-minute. Unexpectedly, it's the broadsheets that made it to the Internet first, and they've made a surprisingly good job of combining content, style and usability.

Let's take The Times (at **http://www.the-times.co.uk**) as an example. As soon as you arrive at the site's front page you're faced with clear icons that take you to the Times ' newspaper' itself, The Sunday Times, the Education

▶ Click any hypertext headline at The Times to read the complete article, or browse some of the stories from earlier in the week.

supplements, and the Interactive Times. The latest news stories are easy to find: selecting the link to The Times presents summaries of the major stories in several categories, with hypertext links to the related articles if you'd like more detail, plus TV and weather. In true newspaper style, you'll also find links to classified ads, cartoons, crosswords and puzzles, and more hypertext-linked news summaries by visiting the Interactive Times.

So, it's all there, and it's easy to navigate. But what makes it better than an ordinary paper version? In a word – storage! The Times and all the other online newspapers are building ever-expanding databases of news articles. With a quick keyword search, you can retrace the path of a news story you missed, track down articles on, say, a particular aspect of business, or find out what made headline news on any particular day. And, of course, it's a lot easier to save and store useful articles on your own hard disk for future reference than it is to keep a stack of newspaper clippings!

Information swapping

BY THE WAY

Although access is usually free, when you first visit many online newspapers and magazines, you'll have to fill in one of those infamous registration forms, giving your name and address, and a few other details. Provided you're honest, this provides useful marketing information for the publishers which they regard as a fair exchange for the information they're giving you.

Newspaper	URL
The Times	http://www.the-times.co.uk
The Financial Times	http://www.ft.com
The Daily Telegraph	http://www.telegraph.co.uk
The Guardian	http://www.guardian.co.uk
The Independent	http://www.independent.co.uk
Wall Street Journal Europe	http://www.wsje.com
The Economist	http://www.economist.com
International Herald Tribune	http://www.iht.com

So where can you find your favourite paper online? Perhaps it's one of these:

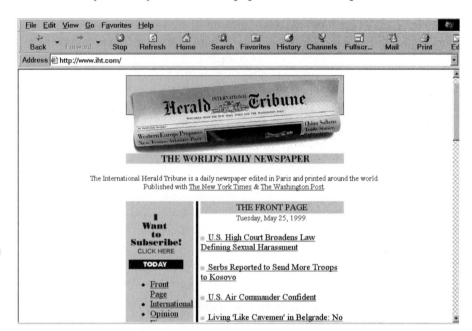

▶ For the latest business news, you might want to try the International Herald Tribune site.

Some journals charge for their service. For instance, the Wall Street Journal Interactive Edition costs $49 per year after the first fortnight's free trial.

Create Your Own Custom News Page

Your business probably has several newspapers delivered every day, and perhaps weekly or monthly trade journals of some sort. But do you actually read them all from cover to cover? The chances are that you glance at the headlines or the contents page, read the articles that interest you, and ignore the rest. Wouldn't it be great if there was one publication you could buy that gave you just the stories that appealed to you, and left out everything else? Well there is. In fact there are quite a few, and you don't even have to pay for them!

The 'personal page' is a recent arrival to the Web, but more and more online publications are building the option into their sites. If you find a trade journal that covers one of your areas of business or interests, take a look around the site to see if they offer the service, or send them an e-mail to ask if it's in the pipeline.

The best of Times

The Times Internet Edition lets you create a personal news page by choosing the types of business, arts, national and world news that interest you. Click the **Interactive Times** icon, then **Personal Times**, and check the boxes to specify your preferences.

One of the best non-specialist services is provided by Yahoo, the Web-search directory, and it takes only a couple of minutes to set it up. Point your browser at **http://edit.my.yahoo.com/config/login**, and click the **Sign Up Now** link. On the next page you'll have to fill in another of those registration forms – although this is a free service, Yahoo needs to assign you a unique username and password to personalise your page. When you come to choose these, make sure you pick something that's easy to remember; it doesn't matter if it's easy for someone else to guess, since there's no security issue at work here.

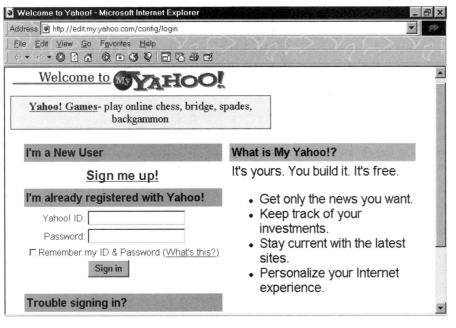

◀ Login at My Yahoo and read your own customised news pages.

As soon as you've filled in the registration form you can start to build your own page by checking boxes in all sorts of categories covering news, financial markets, sports and leisure activities, and then click the button to confirm your choices. From now on, whenever you visit the main My Yahoo page at **http://my.yahoo.com** you'll see your personalised page. Your browser should store and send your username and password to save you the bother of entering it every time, but make sure you keep a note of it somewhere, just in case!

Hot News Delivered Straight To Your Desktop – A Push Too Far?

In the busy hurly-burly of modern life, the personal news page is a great time-saver, but you still have to visit the Web site to read it. By today's technological standards, that's much too inconvenient! Instead, the news could come to you, and it should do so without even being asked.

One of the latest Internet innovations is **push technology**. In a nutshell, any type of information you could find on the Web can be sent straight to your desktop – text, pictures, sounds, video, and more – without the need for surfing and searching. You simply install the software, set a few preferences, and then sit back and watch as your personalised content streams down the line to you.

JARGON BUSTER

Push technology

This is also known as *server push*. Instead of your computer 'pulling' the information from the Web when you ask for it (*client pull*), the Web literally 'pushes' the information down the line to you and keeps it updated automatically. With 'push', you can already receive regularly updated world news, sports results, weather, share prices and leisure information.

Despite the fact that this was developed by computer technicians, some business aspects were overlooked. Even if you set up your own personalised news and information to be pushed to you, when you receive additional emails and messages on a regular basis they can become the straw that breaks the camel's back as far as workload is concerned.

As this technology has been around for more than two years now (old in Internet terms) it has become increasingly clear that people resent information being pushed at them. However there are some facilities that it offers which are invaluable. Suppose for instance that you run a car dealership. Instead of the manufacturer posting his prices on his Web site for you to look at – which involves your logging on regularly to check for any changes, wouldn't it be better if the price changes were 'pushed' to you whenever they occurred? A number of car manufacturers do just that.

In order to make sure that you don't have an uprising on your hands you must plan any implementation of 'push' technology within your business very carefully. Only the absolute essentials should be 'pushed' and the staff should all understand why you are bombarding them with this information. This ties in with the move away from top-down hierarchical business structures to the more people-rich flatter structures of tomorrow's company.

The main program that everyone is talking about for personalised news is called the PointCast Network (shown in the next screenshot), and you can download it free from **http://www.pointcast.com**. Its main drawback, at the time of writing, is its heavily American content, but the company is working hard at providing localised coverage. Getting up and running with PointCast is quick and easy – just follow these steps:

1   After you've installed the software, click the **Personalize PointCast** button that appears, and fill in a few personal details. You'll also have to select the method you use to connect to the Internet.

2   Next, you'll see a set of tabbed pages. These are PointCast's channels, following a television metaphor. On the first page you can select up to eight channels to follow from a list of categories such as news, weather, sports and lifestyle. Clicking the other tabs lets you fine-tune the content to be included in each channel.

3   Finally, click **OK**, and PointCast will automatically download and display the information you selected. You can move between channels using the buttons on the left of the screen, and click on tabs and stories to view them on the right.

GOOD QUESTION

Why is the PointCast service free?

PointCast makes its money through advertising, and a small area of the PointCast viewer is devoted entirely to displaying ads. The software works on the assumption that you'll be so tempted by an advertisement that you'll click on it to visit that company's Web site.

You can change the content to be downloaded and add or remove channels any time you want to, by clicking the **Personalize** button to return to those tabbed pages. Selecting the **Options** button lets you choose whether PointCast should dial-up and retrieve information automatically at regular intervals: you can set the frequency of these updates, or (as a more practical method for UK users) bypass the automation and just click **Update** when you want to download the latest batch of news. By default, PointCast also sets itself as your screensaver – if you haven't read the Help file, this could come as a bit of a shock, especially if you don't know how to override it!

If you're less than enthralled at the prospect of American content, Yahoo offers its own alternative. After setting up your My Yahoo personal page, click (as described on page 201) the **News Ticker** link to download and install Yahoo's own software. This is a small program which attaches itself to the Windows taskbar or the title-bars of your applications, and scrolls the contents of your personal page through its compact viewing area. A word of warning, however: unless you particularly need real-time share prices or news headlines, having a News Ticker on your computer screen is liable to drive you to distraction in a very short time!

In a similar way to PointCast, the News Ticker can be set to grab updates regularly by itself. If you see a headline that looks interesting you can click it to open your browser and download the related story, and (of course!) you can type keywords into the ticker to start a Yahoo search.

All-in-one news & weather

BY THE WAY

If you prefer to find your news, weather and sports information all in one place, go to **http://www.yahoo.co.uk/headlines** and choose news headlines or summaries in several categories together with UK, Irish and worldwide weather forecasts.

Open for Business, Gov?

Whether you want to explore 10 Downing Street, delve into government archives, read press releases and speeches, or check electoral and constituency information, the Internet has all the resources you need. But let's start with the obvious – if you're interested in politics, the first place you'll want to visit is one of the major parties' own Web sites, so consult the table below and pay them a visit.

Political Party	Web Site URL
Conservative Party	http://www.conservative-party.org.uk
Green Party	http://www.greenparty.org.uk
Labour Party	http://www.labour.org.uk
Liberal Democratic Party	http://www.libdems.org.uk
Plaid Cymru	http://www.plaidcymru.org
Scottish National Party	http://www.snp.org.uk

If you're more interested in the real workings of government, head for the Government Information Office at **http://www.open.gov.uk**. This is a huge site containing thousands of documents and articles, but there are several choices of index to help you find your way through it. The easiest method is probably to click on **Functional Index** and scroll through the alphabetical list looking for keywords relating to the subjects you want. Another well-organised and informative site is the Central Office of Information at **http://www.coi.gov.uk/coi/depts/deptlist.html**, which provides a comprehensive hypertext list of the many government departments on the Web.

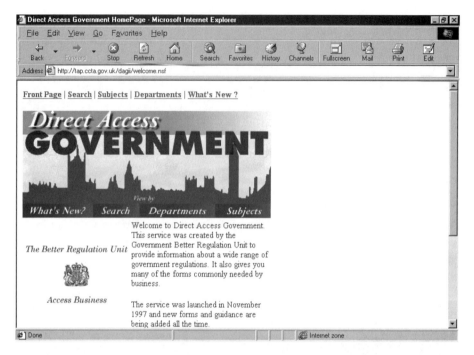

▶ Part of the **open.gov.uk** site is dedicated to business users...

For all the government departments and official bodies on the Web, one of the most useful and informative sites is actually unofficial. The British Politics Page (**http://www.ukpol.co.uk**) is a veritable goldmine that includes local and national electoral information, constituency lists and analyses, local government details, and a useful Basic Information section. There are even lists of MPs' personal Web pages and e-mail addresses!

Oil The Wheels Of Government Yourself

Getting your voice heard in the crowd isn't easy, but if you can find a few people who share your views you can improve your chances. The newsgroups provide one of the few resources available anywhere that allow you to discuss your political opinions with people from all over the world. Indeed, they could even act as a springboard for launching pressure groups and petitions, or organising online 'conferences' using programs like NetMeeting and PowWow. The three major political newsgroups in the UK are **alt.politics.british**, **alt.politics.europe.misc** and **uk.gov.local**, but you'll find many more under the **uk.politics** hierarchy. Or try filtering your list of groups by entering **politic** to find related groups in other Usenet hierarchies.

As an alternative to the newsgroups, a recent newcomer to the Web is UK Citizens Online Democracy at **http://www.democracy.org.uk**. This is a discussion site that works in a very similar way to the Usenet groups: you can post your own messages by e-mail, and follow discussion threads by clicking on hypertext links. The major difference between this site and the political newsgroups is that UK politicians actually take part in the discussions. In the words of the site itself: 'We hope it will become a place to make things happen – an exciting new interface between the public and politicians.'

Tracking Money Markets Online

There's little that can't be done on the Internet, but a few things cost money, and share dealing is one of them. Because the sort of information you're looking for is worth money, you'll have to whip out your credit card and cross palms with silver before you can trade or even reach the information you're after. Nevertheless, there's no shortage of companies on the Internet holding their palms out expectantly, and one of the better known is Electronic Share Information (ESI) at **http://www.esi.co.uk**. Alternatively, nip along to The Share Centre at **http://www.share.co.uk** – this is a good, easy-to-follow site for new investors, offering plenty of straightforward help and information on the financial world.

For stock-market information which is updated every couple of hours look on **http://www.ft.com** but you'll have to subscribe. If futures are your business then Liffe has an information site which you can find on **http://www.lce.co.uk**. And if you need to have real-time figures, a good place to start is at **http://www.yahoo.co.uk**.

For small businesses where the divide between business and home is more of a grey area you can get information on a wide range of money matters at MoneyWorld (**http://www.moneyworld.co.uk**). This is a huge and popular site covering every aspect of personal finance you can imagine – homebuying and mortgages, ISAs, unit and investment trusts, and company performance, to name but a few. You can read the London closing business report, check the FTSE 100 and 250, view regularly updated world prices, and consult the glossary to find out what everyone's talking about. And if MoneyWorld doesn't have the information you're looking for, you'll find links to other financial services and organisations in the UK and abroad.

▶ Yahoo contains links to loads of share prices and financial news.

Money talks

Usenet has several newsgroups for people wanting to give or receive a little financial advice. A good starting point is **uk.finance**. For more international input, try **misc.invest** and **misc.invest.stocks**, and have a look at the **clari.biz.stocks** hierarchy.

Online newspapers such as the Electronic Telegraph, mentioned earlier in this chapter, also provide city news and prices just like their disposable counterparts, but if you need in-depth analysis, you can find the major finance publications on the Web too, although you'll have to subscribe for some of the more in-depth information.

Financial scandals

BY THE WAY

The financial world has caught a few hands in a few tills in recent years. To find out more about financial scandals and the unfortunate owners of those hands, hurry along to **http://www.ex.ac.uk/~RDavies/arian/scandals**.

Go Away On Business

If you have to travel on business and need to find a hotel, you could wander over to Expotel at **http://www.expotel.co.uk** where you can choose between several search options such as a region of the UK or Europe, or the name of a particular hotel, or select from a list of forthcoming events and conferences to find accommodation in the right area. Every hotel listing gives prices and facilities and **First Choice** and **Second Choice** buttons: choose two hotels and set one as your first and one as your second choice, and then click the **Book hotel choices** button to fill in the online booking form.

Having found a hotel you could even check them out by viewing their own Web site where you might find more detail than is listed in Expotel's pages. For instance, if you had to go to a conference in Harrogate and wanted to stay in a small hotel Expotel would make some recommendations. However, their detail is basic. But if you found Foxfield through a search engine (**http://www.foxfield.demon.co.uk**) you would see pictures of the rooms, special menus, information about corporate facilities and much more.

If you can't find what you're looking for at Expotel, try the UK Hotel & Guest House Directory at **http://www.s-h-systems.co.uk/shs.html**. This uses handy clickable maps to pinpoint a location (along with ordinary hypertext links for the geographically challenged!), and gives all the important information about each hotel along with photographs. Booking isn't quite as nifty here – you send an e-mail which is delivered to the hotel as a fax, and they should then get in touch with you to confirm the details – but this does have the advantage that you can use the Net to reach as yet un-Netted hotels.

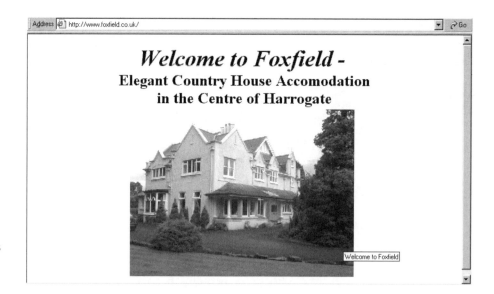

▶ A warm welcome awaits the corporate traveller.

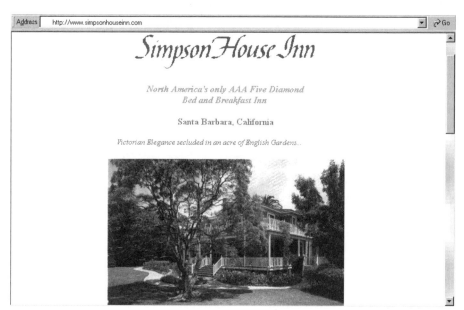

▶ Victorian elegance in delightful Santa Barbara.

If you are travelling abroad, there are myriad sites devoted to travel and accommodation. If you want to go to California, for instance, you could use a search engine to look for the words ' hotel' and, say, ' Santa Barbara' whence you might be directed to **http://www.simpsonhouseinn.com**, the only five diamond AAA B&B in the US.

For sorting out those travel arrangements within the UK there's one magical Web site that handles the lot – the UK Online All-In-One page, at **http://www.ukonline.co.uk/UKOnline/**. From here, you can access dozens of European and international airlines and airports and check flight information; find the departure and arrival times of trains and National Express coaches; and book seats on planes, trains and buses. If that isn't enough, you can hire a car from one of four companies, check the latest news on motorways, London traffic and the tube, track down a taxi or look at the World Ski Report. And that's barely skimming the surface of this huge site! You could also try the RAC at **http://www.rac.co.uk** for live traffic news, another hotel finder, and a route planner.

How About A Night At The Opera?

Or not necessarily an opera. Perhaps a ballet, an ice show, or the latest Andrew Lloyd Webber musical? Many companies nowadays are looking for different kinds of corporate entertainment. Make your way to What's On Stage at **http://www.whatson.com/stage** and run a simple search for live entertainment in your area. You can select a single region or the whole of the UK, and choose one of 17 categories of stage show if you're looking for something in particular. You can even confine your search to particular dates, or use keywords.

Finding more culture

UK Calling (at **http://www.uk-calling.co.uk/frame.html**) is a very attractive site with extensive listings in eight categories including Classical Music, Art Galleries, Dance, Theatre, and Leisure Breaks. Or visit Events Online (**http://www.eventsonline.co.uk**) and click a category, or browse by event type or venue – whatever is most suitable for your corporate occasion.

When you've found a show you'd like to see, you can usually book tickets online. Click the **Order Tickets** link, fill in the form, and you should receive e-mail confirmation.

▶ Stage show news, reviews and easy ticket booking at What's On Stage.

Let's Talk About The Weather

The weather is officially the most popular topic of conversation in the UK, probably because we have so much of it. And the Internet has a solution to that centuries-old problem, *What can you do when there's no-one around to listen?* Just start up your newsreader and head for **alt.talk.weather** or **uk.sci.weather**.

To become a real authority on the subject, though, you need to know what the weather's going to do next. One option is to consult the online newspapers mentioned above, but here's a better one: head for **http://weather.yahoo.com/Regional/United_Kingdom.html**. On this page you'll find a hypertext list of almost every town in the UK – click on the appropriate town to see a five-day local weather forecast. (You might want to add the forecast page to Internet Explorer's Favorites menu or create a shortcut to it on your desktop for quick access.)

For more detailed weather information, including shipping forecasts and meteorological data, visit the Met Office site at **http://www.meto.govt.uk/ sec3/sec3.html**.

◀ The weather site – but make sure you update your cache for the latest details.

Portals – The Best Of The Web In One Place

Don't forget what we said in Chapter 7 about **Portals**. If you want to find a representative selection of accessible information and e-commerce on a wide variety of subjects and products, portals are some of the best sites to access.

BUYING & RESEARCHING ONLINE – THE CUSTOMERS' VIEW

In This Chapter...

▶ **See how to buy goods online**

▶ **Order your groceries online**

▶ **Slippage problems**

▶ **Recruitment online**

▶ **Research online**

The Internet connection is starting to look like the Swiss army knife of the 21st century. In the last few chapters we've seen how the Net has tools to replace the telephone, answerphone, radio, TV, newspapers and magazines, fax machine, and a fair bit more. With the arrival of secure transmission on the Internet, you can use your credit card at thousands of online 'cyberstores' offering most of what your business can possibly need to buy. It's quick, it's easy, and in this chapter we'll look at some of what's on offer out there in cyberspace.

Are These The Stores Of The Future?

So will everyone be shopping in cyberspace in the next couple of years? Definitely not. However, there are many exceptions, starting with items such as computers and computer peripherals and stationery, as well as 'FMCG' items, including books and CDs, for example.

Despite the fact that you'd think that there are few purchases you'd want to make without first seeing, touching and testing the goods, there are many items which are now selling well online. For instance, during the second half of 1998 the rise of online auctions selling anything from really expensive items to the equivalent of the contents of a virtual car boot sale indicates that people just like to have the access to buy – in their own time. The initial resistance to something that was unfamiliar appears to be crumbling as people begin to regard their access to the Web as part of everyday life.

How Do We Buy Stuff Online?

Before we look at the advantages to business of selling on line – or e-commerce as it has come to be known – let's look at it from the consumers' point of view; after all, they are your customers. (We'll be examining the business benefits of e-commerce in the next chapter.) In almost any cyberstore you visit, the routine will be pretty much the same. The names of the options and buttons will vary of course, but most online stores use a readily-accepted 'shopping' metaphor that involves placing items in a basket or trolley and then going to the checkout to pay.

As an example, let's buy a laptop computer from Dell using what is probably the most successful online shop in the world, showing increases in worldwide online sales for instance from $6m per day in December 1998 to $8m per day in March 1999.

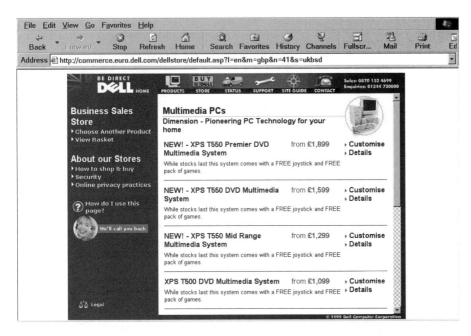

◀ The site offers a wide selection of computers.

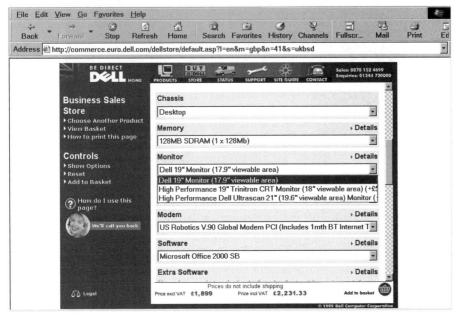

From Dell's front page we can choose a link to take us to the type of computer we are interested in purchasing. Every part of the computer can be configured online to your own specification and a running total of the costs is shown at the bottom of the page.

By clicking on the *Add to Basket* button to the right, we can add as many items as we like to our virtual shopping basket. Once we have added everything we want, the next stage is to look at the contents of the basket to check that it represents what we have ordered.

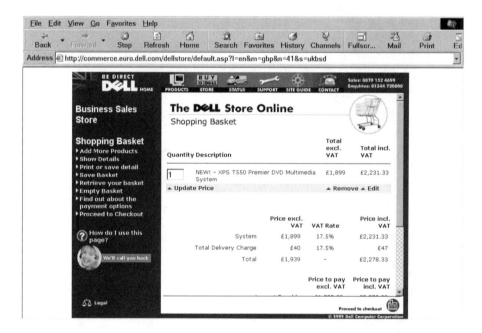

▶ The basket shows the contents of our order, together with VAT added automatically.

You will notice that we can also, if we want, save the contents of the shopping basket and come back later to retrieve it. But for now, assuming we want to go ahead with the purchase, we can choose the option to *proceed to checkout* where we will be asked for our credit card details.

At this point you will notice a little padlock symbol appears at the bottom of the browser.

This indicates that we have entered a secure zone where details of credit cards and transactions are secure from prying eyes. The final step, which commits us to the transaction, is to click on **Submit Order**. At this point, all these details are passed to Dell and one last page appears giving us a reference number for the order and an e-mail address to contact in case of queries.

Take A Tour Of The Shopping Malls

Where do you go when you want to find the biggest selection of stores and merchandise quickly and easily? A shopping centre, of course! The theory behind shopping malls in your local town translates perfectly to the Internet – not only are all your favourite stores within easy reach, but while you're there you might be tempted to do a spot of 'window shopping'.

One of the first shopping sites to hit the Internet was a UK site called BarclaySquare. It's still there, and still growing, at **http://www. barclaysquare.co.uk**. The site is hosted by Barclays Bank, which gives it the pulling power to attract some of the best-known high street names in the country.

The entire site is secure, well-designed, and above all, easy to navigate. Its one drawback is that if you're looking for a particular item, it isn't always easy to find when browsing through store names.

The trouble, though, with shopping malls is that most people go onto the Net to find something specific, rather than wander aimlessly through a virtual store looking for ideas of things to buy. So these online malls really come into their own when you are looking for a birthday or Christmas gift or if you are searching for a generic item rather than a particular brand of something.

▶ And a cash till rang in BarclaySquare.

Groceries In Cyberspace

Ever the innovator, the Tesco superstore chain was the first in the UK to add a new dimension to Internet shopping: the online supermarket. At the time of writing, this service is available in only a few areas, but it seems a certainty that the entire country will soon be covered, and your own area may be served already.

To find out, visit **http://www.tesco.co.uk**, click the Internet Superstore link and follow the registration process. If your postcode falls into one of the areas covered you can order your groceries online, pay by credit card and arrange delivery for a time that suits you best.

Shopping for your groceries online is something that is likely to become ever more popular. Pity the poor manager at Sainsbury's, however, who designed the idea behind their online shopping experience. If you want to see what goods they have and order something quickly and easily, then forget it. Sainsbury's insist that you physically visit the store and build your own catalogue before you can order anything online. So what's the point? Surely the whole ethos of shopping on the Web is that you can do just that without having to leave your office or home.

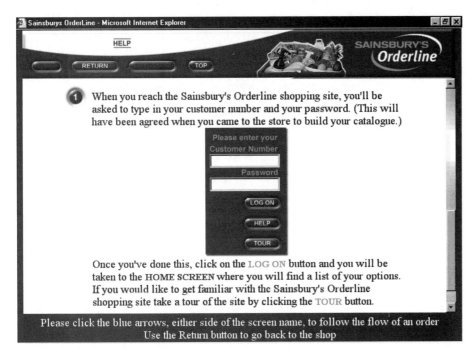

◀ Sainsbury's – for determined online shoppers only!

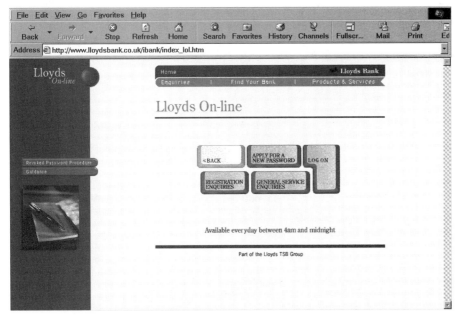

◀ Online banking requires patience if you're a Lloyds Bank customer.

These follies are not just committed by supermarket chains. Even the High Street Banks have their foibles. Try getting any online information from Lloyds Bank in the wee small hours and you'll be met with a notice that tells you that you cannot log on between midnight and 4am. Once you do manage to log in during the day, however, you'll then find it takes two weeks to get your registration sorted out.

What this indicates is that businesses are trying to get up-to-date and provide online services; but having to try and integrate them with lugubrious legacy systems – which have grown up over a number of years – shows up the amount of work that needs to be planned for when trying to take a quantum leap.

Recruit Online

Just as you can shop for goods and services on the Web, you can also shop for staff! We all get involved in the employment market at some time in our lives, and it's usually a frustrating, hit-and-miss ordeal. Although the Internet can't give you any firm guarantees, it can give you access to resources that your 'unwired' competitors don't have, and it puts all these right on your computer desktop to take some of the drudgery out of job-searching and self-promotion. The converse is equally true. If you are searching for new staff, it could be that putting an advertisement either on your own or on someone else's site could be one of the most cost effective methods of recruitment you will encounter.

If you're offering full or part-time work, two UK sites are head and shoulders above the rest, between them offering many thousands of vacancies. PeopleBank, at **http://www.peoplebank.com**, gives its services free to jobseekers, but makes a charge for companies posting their search requests . WorkWeb (**http://www.workweb.com**) splits its vacancies into 25 searchable categories, and also provides support services for jobseekers and information about employment agencies.

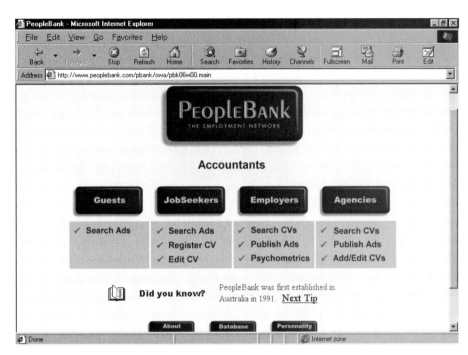

◀ Pick a category
and then search
PeopleBank's
database.

Newsgroups provide valuable methods of 'meeting' potential employees, employers, collaborators and customers. If you filter your newsgroup list with the word **job** you'll see a number of useful groups, including **alt.jobs**, **alt.jobs.overseas**, and an entire **uk.jobs** hierarchy that includes **uk.jobs.offered** and **uk.jobs.wanted**. It's well worth looking for newsgroups catering for your particular profession or vocation too: sometimes the only way of letting the right person hear of your particular job is to be on 'speaking terms' with the type of people who can point you in the right direction.

Research On The Internet

Whatever you do in your daily business life, the Internet can help, whether it is the purchase of products and services or the harvesting of information. It can provide you with vital reference and research materials; supply information about complementary or competing companies; enable you to work or study from home; and put you in touch with other users working in a similar field.

Put simply, the Internet is the most comprehensive market research tool you can get. And as you get used to using it you will find ways to get through to your target information quickly. We, for instance, were doing some market research for a client who knew very little about his competition and had no idea where to start getting information. Within a very short time, putting in keywords identifying the products he manufactured, we found out his major global competition who had a Web presence, their full product ranges, their pricing structure including discounting, as well as their geographical and target markets. This greatly augmented the information gleaned from other market research processes and enabled the strategic marketing plan to become extremely focused.

Resources For Business

There are myriad other sites of particular use for business research, and it would be well nigh impossible to list every type in this book. Many of the Business Links, TECs and Chambers of Commerce have their own sites offering local business advice.

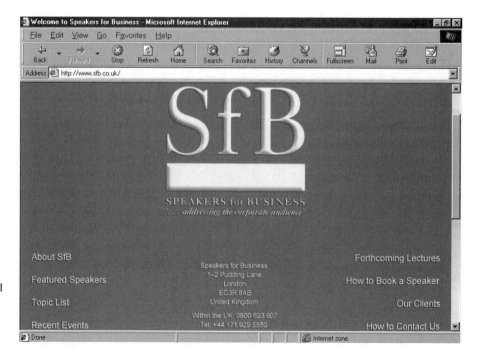

▶ The SfB site will help you make your corporate event a success.

If you have a particular business need – such as finding a speaker for an event – you can't do much better than to visit Speakers for Business on **http://www.sfb.co.uk**. For the big boys there is the CBI at **http://www.cbi.org** but the Institute of Directors site at **http://www.iod.co.uk** is, disappointingly, still in need of some work and customer focus.

Accounting firms and consultants such as Arthur Andersen and KPMG are highly visible on the Web and can be found easily through the search engines. Banks too have not been slow in appreciating the benefits of a Web presence. Some, though – as we have already seen – have sites of questionable value to the visitor, but we'll leave you to make up your mind about them.

An enterprising bunch of entrepreneurs north of the border has a gathering of like-minded individuals called the Entrepreneurial Exchange. They can be found at **http://www.entex.co.uk**.

And help for UK-wide entrepreneurs can also be found at **http://www. entrepreneurs-exchange.com**.

4

BUSINESS ON THE WEB

In This Part...

BUSINESS OPPORTUNITIES & APPRAISING WHAT OTHER PEOPLE ARE DOING

In This Chapter...

▶ **Can you virtualise any aspect of your current business?**

▶ **Can you reduce your overheads if you use the Net?**

▶ **Do you need an info site?**

▶ **Do you need an online shop?**

Just think about it – how do you do business? Has your organisation grown by traditional processing methods or can you see yourself embracing the new technology? With a little capital to spend and a learning curve can you hike your business up to a faster way of working which also saves on administration costs and reduces the likelihood of error by a one-touch input system? Depending on your line of business, you can do all of these things using Internet technologies.

Take, for instance, a trade that in Britain alone is worth £30m per year. Bull semen may not be the most glamorous commodity, but dairy farmers have traditionally had to look through bulky catalogues in order to end up with the right type of calves they need for their milk herds. Now the majority of artificial insemination companies are turning to the Internet as the perfect way to get their product to market. Bull semen, it appears, is highly variable and dairy farmers get different prices for their milk according to whom they supply. Some look for maximum milk yields, whilst others have to watch the fat or protein content of the milk. By typing their requirements into an online database they can exercise their preferences regarding all these variables in addition to cow stature, rump angle, udder depth, teat placement and a whole lot more besides. The time saved on searching for different criteria from catalogues is enormous. In short, dairy farmers are all agreed that the Internet is likely to play an ever increasing role in their particular business sector.

Virtualise Your Business And Fly!

The only real way to benefit from the Internet is to take a step back and make a few objective assessments of your current business and what you can do with it to virtualise it. The best way to do this is to get an idea of what other people are already doing and, having grasped the concepts of a virtual business, develop your own ideas beyond that.

This, then, is a great opportunity for us to whizz through a number of business scenarios, get the picture as to who is doing what, reckon how it could relate to our own businesses and also – and here's the added value – make judgements as to what works and what doesn't, as well as what we like and what we would not go looking at again.

What is a virtual business?

GOOD QUESTION

Basically, a virtual business is one that has no physical shops, that has its 'shop window' solely on the Internet, and that trades on the Internet. The offices and back office systems exist to support the virtual trading site and the focus is on marketing the Internet presence.

So how do you virtualise? It is quite difficult to change what you, your staff, suppliers and customers are all used to and it feels like a leap of faith. However, let's look at some of the types of business organisations that can have some, or all, of their parts virtualised and then we'll look at the potential benefits. There are two types of business which are ripe for virtuality:

▶ businesses that can operate with credit card sales and mail or ship the products; and

▶ information providers.

Mail Order Sales...

... for instance, products that are well known to their target market and can be selected in sizes, colours and styles. You know the frustration of finding a shop doesn't have your particular size in stock when you happen to want it? Take underwear, for instance. For women whose bra size is 36B, there are loads of styles and plenty of colours. But if you're a 40DD or a 32AA where should you turn to get more than a few choices?

Try Bras Direct at **http://www.brasdirect.co.uk** – a virtual company that sells underwear on the Net. They have a display which enables you to search for different items of underwear, view them on a model, change the colour and style, select, change your mind, reselect, put in the shopping basket and pay through secure payment methods – all online.

File Edit View Go Favorites Help

Back Forward Stop Refresh Home Search Favorites History Channels Fullscr... Mail Print Ed

Address http://www.brasdirect.co.uk/bras/default.asp

▶ Should we be surprised that some 40 per cent of the visitors to Bras Direct are men?

GOOD QUESTION

Can your products be selected by parameters like colour, size and style ?

Whether you sell bras or artists' equipment, perfume, shoes or stationery, your business could be more virtual than it is – or you could set up a new virtual business altogether.

Business Travel

What about a flight ticket? Do you want to go to a travel agent or phone up and wait? Neither. Just look online. After all what is an airline selling and what does it have to provide for people to be able to buy its products? Things like timetabling, availability of seats, discounting, cost and online booking. And, of course, a loyalty card which enables the process to be completed faster.

Look up Virgin Airways at **http://www.virginairways.com**. This again offers the details that the customer wants. It is entirely customer-driven and has to provide information quickly and easily or the visitor will get off their site and on to another vendor's site without so much as a by-your-leave. Other travel sites are also available and it would be a good idea to compare them and see which of them work and which do not. Just take a look at the following and judge for yourself by asking the questions that you would normally ask if you wanted to find out flight times, availability, cost and so on:

▶ British Midland Airways (**http://www.britishmidland.co.uk**)

▶ British Airways (**http://www. britishairways.com**)

▶ EasyJet (**http://www.easyjet.co.uk**)

▶ Go (**http://www.go-fly.co.uk**)

Well, what did you think? Which site made it easiest for you to get all the information you needed to be able to make a judgement and book a flight?

Books & CDs

This kind of product needs to be searchable by a variety of different routes – author, publisher, title, hardback, paperback, fiction, non-fiction etc. in the case of books; and artiste, label, category (classical, country, rock, jazz, opera etc.) in the case of music. Take a mosey across to these sites and see what you think of them:

▶ Amazon   **http://www.amazon.co.uk**

▶ Bookstore   **http://www.bookpages.co.uk**

▶ CDNow   **http://www.cdnow.com**

▶ HMV   **http://www.hmv.co.uk**

The sheer breadth of stock available, combined with the amount of information that can be provided, could make the difference between visitors coming back to the site and never visiting again.

So you can see that if you can visualise a virtual warehouse, then there is a potential for explosive growth with minimum overhead costs. The other immediate advantage is that you would not have to keep a large stock. Indeed, you may well be able to organise it so that your suppliers supply you on a single item basis so you therefore only need to order products from suppliers when you have received orders from your customers – together with their payment. Wow! Positive cash flow, as many of the virtual book stores and CD suppliers know only too well.

Information Sites

Many sales sites attract visitors in the guise of being an information provider. For instance, in the next chapter we'll be looking at a nice little site, based in Yorkshire, that belongs to a mattress cover company. It provides loads of information which is pertinent to the products – and also to the reasons why those products may be purchased. It is very much a case of *who* needs our products and *why* they do. So information is given regarding not only the medical reasons why the products might be a good thing, but also the legal reasons – and these are substantiated by references to guidelines and specific requirements within the industry – all of which are viewable on the site. This is a good way to get visitors to come to the site. See **http://www.sidebottom-covers.com** and you'll see what we mean.

Pure information sites are offered by bodies like the British Helicopter Advisory Board who are a non-profit trade association within the UK helicopter industry. You can find them on **http://www.bhab.demon.co.uk**. They're not trying to sell you anything (except, perhaps membership of their organisation) but they can reduce their administrative overheads by posting the answers to questions that they are asked day in and day out, over and over again – their FAQs.

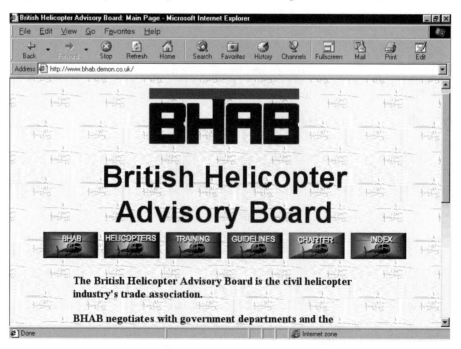

▶ If you like whirlybirds, you'll love this site.

Time-Warner offers a great site that we first found in May 1997 when 'Virtual Chelsea' was launched at the Chelsea Flower Show. As well as listing all the Royal Horticultural Society Events, benefits of membership and so on, it hosts discussions on particular and extremely specific plant ailments which keeps interested parties revisiting the site again and again. Why not dig up **http://www.vg.com**?

Yet others take a totally different stance from what you might expect. Whereas you anticipate Disney to be, well, *Disney*, you don't necessarily expect solicitors to do much more to their site than list their services, say what good eggs they are and keep their client list and extra-curricular activities fairly quiet. After all solicitors were only allowed to have entries in the telephone book in bold type about 15 years ago, and after years of having to look restrained, the legal profession burst into coloured letterheads and even *advertised*. These old fashioned mores have been abandoned by many legal firms now, and one of the best legal Web sites in the UK can be found at **http://www.olswang.co.uk** which is not only a joy to behold, but where there is a wealth of information.

◀ Where are the stuffy legal briefs? No moths on this site!

The site includes not only information on what the practice does, but has fun elements from their Home page onwards. This Home page has a seasonal change in the top left-hand corner, where in summer a rabbit lollops down a hole in verdant grass under blue skies; and in the autumn the change is to a scene of a squirrel collecting cob nuts and burying them under a leafless tree.

Within the site there is information, not only about the firm and its lawyers, but also sections on 'Clients alive', 'Thinking about a career in the law', 'Not just grey suits', 'Diary' and 'Publications'. They are high profile and we first found their Web site when they were acting for the Guardian against Jonathan Aitken regarding that Paris hotel bill... So whilst Olswang are promoting themselves and their professionalism by stating what they do and who they do it for, they are also well into touchy–feely-land, with their human faces showing through with their humour and fun and explanations of what the people do when not working.

One of the most elegant online sales must be computer software and upgrades. Microsoft has for several years offered upgrades online. The sheer ease of getting your software this way has to make this the perfect Web sale. However, because of the size of the files involved, the download times can be horrendous depending on the speed of your modem and the less controllable telephone connection. We'll be covering the practical and business considerations in the next chapter.

DRAW UP THE BATTLELINES (BUT AVOID THE PITFALLS)

In This Chapter...

▶ **Sort out your objectives**

▶ **Involve your staff**

▶ **Understand some of the security concerns of Web trading**

▶ **Ponder some of the multi-currency issues**

▶ **Methods of e-payment**

▶ **Explorers beware!**

E-commerce, or e-business, is taking off. As you read in the last chapter, you can now buy practically anything over the Net and not a day goes by without a new cyberstore opening its doors to new customers.

The problem is that at present there are relatively few British companies using e-commerce software. The statistics are instructive. At the time of writing, around 54 per cent of SMEs and 33 per cent of small companies in the UK are online. Online purchases have increased dramatically in the past three years to the point where, world-wide, some 43 million users are ordering with their credit cards. Predictions, of course, vary, but some estimates put the amount of world-wide e-commerce to have reached $400 billion by 2002, primarily in the business-to-business market.

GOOD QUESTION

Where do these statistics come from?

There are very many research organisations specialising in Internet statistics. Some charge for their information, whilst others make it available for free. Most specialise in the American model since that's where e-commerce is really in its element. But for a world-wide view you can't do much better than make your way to the Graphics Visualization and Usability Centre at the Georgia Institute of Technology site at **http://www.cc.gatech.edu/gvu/user_surveys/** .

So You Still Want To Sell Online?

The Internet offers businesses a new way of reaching markets previously undreamed of. At first glance it all seems too good to be true. Apart from the fact that your potential customer base is simply enormous, there's no need for a physical presence in Tampa, Tenerife or Timbuktu if you're based in Torquay and your channel is immediately responsive to change, as long as you still produce the jelly beans and keep the customers happy.

Most businesses with a Web presence will be on the lookout for new clients, even if they are still trading within the same geographical area over which they have already been trading. The real question is, how will you deal with new clients who come to you from all four corners of the globe? It's a truism that your Web site is one of the guardians of your brand image and reputation, and you certainly don't want to upset potential clients before they have even started to have any dealings with you.

The fact is that having a Web presence is not an easy way to reach foreign markets, and when you start thinking about dealing in different currencies, in different languages, with customers used to different customs, in territories with different tax regimes, it might seem a wonder that anyone bothers at all!

But let's move into positive territory. Despite the apparent pitfalls, and the learning curve for everyone in your business, we think it's more a case that you simply cannot avoid going online if you are to survive and prosper in the new millennium. This chapter will devote itself to the many factors that you need to consider for business success.

Let's go back to basics. What are you trying to achieve? Why should you have a website at all? The primary reason has to be both to save money and to make money, whilst providing excellent customer benefits. That is, after all, the whole point of being in business.

BY THE WAY

It is a truism that on the Net, no-one knows how big your business really is. Big or small, you can compete on an equal footing with the major corporates – and better still, because of their in-built inertia you could even have the edge on them.

Who will you aim your site at? Surely not any old passing Tom, Dick or Harry? For a successful business Web site, it is imperative to know who your audiences are and to target your site ruthlessly at them.

Do You Aspire To Being Upwardly Mobile?

Because of the opportunities offered by the flexibility and ever-improving technologies of the Web, every business can begin with a Web site that it can cope with – knowing that it can always grow that site to incorporate new capabilities and cope with new demands as the business grows.

It may well be that you will move into the realms of inclusive computing, to the extent that you will want an internal Internet (an Intranet) – or even a private Network that outside suppliers and distributors can access (an Extranet). We'll be taking a look at the business case for these in Chapter 21, but we'll stick with the business case for the Internet for now. They all use Internet technologies which is the basis for inclusive computing so let's learn to walk before we fall over our feet in the rush!

As you move along the upward growth path it is vital that – just like any other business function – you stop to review progress *on a regular basis*. You don't have to change anything when you have a review, but you *do* have to review it. After all, you reviewed the situation before you decided to have a Web site at all. Didn't you?

Marshalling The Troops

Change is, for some people, extremely difficult. It brings threats – as well as opportunities – and, as with any other change in your business, it is important to win the hearts and minds of all your troops. There are many aspects of a prospective Web site to which all the different people in the organisation can contribute. For instance, when you go through the process of identifying all the elements which have to be on the Web site you will have a much smoother ride through the whole Web site development if you get everyone together to define the elements. (We'll be looking at this in detail in the next chapter.)

It will be fairly obvious which of your people would hold the different responsibilities that having a Web presence carries. The act of owning responsibilities at an early stage, with the enthusiasm that a new project can bring, lends its own rewards. The tasks include:

▶ There will be a need to update the site on a regular basis. Who will do it?

▶ Agree review format and frequency.

▶ Analyse the effectiveness of the site and feedback.

▶ Who should be the Webmaster?

▶ Who will be responsible for the text?

▶ Who will have final sign-off?

Don't forget to take into account:

▶ colour-blindness of visitors

▶ dyslexia of visitors

▶ ease of navigation around the site

▶ effectiveness of text and graphics

If you intend to sell online you must also attribute responsibility for all commercial aspects.

BY THE WAY

Hooked by his own bait?

We'll mention no names, but there is the cautionary tale of a salmon farmer in Scotland who thought the Web would be a great way to increase sales across the UK. He wasn't prepared for the fact that smoked salmon is a great favourite amongst the Arab nations, and he was totally unprepared when orders started rolling in from the Middle East for his products. The tale has a happy ending, though, because he had the presence of mind to e-mail his potential new customers saying that he was still working on the export and pricing details of his salmon products and that he would get back to them in a couple of days. As you can imagine, he had a very busy weekend!

Choosing & Registering Your Domain Name

We have made many references throughout this book to the fact that any business needs to think carefully about the image it is projecting, both through its company stationery, the way it answers the telephone… and how it is likely to be perceived on the Web.

Choosing a domain name is not something that should be rushed. Like the naming of any company, it is something you will be living with for some time and not something that is easily changed.

So let's reiterate. When choosing your domain name the choices facing you may not be as simple as at first they appear. At the first level you are likely to want one of these:

- ▶ www.mycompany.co.uk

- ▶ www.mycompany.com

- ▶ www.mycompany.accessprovider.co.uk

- ▶ www.accessprovider.co.uk/~mycompany

or variations on these themes.

However, you may well find that your company name has already been taken by someone else. What then?

This is where your fellow workers can be invaluable in brainstorming suggestions that could be suitable. Think laterally. Do you have to have your name in there? For instance, the British Greyhound Association has their Web address as www.thedogs.co.uk. Very simple, very memorable and quicker to type out than their full name.

OK. So you've decided on the killer name to end all names, but how do you tell if it has already been grabbed? Go to **http://www.internic.net** to investigate names with *.com*, *.org* or *.net* endings, or **http://www.nic.uk** for *.co.uk* endings.

You can also use these sites to register your chosen name or you can register through your chosen IAP, although sometimes they may charge a small premium for the privilege.

Taxing Times

It should come as no surprise that the majority of e-commerce sites are US-based. Pricing and taxation are relatively simple affairs and, as the whole world is happy to deal in US dollars, the currency problems are minimal as well. Perhaps not so obvious is the fact that, of the US online stores, the majority are based in Delaware. This is explained simply by the fact that here there are no sales taxes, so prices to the consumer are proportionally cheaper. Sure, there is the little matter that something should be paid sometime between goods being despatched and being accepted by the buyer, but in practice this rarely happens and the whole process is very difficult to police.

Translate this process to Europe, though, and things are very different. There are 15 different currencies and a whole heap of local taxes and, although the

Euro is now riding in on its white charger to save Europe from the Babel that is its system of commerce, in the first instance it simply means that pricing will become even more complicated as currency triangulations will have to be set up. Eventually, though, the Euro should help to simplify world commerce at all levels.

Er, Pardon Monsieur?

But what about dealing in foreign languages? What's the point of trying to deal with the rest of Europe if none of your staff speak French or German, let alone Flemish or Greek? True, there are now some software packages that will translate English to and from a variety of European languages – and quite well too, in some cases – but then what will you do about local laws which specify what you can and cannot offer over the Net?

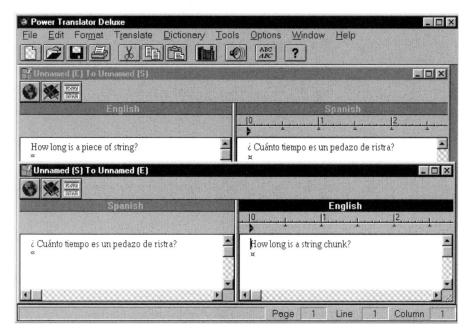

◀ ....and it looked so easy too!

And what do you do if your site is viewed in France where language laws dictate that your site *must* be able to be viewed in French if you intend to trade there? The argument used is that if you are trading in France then you should also have a French language version or you will be in contravention of French law. Of course, trading *from* the UK with French customers is another matter!

The fact is that, whatever you want to do with your site, you should stick to a few simple basics and first establish your ground rules for playing the Internet commerce game.

▶ Should your site be priced purely in sterling, or in a more widely acceptable currency such as US dollars or Euros; or should you go for some of the more popular currencies as well – say Yen and Francs, for example?

▶ If trading in multiple currencies, how will you cope with shifting exchange rates? How often will you update your prices?

▶ Will your customers pay mainly by credit card and, if so, will you explain that the final amount on your customers' credit card bills may vary according to the prevailing exchange rate?

▶ How will you cope with packaging and delivery charges, and will varying time zones mean that you have to be more vague with expressions such as '24-hour delivery'?

▶ Will you be able to provide multiple language support, or stick to English as 'the language of the Internet'?

If you are planning to trade cross-border, then there are software vendors who have the tools and experience to help you in this area. As you can see, things are not always as straightforward as they seem and you should not go into cross-border e-commerce without thinking things through in great detail. So even though your company is UK-based you still have to think of the implications of your Web presence across the globe.

E-payment Systems

One of the questions that baffles most businesses sooner or later when they have taken the decision to trade on the Net is how to charge for their products or services. There is a plethora of payment systems to choose from and it is daunting to know where to start. So-called e-cash systems fall primarily into one of two categories: 'open' or 'closed'. Pre-payment cards for telephones are a good example of a closed scheme since they cannot be used for anything else other than to make a phone call using the equipment of one particular operator.

Open e-cash systems are like ordinary money, being exchangeable anywhere for any goods. The Mondex (**http://www.mondex.com**) payment card is a good example of this, albeit that it never really took off in the public's imagination as a viable alternative for cash or credit cards.

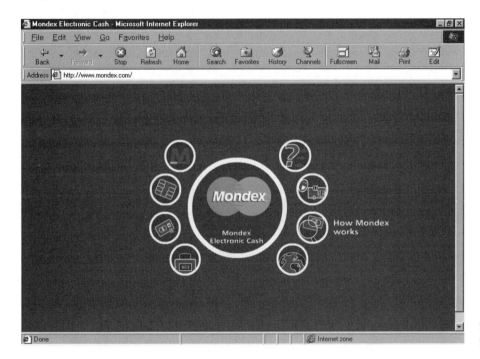

◀ Mondex – still going strong on the Internet.

As far as the Net is concerned there is the obvious need for something which is secure, and enables online transactions to be carried out easily. For such a system to work, the following four conditions need to be met:

▶ No-one, apart from the parties to the transaction, can read the details.

▶ No-one can have access to, or be able to tamper with, the transactions *en route*.

▶ Both parties should be able to positively identify one another.

▶ Evidence that a transaction has actually taken place can be provided.

Confidentiality

As long as no-one apart from the intended recipient can read the message, it can be classified as confidential.

In order to ensure that a message remains confidential, there has to be a method used to encrypt the data. There are plenty of encryption routines, some of which involve the same key for both encrypting and decrypting the message, whilst others work using the public key process whereby the message can only be decrypted by the recipient using a private key.

Integrity

Provided that no-one can tamper with a message *en route*, then integrity is maintained.

Integrity of a message can be provided by generating a digest rather like a checksum. What normally happens is that some kind of algorithm is applied to the text which generates what is known as a *hash number* that describes the message. If the original message is tampered with in any way, the checksum will be different, and so the recipient can check that all is as it should be. Naturally for this to work the checksum needs to be sent separately from the message; it should also be sent encrypted.

Authentication

Only if both the receiving and sending parties can prove each other's identity can authentication be achieved.

In order for both parties to have faith in each other's identity they can make use of a trusted third party who issues a digital certificate confirming a link between a person or company and a public key. This way, when someone receives a public key, they can tell exactly who it is from. These trusted third parties are known as Certification Authorities and there are several, such as Interclear in the UK (**http://www.interclear.co.uk**) and Verisign in the US (**http://www.verisign.com**).

Non-repudiation

If there is evidence that a transaction actually took place, then neither party is able to repudiate the transaction at a later date.

Non-repudiation is the most tricky of the four secure conditions to meet and relies itself on four more requirements to be met:

▶ An underlying protocol such as Netscape's 'Secure Socket Level' (SSL) provides authentication between the server and client and requires digital IDs to be sent backwards and forwards before a secure connection is finally made.

▶ Both parties must synchronise their exchanges.

▶ Evidence tokens are exchanged noting the results of the transaction.

▶ The status of the transaction must be clear at all times.

SET

BY THE WAY

As well as SSL, which we mentioned above, another common security standard is the Secure Electronic Transaction protocol which has the backing of such stalwarts as MasterCard International and Visa International. It differs from SSL in its use of time stamping and digitally signing to offer non-repudiation.

SET is likely to form the backbone of many credit card dealings on the Net. However, tiny transactions, known in the trade as micropayments, would attract disproportionately large amounts of commission and so to deal with this problem a number of electronic currency payment systems have been developed.

WorldPay (**http://www.worldpay.com**) is one of the best known but there are more than 50 other systems which each offer a slightly different arrangement, but can take care of the back office accounting systems for you. They work like this: the bank gives its client a password in exchange for their payment card details. The purchaser uses this password to authorise the payment. The bank then charges the user's payment card and transfers the funds, minus commission, to the vendor.

The Practical Solution

If all the above sounds overly technical, then rest assured that you are not alone in feeling this. If your site is going to be used primarily for business-to-business purposes, then an appreciation of the basics of payment systems will be necessary, but the good news (or bad news, depending on your point

of view) for business-to-consumers site owners is that the majority of
e-shoppers will expect to pay for goods via credit card and this is probably
the easiest payment system to set up for a small business.

Let's assume then that you want to set up an online shop or some other kind
of e-commerce site. As we have already said, e-commerce can offer
tremendous savings in administration costs as well as offer goods to a much
wider audience. But you have to have the logistics in place to process the
orders, or you will be letting down your customers which, in today's ethic of
customer-is-king, is the last thing you want to do.

Probably the type of business best suited for e-commerce is one that could
sell its products using a catalogue. We met some of these businesses in the
last chapter, and they make up a very diverse range. In many cases they
already have a business model that is similar to that of an online store; in
other words, they already have a distribution channel set up and they have a
system that can handle incoming orders.

In its simplest form, you could have an e-commerce system that relies on
orders being received via text files coming in on e-mail. Somewhere on
your Web site you will have displayed an order form into which your
customers will type their requirements. It's easy, it's effective ... and it's also
a bit dull. It won't do an awful lot for your corporate image, and if you are
hoping that your customers will go back and forth across your site
returning to the form every time they come across a particular product that
takes their fancy, then think again. However, it is simple, and if you do not

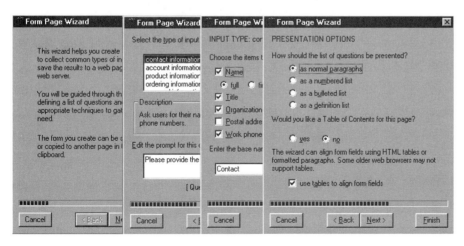

◀ FrontPage
wizards take the
guesswork out of
form creation.

249

have a wide range of products it is a highly workable solution. Many HTML editors such as FrontPage and Hot Metal can generate forms very easily along with the rest of a Web site.

However, sooner or later you may want to set up shop using one of a number of proprietary software products that take all the hassle out of building an online store. Some, such as IBM (**http://mypage-products.ihost.com/uk/index.hpc**) and Yahoo! (**http://store.yahoo.com**) allow you to enter a few company and product details, pay a monthly fee (typically £15 for up to a dozen or so items) and sit back. Others are more suitable for companies offering more than a small handful of products, and we will be looking at setting up our own store, complete with a shopping basket system, using one of these software packages in Chapter 20.

Doing The Biz

Whether you have a large or small cyberstore, the golden rule is to remember the old acronym KISS – Keep It Simple Stupid! You don't want to overwhelm your visitors with too many choices, and if you have a number of different categories or products the best bet is to categorise them into several groups. Use different product shots on each category page, but don't overdo the graphics.

Because buying over the Net is a novel experience for many users, remember to keep your order form simple to use. Only ask for the minimum of details necessary and – if possible – offer your customers a choice of payment system. Many are still very wary of giving out their credit card details over the Net, despite the different security systems in place, so you could, for instance, allow your customers to print out the order form and post it to you complete with a cheque.

If you are going to offer a secure system for credit card payments, such as SSL – which we referred to earlier – then you first need to check with your IAP what its procedures are for dealing with this. Normally the IAP will have to set up your site with a trusted certificate from a third party company or Certification Authority such as we mentioned earlier and this will probably cost you between about £400 and £1000.

An alternative, cheaper way of doing this is to use an IAP who already has a Web server that is already certified and who will allow you to put your site on its server for a much smaller cost than you would have to pay otherwise. The disadvantage here, however, is that the certificate will have the IAP's details rather than your own.

Doom & Gloom Merchants

If all this has fired you up so that you can't wait to get your store up online, just wait one second. As in all areas of business, there are the doom and gloom merchants who, if they had their way, would ensure that nothing ever got off the ground. But it's still worth noting what they have to say since although there could be a great deal of money to be made out there in cyberspace, you could just as easily lose your shirt.

Research has shown that two out of every three businesses on the Net fail. Most of the virtual malls that have sprung up in their thousands have failed. Even the likes of the mighty amazon.com – which has become a byword for successful Net businesses, having become one of the largest book stores in the US since its start in 1995 – continues at the time of writing to be making a loss.

In essence, most of the big-name researchers have concluded that retailing to the public over the Net is likely to remain small and largely unprofitable for the next ten years. The combination of software bugs, limited selections, and slow download times have even led some to describe the Internet as the High Street from Hell!

But those same researchers also conclude that e-commerce will get much better in ways that we can only guess at now. You have to remember that a mere five years ago none of what you can now find on the Internet could be envisaged by the majority of its users. And the big money will be where it always has been – in business-to-business commerce where, just as in the real world, business transactions are worth about ten times as much as consumer sales.

Trade Marks, Copyright & The Law

Although the Internet has broken down the geographical barriers to trade, it does not mean that copyright does not apply. In this country the copying of copyright work in any medium by electronic means is treated as copying under the Copyright Designs and Patent Act of 1998 – unless the copyright owner has given his permission. Therefore, in theory copying any graphic image from somebody else's website could technically put you in the position of having committed an offence.

Therefore if your company Web site includes text and graphics that have been copied from elsewhere on the Web then your company could be in breach of the act as well. However, many companies have made copies of other people's components and put them up on their own site and now all we have to do is to wait for the lawyers' bonanza!

Bearing in mind that cyberspace is subject to the laws of some 200 nations, there is a programme of meetings between states to formulate how cyberspace law will operate. If the precedent of domain names is anything to go by, however, this may take some time.

Stand & Deliver

Since the dawn of civilisation, certainly since the dawn of commerce, man has looked for ways to perpetrate fraud on his fellow man. It became a national obsession and sport in 1720 with the bursting of the South Sea Bubble, but with the coming of the Internet, the opportunities for scams and frauds have multiplied in leaps and bounds.

Many people believe that stolen credit card numbers are the biggest security worry on the Web; but there are several ways in which highly organised fraudsters can breach the company defences once it enters the electronic marketplace.

The majority of scams are simply extensions of long established frauds wrapped up in new clothing. Pyramid selling – sometimes under the guise of Network selling – tops the list of get-rich-quick schemes. You know the kind of thing: in the most basic chain letter, you send £5 to a name at the top of a list adding yours to the list and pass it on to ten other people who in turn pass it on to ten others. It sounds a great idea, until you try out the maths. By the ninth generation letter you will have involved one billion people, and (so far) there aren't that many people out there in cyberspace, even supposing they were all daft enough to take part in the project in the first place.

The stock-markets have always (allegedly!) been home to insider dealing, and the Internet has proved to be the perfect vehicle for hot stock tipsters talking up – or down – a share price so as to make a killing selling – or buying – that particular commodity. Newsgroups are saturated with self-styled experts who 'only want to share their experience' with friends on the Net. If you come across someone with a hot tip about a share price that is poised for rapid growth, be extremely wary.

The Securities and Exchange Commission is now so worried by Internet fraud that it has launched a 'cyberforce' of 125 officers to search the Net for scams. However there is a limit as to what financial watchdogs can do about Internet fraud since the Net is essentially unregulated.

Phantom Of The Internet

More of a danger to businesses is the case of phantom Web sites that have started to appear. This involves a Web site literally passing itself off as another one, and stealing any income generated. It needs the skills of an accomplished hacker to set up, but in its simplest state it might just be someone getting into a site and changing a phone number so that any orders go to a rival company, betting on the fact that the owner of the site won't check such a detail that often.

It's not just the company who loses. The customer is unlikely ever to return to that site again and they could even have their credit card details misused in a number of other ways as well.

BY THE WAY

If you think hacking is for professionals only, a quick visit to the **alt.hackers** newsgroup might give you something to think about!

When looking at the risks that hackers could pose to the security of your company, it is worth noting the findings of several surveys that note that most hacking is carried out by people known to the company – be they ex-employees, or even suppliers and subcontractors.

Hacking tools are widely available on the Internet and allow the hacking of passwords and the opening of 'back doors' into Web sites of unsuspecting companies. They allow even total novices to penetrate corporate networks. Without some kind of protection such corporate networks are highly vulnerable to damage and loss of corporate assets. This is particularly true when the company Web site is connected in some way to the corporate network (such as via a database link). Here the Web site is a potential gateway for any kind of external attack and it's here that the importance of firewalls becomes so apparent.

JARGON BUSTER

Firewall

A system designed to prevent unauthorised access to or from a private network. Firewalls can be implemented in both hardware and software – or a combination of both.

So, You Have Been Warned!

Everybody knows that it's always some other guy whose business burns down, who gets fleeced or gets knocked down by a Manchester tram.

So be bwave, intwepid cybernaut, and turn that page!

BUILDING YOUR SITE

In This Part...

19

YOUR OWN WEB SITE –
THE BUSINESS BASICS

In This Chapter...

▶ **Things to bear in mind when setting up a business site**

▶ **Who should develop your site?**

▶ **What to ask your potential developer**

▶ **Marketing your site**

▶ **Who should host your site?**

Up to this point in the book, you've learnt how to use just about every area of the Internet – the major (and not-so-major) services, the search engines, plug-ins and multimedia, interactive pages, shopping, the whole shebang – but it's still everyone else's Internet you're using! Sooner or later you'll want to grab a little corner of it and give your business a presence.

You should approach this from the viewpoint that you would approach any other business venture. Do you service your company vehicles or do you get an expert in? Do you design your company stationery and marketing brochures or do you leave it to the professionals? In the same way, there is a very strong argument for leaving the design and development of your Web pages to the professionals.

But before you can do any of that, you have to decide what you actually want a Web site for. Only then can you give a proper briefing to your Web developer to get the content just right.

A professional attitude will enable your Web site development to enhance and reinforce your business presence in the marketplace as well as introduce the possibility of it being used for online trade, either straight away or as part of a later development.

Things To Bear In Mind

So that your company Web site will really work for you and play the right role in the suite of business tools you use, it is important to plan it properly, developing it in stages. Bear in mind that, even if you are only thinking of a marketing site, there should be a continuity of message with your other corporate literature and that the site should be easy for visitors to use. Another helpful virtue of Web sites is that they are not finite. Unlike corporate literature, business cards and headed paper which can't be changed once you've signed them off to print, you can go back and tweak your Web pages for any errors or with updates with minimal cost. This could engender sloppiness but we would advocate that you insist on thorough proof-reading and then signing off anything to be published on the Web in the same way as you would with any corporate brochure text and design.

Structure

Planning the structure of the site is of paramount importance as this can make or break it. When dealing with your own organisation, it is all too easy to try to make things too complicated. The objective should be to create a structure that enables visitors to jump from one area of information to another using a hyperlink, which will make it easy for them to get the information they want, and get off-line as soon as possible.

Elements Into Balloons!

We normally suggest that the best way to do this is not to write a hierarchical structure from the first but to list the elements which need to be on the Web site – in this phase – in an apparently random way, rather like this:

For this example, we've looked at a company we worked with in Leeds which supplies the NHS and others with removable covers for mattresses and other items. We started by sitting down with the MD of Sidebottom Ltd., and brainstorming all the different elements of his business and how it would impact and be impacted by having a Web presence.

These elements are anything, whatever the relevance to the business or product, that needs to be included within the Web site. If you use this brainstorming technique, you will not forget any elements, and grouping them afterwards into a hierarchical structure is likely to be most successful. This is also a very good way of sorting out what would be better to go into the second phase. You can also start working on the text and graphics that have to be included – although you might find that it is better to do that when you have finished the next two phases.

Groupings

To create some order and logical flow in a Web site the next step is to group the subjects, such as products, target market and so on, as you can see below. From what we've worked on so far you will know how easy it can be to get around a Web site if the navigation buttons and hyperlinks are well planned. We're grouping the Sidebottom information into:

▶ Homepage.

▶ Reasons why people might want to talk to us and buy our products.

▶ Our target markets.

▶ Who we are and what references and history can we write for people to feel comfortable with us.

▶ Products and everything that makes our products different and better than others.

From this it is easy to set up hyperlinks from one part of the site to any other part of the site and these can be planned from this:

Don't forget though, that you can set up a hyperlink from anywhere to anywhere and so if we were to draw the links all over this scheme you wouldn't be able to read the words at all for all the lines that would be there!

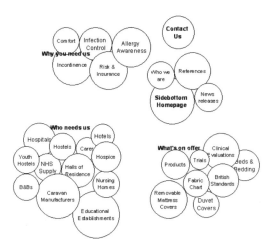

These groupings now give you the wherewithal to define your click buttons and the contents of the pages that they link to (plus Home of course!):

Click buttons

Images used in the same way as hypertext to transport you to different parts of

Who Would Be Right For Developing Your Web Site?

Now we come on to some questions you'll need to find answers for. There are loads of people and companies out there who claim to design Web sites.

Some of these have sprung from design houses and some from technically driven companies and, of course, some are from marketing and PR origins and offshoots. Some charge like a wounded rhino whilst others charge modestly. Many undercharge and don't do a good job for business, and others charge too much for what they deliver.

Here's the knotty problem – who do you go to for your company site?

Let's list some of the possibilities:

1   Ask around for recommendations.

2   Look on the Web for sites you like and hope they list the developer.

3   Look at the advertisements in Internet and PC magazines.

4   Approach design, marketing and PR companies with whom you already do business.

5   Ask one of your IT people in the office or someone who is technically minded.

6   Ask your neighbour's techie wizard of a child.

7   Do it yourself.

All of these have their good and bad points. To end up with a Web site that is going to suit you and your business you need to have clear objectives and an open mind because the Web behaves – and is perceived – differently from paper-based corporate representations.

1   **Recommendations.** The problem with seeking recommendations is that relatively few businesses at present have established a viable Web presence. There are lots of Web sites out there, some on shopping malls where they may not be found easily, and some totally inappropriate for the medium. Many appear totally inappropriate for the business they're meant to represent. Nevertheless recommendation is always a good starting point if you're lucky enough to be in this position. If you don't know of anyone who has already put up a Web site, then don't worry: you are like the vast majority of Web 'newbies' who are looking to establish a Web presence.

2   **Sites-U-Like.** Something that we preach passionately to people about to make that first jump is to urge them to look around the Web for any sites

they particularly like (or dislike). Design is a very personal thing. If we all liked the same things, then just think what a boring world we would live in. The fact is there are no rights and wrongs over what constitutes good design. Your Web site should reflect the message you want to put across about your business. Choosing a designer who is in sympathy with what you are trying to project is therefore absolutely essential. So, if you find a site that you like and you can get the name of the developer, and he is relatively local, then perhaps you are on the right road.

3 **Advertisements.** Another good source of Web designers can be found in the myriad advertisements in Internet and PC magazines that fill the shelves of your high street stationers. Pick out advertisements that you like the look of as you may well then find a synergy of approach between your business and the development company. However, you should always ask for references and reference sites to view before going further.

4 **Marketing company.** If you were to approach your regular PR or marketing company to ask for their advice, then you should find that there is an area of comfort in dealing with people who already understand what your business is about so that this has to be a preferred starting point. They, of course, should already have addressed the question of Web site design and, even if they do not have their own in-house developers, they are likely to know of someone they can recommend. But again, do ask for reference sites so that you can have a good feel for what they do.

5 **The IT whiz.** In our experience, despite the fact that some of our best friends are technological wizards, the last person you should give a Web development project to is a techie. Granted, they will probably come up with all manner of bells and whistles and zappy applets to add to your site but will that fulfil the main criteria for your business? It might be tarring everyone with the same brush to suggest that techies – in the main – have trouble in spelling, and do not focus on the main requirements of the business. As with most corporate image needs, the design perspective needs to be brought in. Another word of warning: many small companies get someone in-house with a modicum of technological knowledge to design their first Web site and create a potential management and motivation problem when that Web site expertise is exhausted and outside developers then have to be brought in.

6   **The kid-next-door.** This could be worse. Superficially, it may sound like a good deal and quite often you'll find that younger people have the edge when it comes to what works well on the Web, since it is such a dynamic medium. However, kids-next-door will have almost no business knowledge and 'play' with computers as part of their learning experience. Things like continuity of style, corporate font and business message will cost you more time than if you were involving a business professional – and if you're dealing with your neighbours and you end up rejecting the site, you could end up with your neighbours rejecting you!

7   **DIY**. They always say that if you want a job done well, do it yourself. Well, maybe you can afford the time and have the talent in all the areas needed – that's for you to decide. In the next couple of chapters we will be talking about the basics of writing in HTML to help you on your way. But there is also a halfway house. If you don't want to get your fingers dirty with all that HTML, then there are software companies that have taken the pain out of creating both zappy and professional-looking business sites by providing 'idiot-proof' software. We'll be walking you through the development of one in the next chapter.

BY THE WAY

Don't accept as gospel everything that an 'expert' tells you about the Net. The technology is changing so fast that no-one is an expert on every aspect of the Web.

Essential Questions To Be Answered Before You Embark On Your Business Web Site

Unfortunately an awful lot of companies seem to lurch into developing a Web site without applying the normal business practices. If you were launching a brand new product, you would do all the following:

▶   write a business case

▶   cost the development time

▶   cost the packaging

▶   cost the literature

▶ cost the marketing

▶ cost the delivery etc.

You need to do precisely the same with a Web site. You can see from the amount of time involved in just identifying the balloons mentioned earlier in this chapter that this could take a lot of time, as there will always be room to improve on the current state of affairs.

In order to provide the best business case for your company, running through the following questions – both with your own staff and potential developers – will help you to identify the cost factors for in-house and outsourcing so that you can judge the up-sides and down-sides clearly:

▶ What are our realistic deadlines? First, to get the main concept work agreed and, second, to have it ready for approval and publishing it on the Web?

▶ Can our deadlines be met?

▶ Who will do the actual site creation? It's very important to get on with the designer because this relationship should be long-term.

▶ What sites have you already designed?

BY THE WAY

When speaking to a potential developer, look for different design techniques rather than the same design which has been altered for different sites.

▶ Have you already designed sites for our type of company?

▶ Can we speak to the owners of two reference sites and see some of your work?

▶ What do you charge for updates?

▶ How much will the whole project cost?

▶ Do you accept stage payments?

▶ How much of our business time will be involved?

▶ Which of our staff will be involved?

▶ Who is going to sign it off, and at what stages of development?

As different types of business will offer different types of Web sites, you have to identify your objectives clearly. For instance, if you intend to provide customer support then information on your products and their areas of use, combined with other general information, will probably be appropriate, whereas if your intention is to set up a mail order business, then an online store is your obvious route.

To make your Web site compelling, you should always:

▶ Make an impact on first-time visitors so that they remember the site and come back.

▶ Keep abreast of current Web culture.

▶ Ensure that you do not just provide pages of content that look as if they have been lifted straight out of a catalogue.

▶ Update your site regularly, giving visitors a reason to return and stopping them from leaving early because you are out of date.

▶ Make the site easy to find by registering it with search directories and key-wording it for the search engines.

▶ Make your information easily accessible as it is more important than showing off the zappy skills of some graphic designer.

▶ Make the home page easy to use with good, well-signposted hyperlinks, and give a good flavour of what's on offer in the various sections.

▶ Give the visitor an opportunity to feed back with an automatic e-mail link.

▶ Keep graphics small and simple so that your visitors will not leave your site before getting the information you want.

▶ Practise the Three Clicks rule: no single piece of information should be more than three mouse clicks away from your home page.

If you can incorporate the factual answers to these questions into your Web site plan, then you have the potential for a formidable site and one that will be valued by your customers.

Marketing Your Site

Now we come to the bit that so many people forget to do. If your Web site is to have any impact at all then you need to market it. This sounds simple and obvious, but it is often overlooked.

There are some basics – so please excuse us if we're teaching your grandmother to suck eggs!

Continuity of image

In developing your site the genre of the Web must be enjoyed but that doesn't mean that you should not have a continuity of image with your other corporate marketing tools and company literature. The Web site must *fit in* with your company as well as within the immediacy of the Internet.

Holistic image

Just as you wouldn't dream of printing your company stationery without phone and fax numbers, nor should you, from here on in, neglect to tell everyone both your e-mail address and Web site URL. This means that you should update your:

▶ headed paper

▶ business cards

▶ complements slips

▶ fax headers

▶ product packaging

▶ other corporate literature

▶ technical literature

▶ advertising

▶ other gismos that you give out.

Assumptive marketing

With the arrival of your 'new baby' will come the opportunity to change the ways in which you normally tell the world about new products. No longer will you be forced to produce expensive brochures, backed up with telephone support; now you can refer your potential customers to your Web site for all the information they require – saving your company time and money whilst offering better customer support.

Target marketing

With all the different target audiences your company has you will already have assessed the U.S.P. (unique selling point) that attracts them to your products. Your new Web site is a splendid opportunity to reinforce the varied messages for your various target audiences, rather than having to rely on one printed piece of material to satisfy everyone.

E-mail marketing

You can use the launch of your Web site to send an e-mail to every business whose e-mail address you know, trumpeting its arrival and the wealth of useful information available on it.

When you add more Web pages you can target specific market areas in the same way. And as your database of e-mail addresses grows, you will be able to increase the number of targeted businesses without it costing you a penny more in processing costs.

BY THE WAY

Many people are so relieved when they have 'finished' their Web site that they overlook the organic integration of the site with the rest of their business. Having built the site is just the end of the beginning; please don't regard it as the beginning of the end!

Who Should Host Your Site?

Although it is perfectly possible for your company to have its own web server with which to house your own site, there are many advantages in having your Internet Access Provider to host your site. For instance:

▶ The costs are very much lower than paying for the hardware and leased lines needed.

▶ The IAP will take care of maintenance 24 hours per day, and 24-hour monitoring is the norm.

▶ You can buy a package that incorporates domain name registration and e-mail forwarding.

However, there are some things to note that should be thought about carefully before you embark on a relationship with any one Internet access provider.

▶ Some IAPs may not permit the use of certain types of scripts in your coding. For instance Active Server Pages (ASPs) – which interpret code in a page as it is being served, perhaps inserting live information from a database – cannot be handled by all providers. It is essential to check with your provider about any restrictions in this area.

▶ You may not get as much information as you would like about the people visiting your site. Some IAPs can, however, provide full access logs.

CONSTRUCTING AN ONLINE SHOP – THE EASY WAY

In This Chapter...

▶ Construct an e-commerce site without understanding a word of HTML

If the thought of constructing a Web site in HTML leaves you cold and you feel like running away screaming and gibbering from anything that smacks of those dreaded letters, then worry not. Some awfully clever programmers have woken up to the fact that there are many just like you who would rather not get their fingers dirty with the detritus of page coding. After all, most of us are happy to drive our cars without understanding the relationship that the HT coil has with the spark plugs. So why should e-commerce be any different?

Flat-Pack Shops

Just as there are packages – such as Microsoft's FrontPage and Adobe's Page Mill – that make the development of a Web site a relatively painless process, so there are now a handful of packages that make the entire creation of an e-commerce site a doddle. If you can cope with the basics of using a computer, then these packages can lead you through the creation of such a site step-by-step to give you a site that can cope with online shopping baskets, currency transactions, visitor tracking and a whole lot more besides. These all-in-one solutions can start from under £100 for a shop with only a few items to sell, but even the top end solutions are likely to be a great deal cheaper than paying someone to make your site up for you.

In this chapter we're going to put together a site for a typical shop using one of the leading packages called Shopcreator, but others you could also try out are:

▶ Shop@ssistant (**http://www.floyd.co.uk**)

▶ Maximizer (**http://www.maximizer.com**)

▶ QDCat (**http://www.pcl.ndirect.co.uk**)

▶ ITS (**http://www.marketingsense.co.uk**)

▶ Actinic (**http://www.actinic.co.uk**)

Time To Unleash Some Artistic Licence

Let's assume for this example that we want to virtualise a store selling artists' supplies. This shop has a wide range of product lines such as brushes, paints, paper, frames and even some finished framed prints. We're going to call it Barbers. (Why not? We know of a fishmonger called Baker!)

Because Shopcreator uses some pretty sophisticated programming, the site has to be built up whilst you are online, sending information backwards and forwards from your computer to Shopcreator's servers. (We understand that the next version, which may have been released before you even read this, will allow site creation off-line with the resultant code being sent to Shopcreator at the end of the compilation process, thereby reducing your online costs. This also gives you time to ponder upon your creativity without the pressure of increasing your telephone costs. Mind you, when you compare the cost of a local rate phone call with the overall cost of setting up a site, then it's not going to set you back much anyway. The creation of this site took only an hour from beginning to end.)

Before we go online, though, we should get everything ready that we are likely to need. That means that we'll need some scans of our company logo, pictures of the products and an idea of any colour schemes that we will wish to implement to tie in with our corporate image, not forgetting the text.

Haven't got a scanner?

BY THE WAY

If you haven't yet got a scanner to get those pictures onto your computer, then you really have little excuse for not getting one. These days you can get quite reasonable scanners for around £50. Look in any PC magazine, available at all newsagents, for a plethora of adverts.

Before you start working on your new Web site, you can print off Shopcreator's helpful user guide. It takes you through the setting-up process in words and pictures, explaining all Shopcreator's main features step-by-step. So now it's time to dial up Shopcreator. Their Web address is **http://www.shopcreator.com** and once you are logged on you will be able to click on the option of creating a new store. Via a series of nine screens you give Shopcreator enough information to set up the store shell for you on its computers, and then you are led through the compilation of the site itself.

So let's start with those initial nine screens. This is where you supply information so that Shopcreator can set up your site both with the correct contact and billing information for your customers – and also so that it knows your credit card number for your bill, after the initial trial period (10 days) has ended!

It is also at this point that you can specify whether the site will feature all three indexes of your products by product type, by supplier or author or manufacturer, and by topic or area of interest. This is one of the powerful features that makes the resultant site so easy for your customers to use.

You can also specify whether your products are liable for VAT (and if so you can put in your VAT number) and – importantly – whether you wish to allow purchase transactions straight from the site, using the shopping basket analogy that we have already talked about, or whether you would prefer that the customers e-mail you for further information so that you can invoice them separately. This could be useful, for instance, if you were selling cars and you wanted to e-mail your potential clients to allow them to have a test drive.

You now move into the main area of administration where the site creation process actually takes place. As you can see from the following screen grab, there is a menu allowing you to specify your products, suppliers and topics as well as other criteria for the site.

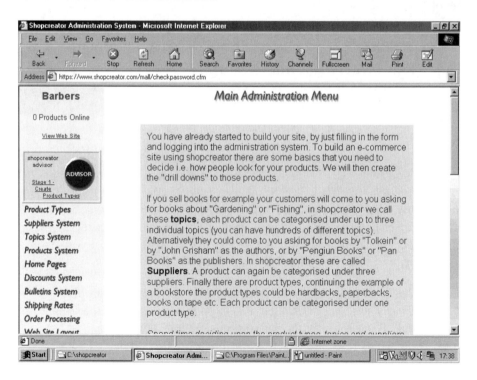

▶ Helpful information is given at every stage of the creation process.

So let's add some information. In the next screen shot we'll type in 'Paintings' as a product type and add some key words: 'paintings, pictures, interior décor' into the second field. These will be used to attract the search engines to point to your site whenever someone is looking up these key words. There is also a field into which you can type a longer product type description – 'pictures to hang on the wall' – which will appear on the actual site itself. As you can see on the left hand menu, you now have the wherewithal to allow product type discounting, allowing you to offer mass discounting – if you have a sale, for instance – as opposed to going into the details of every product and changing the price of each one individually.

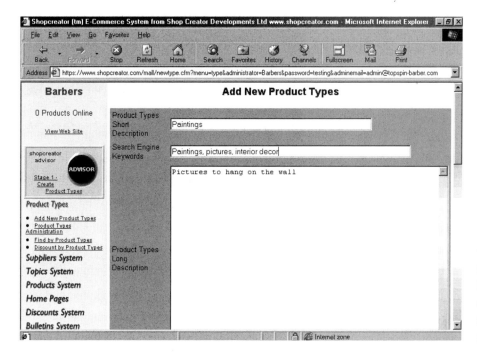

◀ If you think up more key words later on, you can always come back and make any changes you want.

You will be invited to add a picture at this stage to illustrate the category type. (You don't have to if you don't want to). Once again, Shopcreator keeps its beady eye on you and warns you if you are doing anything silly.

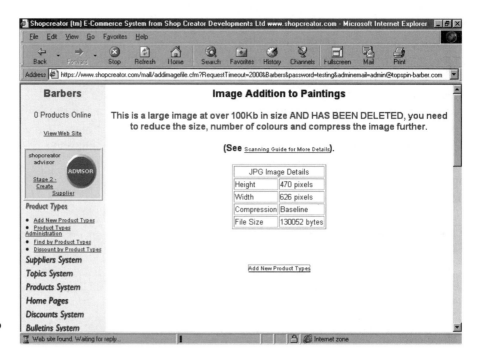

Let's carry on putting in more category types – say, Brushes and Pastels – so that now we have a total of three product types, each with a picture illustrating the kind of product it is. As you can see, we are given the options of amending the details, adding new images or even deleting the categories altogether.

Now that we have entered the product categories, we are invited to give some information about suppliers. We'll enter two manufacturers' names – 'Daler-Rowney' and 'Winsor & Newton' – and again we can give descriptions and keyword entries in case someone using a search engine looks up, say, 'Winsor & Newton'.

The third option on the left hand menu system is to create Topics of Interest. These will be the words that customers may use when searching for that particular item in their mind. It may not be the same as the product type: you just have to help them along a bit. Pictures could also be described as paintings, sketches or canvasses. You get the idea. Shopcreator allows you to add hundreds of different topics, and each product can be categorised under three of these topics.

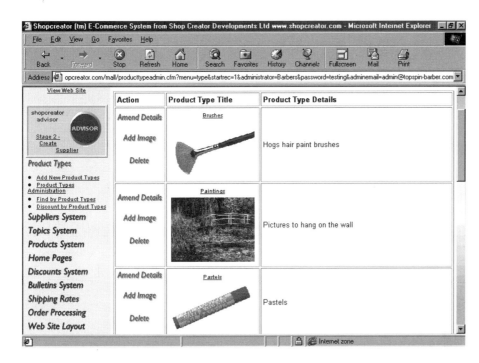

◀ Add as many product categories as you like.

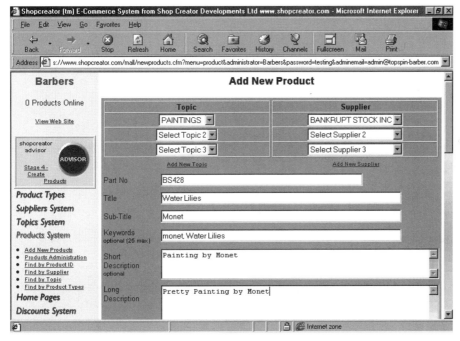

◀ Add as many products as you like.

It's now time we added a few products. So far we've only been dealing in broad brush strokes for the site as a whole, but this is where the nitty gritty is added. Let's add a painting by Monet which is in our catalogue under part number BS428. It came as a job lot from Bankrupt Stock Inc – that well known purveyor of fine art.

We are also invited to enter the price, as well as a sale price, its product type, its shipping weight (to calculate costs of delivery later on), its VAT rate and so on.

Once we have entered all the product details (and if you have many products already entered in a database, then Shopcreator can accept a tab separated value file instead of your having to insert all the details by hand) it's time we gave some details about the company. We can add a number of paragraphs, each of which can be given a separate highlighted title.

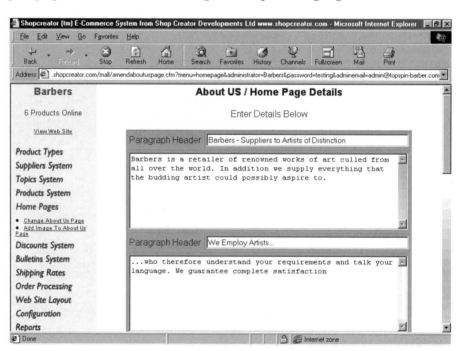

▶ Time to add in details about the shop.

After this comes a whole range of options for applying or removing discounts by product types, by supplier or by topic. You can enter information about the rates you charge for shipping your products, (whether within the UK or abroad), as well as specifying the way in which orders will be handled.

When it comes to Web page layout, your choice is truly enormous. There are templates for buttons which you can use as they are, or import your own designs; you can specify the colours for the background, font, left box, right box, subtitle font, price font and links just by clicking on a grid of radio buttons; you can change the texture of the backdrop from a selection on offer; you can add in a message that will scroll across the status bar at the bottom of the Web page (we chose 'Welcome to the Barbers Web Site'; how original!); and of course you will want to be able to upload your company logo.

◀ You can add or change logos.

Don't worry; we're almost there now. The Configuration menu now gives you control over all kinds of administration areas such as tax and VAT rates, adding real audio files, putting in user-definable fields, stock control, volume discounts, credit card acceptance, response via e-mail, and virtual domain addressing. Let's assume that we've entered all those details; the next thing is to view all that information as a complete Web site. Click the menu option allowing you to do just that and try it out. You want to make sure that the site looks well balanced and works well before you actually post it to the Net. Try, for instance, clicking your way through the site, putting items into your virtual shopping basket and check out your orders as you do so.

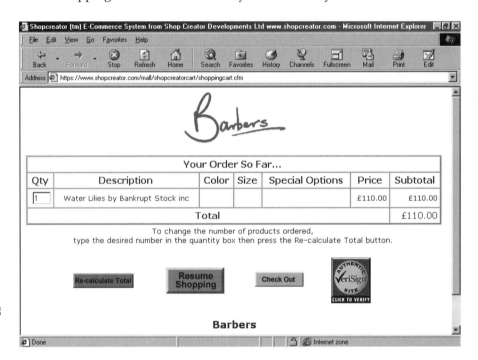

▶ Note the verify Authentic Verisign Site button, giving your customers peace of mind.

Once you are happy with the way it looks then the only thing left to do is to publish your site to the Web.

But Shopcreator isn't about to sit back on its haunches just because you are having a well earned rest. It still has a final ace up its sleeve. For when visitors start coming to your site (and they will, thanks to the 'metatags' it inserts into the pages to flag down the search engines, as well as submitting your details to all the major search engines) it can create reports of user click trails, product page views and your most viewed pages so that you can tweak your site in future to be more responsive to the areas that prove to be the most popular with your visitors.

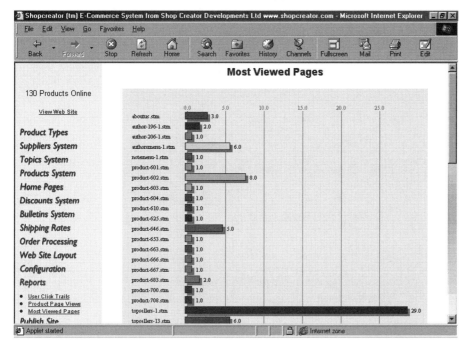

◀ We've had to cheat here as our site has not had any visitors. This is the kind of graph you can expect Shopcreator to prepare for you.

In summary, then, there really is no excuse for you not to be able to get a fully-fledged e-commerce site up and running with the minimum of input from you and your staff. Just what are you waiting for?

INTRANETS & (A GLIMPSE OF) EXTRANETS

In This Chapter...

▶ **How Internet technologies can work *inside* your business**

▶ **Tools for the job**

▶ **Extending the frontiers of your Intranet**

So far in this book we have concentrated on using the Internet for two-way communications with the outside world; and in the rush to get on the Internet many organisations think only in terms of how Internet technology can help them improve their communication with these external audiences.

It's ironic, though, that the very first Web – at the European Particle Physics Laboratory in Geneva, known as CERN – was set up as a means of improving communication with others within the same organisation. In other words, the very first Web was actually an Intranet, designed to distribute information within an organisation to the organisation's own people.

What Is An Intranet?

In thinking of the business advantages of setting up a Web site there are many audiences that we are likely to want to influence:

▶ Current and potential customers

▶ General public

▶ Shareholders

▶ Competitors.

What an Intranet can offer, however, is a far better route to communicating with your own people who might well be interested in what is being said to external audiences, but who have different needs in the kind of information that will improve their working environment.

Typically the kind of information that can be found on any Intranet will include:

▶ Personnel or human resources services, such as employee manuals, pay and health insurance information, expenses, bulletin boards, newsletters and so on

▶ Logistics concerned with the physical services involved in running a business – internal telephone directories, stationery supplies, blueprints of office layouts, availability of fire extinguishers etc.

▶ Information systems – which include Help desks, interfaces with commonly used databases, repositories of documents, spreadsheets and other datafiles

But as technology becomes ever more advanced, these basic Intranet functions are now being supplemented by lots of other add-on functions that get to the very heart of how an organisation runs itself. You could have:

▶ Interactive discussion groups

▶ Customised delivery of company news to individuals

▶ Sales contact tracking

▶ Company-wide diary scheduling

▶ Audio and video communications between offices.

You can even extend the concept of using an internal Web to reach external audiences who are tied in to your own organisation in some way, such as suppliers and distributors. At this point, your Intranet becomes an Extranet.

JARGON BUSTER

Extranet

A term that refers to an Intranet that is partially accessible to authorised outsiders. Whereas an Intranet resides within the confines of an organisation and is accessible only to people who are members of that same organisation, an Extranet provides various levels of accessibility to outsiders. You can access an Extranet only if you have a valid username and password, and your identity determines which parts of the Extranet you can view. Extranets are becoming a very popular means for business partners to exchange information.

Companies that have installed Intranets can invariably make cost savings by no longer having to print staff manuals and other documents; distribution costs are reduced, the need for storage space is diminished and employee collaboration is greatly increased.

In April 1999, the networking company Cisco claimed it was saving typically £30m a year following an investment of some £18m over four years in its system. Its Intranet is accessible by 16 000 staff from 60 000 workstations, PCs and laptops. Over half the savings came from lower operating costs, and around 40 per cent was a direct result of improved productivity and better information flow.

Even within the SME (Small to Medium Sized Enterprise) sector, Intranets invariably prove their worth by allowing the sharing of common information and reducing the need to re-key information by different employees.

However, there is no one right or wrong way to implement an Intranet into your business. Every organisation is different but one thing is crucial if you want your Intranet to succeed.

Interactivity and openness go hand in hand, and only if you are willing to trust your own people will your Intranet succeed!

It's a sad fact that Intranets are often designed by IT gurus with little appreciation of an organisation's needs. But just as with the design of an Internet, it is important to harvest the ideas of your staff and incorporate these into your Intranet planning. At first glance it might seem paradoxical that the implementation of an Intranet is often more complex than setting up an Internet site, but if you think about the advantages offered by the tight integration of Internet protocols into the heart of your business processes, you can see that invariably it requires much careful thought which cannot just be left to your IT department.

And yet, at first glance, designing and building an Intranet seems just a logical extension of building an Internet. Why can't you just link together existing databases and word processed documents using HTML technologies to create an Intranet?

BY THE WAY

Who should control the information on an Intranet?

Should you allow any employee to post information to the Intranet, or should it all be 'moderated' before going live to others in the organisation? There is no hard and fast rule, but if your business runs in an information-rich environment, then it is usually better to allow employees to manage their own information sites and to keep their information up-to-date. It might, however, be appropriate to transfer that power on a gradual basis in the early days as your people get to grips with what this technology offers them.

Well, of course you can if that's all you want to get out of your Intranet, but if you can break away from the traditional ways of working by lifting geographical boundaries and those imposed by hierarchical structures then the resultant improvement in communication will invariably have an impact on the way your company operates in a day-to-day environment.

The problem now comes in finding the right staff to be able to implement an effective solution. An Intranet design must offer ease of use together with controlled access within a secure environment. Your Intranet expert needs to have at his disposal a broad range of skills ranging from general management processing to systems programming, HTML script, CGI or C++ programming and JavaScript coding, database programming, intuitive design, network security expertise and a whole lot more. SMEs in particular are likely to find it difficult to find staff who have these skills – even if they are willing to take them away from their other job functions; and calling in outside contractors may well have a heavy price tag to go with it.

One Saudi Arabian company the authors worked with on the installation of an Intranet in Jeddah had already spent over a year with a team of five people working full time, when they realised that the 'solution' they had come up with was totally useless from the employees' point of view. What they had failed to do was to ask the most basic question before beginning –

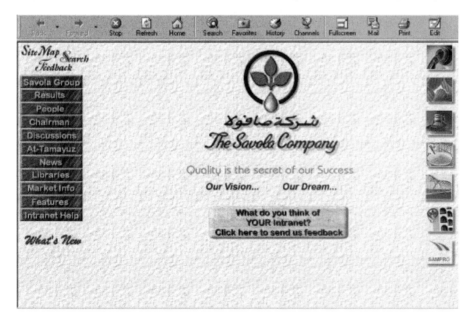

◀ Whilst the left hand navigation buttons hyperlink to general information, the right hand buttons lead directly to individual divisions within the company.

what do we want our Intranet to do? Once we had reassessed that, the building of a new Intranet from scratch took less than three months.

But what if talk of hubs and routers and switches, together with ethernet and token rings, leaves you feeling out of your depth? If, by now, you have become despondent about implementing an Intranet within your business, then this is where the cavalry appears from over the horizon!

Just as with the e-commerce solutions we talked about in the last chapter, there are also Intranet solutions that can be bought 'off the peg'.

Four of the best that we know of are:

▶ Site Solution – **http://www.intrasites.com**

▶ Intranet-in-a-Box – **http://www.intrasites.com**

▶ Merlin – **http://www.focus.net.uk**

▶ IntraNetics – **http://www.b4technology.com**

They are similar in the facilities they offer and, if you are interested in obtaining one of these solutions for your business, it would be worth your while going to their Web sites for more information. If these packages had been around when we were working on the Saudi Intranet mentioned above, installation could have been achieved in about a fortnight, rather than the three months it finally took.

You will still need someone with IT know-how to implement these ready made solutions, but the cost savings can be enormous, as well as giving you peace of mind that after all the hours spent on setting up such a system it is actually likely to work! However, you should still appoint an Intranet development team representing a cross section of managers, so that your finished product will be something that your people will *want* to use, rather than be forced into using.

JARGON BUSTER

Hubs

PCs can be easily networked together using a hub, which is essentially an intelligent switching unit that can route data to and from different machines. Typically an 8-port hub on Windows 95/98/NT can be used for creating a small file-sharing network. Intranets require a larger piece of kit that will also store information as well as connect to all kinds of peripherals such as printers.

Setting Up Your Intranet

We could write an entire book on Intranets, but to give you a flavour of what is involved with these off-the-shelf products, let's take a look at the setting-up of an Intranet using IntraNetics.

For a start, you will need a computer to act as your server – anything faster than 200MHz is required, together with a recommended 128Mb of memory, running Windows NT 4 or above.

You will need someone who understands how to connect up a network of computers using ethernet. If this task is way above your head, it will almost certainly be best to seek professional advice and get the basic building blocks set up before control is handed over to your Web master, or administrator.

It is actually the facilities available to the administrator that makes working with IntraNetics so easy.

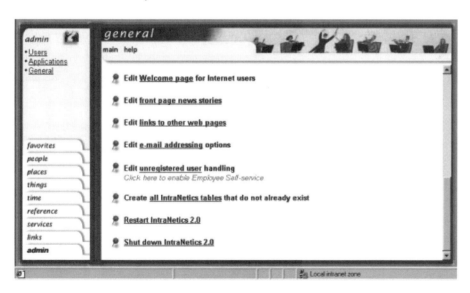

From the screen shot above you can see that the last tab at the bottom of the left hand index is reserved for admin use only. From here the administrator can alter the text, look and feel of the index page to make it welcoming for those using it.

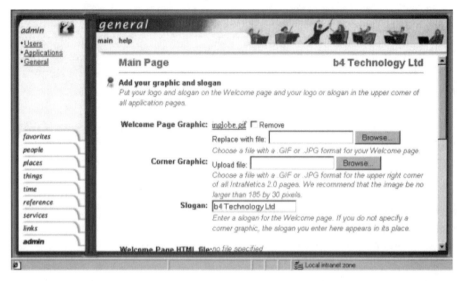

For instance, the administrator would almost certainly want to change the graphics supplied with the package in order to give it the same look and feel as the company's standard logos, and would certainly want to have the company's name displayed prominently. Background colours and textures can also be customised individually.

Of course, new staff must be able to gain access, and this is easily done via a menu accessed through 'Users' at the top left of the screen.

The software includes system security already built in, so you will be able to control access to your Intranet on a user-by-user basis and you can also create field level security so that different information can be accessed only by named individuals. Basically, any employee with a browser can access the Intranet with a password.

There are four levels of access permission:

▶ User – the basic level for all employees.

▶ Moderators – individuals designated as responsible for creating specific content.

▶ Designers – those persons allowed to modify form and structure as well as the content.

▶ Administrator – the individual with overall control of the system.

Because every employee will be listed in the Intranet's main database, this could offer the perfect way of finding anyone in the organisation, together with phone number, departmental information and even a photograph.

In the screen shot above, we have selected to look at the organisation chart in an outline view (it could just as easily have been displayed as a tree, and the number of levels can be chosen, as can be the display for just a certain part of the organisation). Clicking on an individual's name will open up a new window to give more detailed information on that employee.

You will notice that the tabs on the left lead to different sections of the Intranet. Again, these tabs and the fields can be customised to the individual company, depending on what you want included in your Intranet.

For instance, starting with the personnel functions, an Intranet allows anyone to access all the essential documents that are usually only required on an occasional basis. How much better it is to have them all in one place so that you always know where to find them.

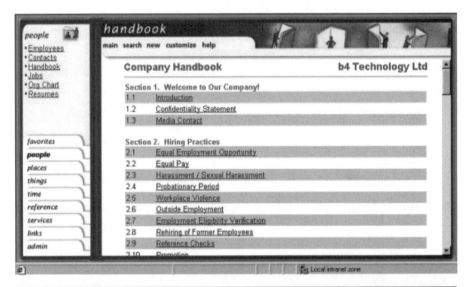

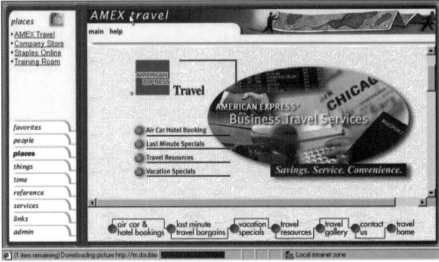

With Intranet access given to your staff, it is entirely possible to offer direct links to Internet pages that are likely to be used regularly. For instance, your people might need access to exchange rates, rail timetables or stationery supplies. IntraNetics allows access through its menu system just as if the information was on your local server.

There are likely to be a number of repositories of data and forms that could all be accessed by different people. Lists of software available throughout the company, expense forms and common documents all fall into this category. Why replicate the information when it can all be accessed by anyone with the requisite permissions?

You can also use the software to build bulletin boards and discussion conferences – very useful for keeping everyone informed, sharing knowledge with one another and allowing the posting of announcements and advertisements.

As we stressed above, for your Intranet to be successful it must have the backing of your staff. It is simply no good imposing a solution on them and telling them to get on with it. So, the design and development stages really are crucial if your project is to succeed.

The best way to promote Intranet usage within your organisation is to make it an essential repository of information. Having the internal phone directory online is an obvious way of getting people to use it willingly. There should also be a help file, support and other documentation available so that it is user-friendly and does not throw up any barriers. A simple, clear user interface can make all the difference to how it is perceived by the end users.

Extending the Frontiers

Once you have got your internal staff on board, it may well be time to consider including external audiences as part of your user base. Most of these Intranet solutions allow the creation of an Extranet through dial-up access.

Amongst your company's business dependencies, the relationships between your partners, strategic alliances and customers can be greatly strengthened by using an Extranet. In e-commerce and the transfer of information, the implementation of an Extranet enables companies to use the speed of Internet technologies to reinforce and develop better relationships, whilst saving time and money.

The role of an Extranet in a business lies somewhere between the Internet and an Intranet, with security and protection provided by passwords and with the usual firewalls. The Internet allows unlimited access because it is a public forum, whereas an Intranet is purely an internal forum and, as such, allows strictly limited access. An Extranet, on the other hand, allows selected business partners and customers into the inner sanctum, so that only companies who have the business equivalent of a 'most favoured nation' status can have access to your company's internal systems. Obviously setting up an Extranet has to be carried out both carefully and properly to work for all the partners and customers involved.

According to Datamonitor in May 1999, the normal business drivers for using an Extranet are:

▶ 46% customer care

▶ 38% supplier relations

▶ 7% network management

▶ 5% sales opportunity

▶ 4% cost reduction.

So, let's take a look at a business case to see how this openness of what would normally be a jealously guarded internal company system can be utilised in a beneficial manner for all concerned.

Within the car industry, Extranets are used to provide information, keep in touch with suppliers and distributors, collect payment and improve the whole process of ordering. Through such a site, suppliers can collect payments, information and documents.

Within the Lloyds insurance market, a syndicate, D P Mann, which deals with brokers throughout the world, has created an Extranet using 'Lotus Domino', triggered by the desire to improve communications with both customers and the brokers through whom they promoted their products.

Whilst their first Web server was installed only in 1998, and then made secure by encrypting with SSL, the syndicate saw the benefits immediately. The connection to back-end databases sped up the information exchange which had, until then, relied on rather long and complicated faxes and telephone calls – actions often frustrated by time differences when dealing in a global marketplace.

In 1998 this Extranet had 240 registered users and supported £3.1m of business, and was expected to grow ten-fold in 1999. Although saving money was not the primary objective, the immediacy of the system allowing documents to be posted on the Extranet immediately saved both time and money.

The new work methods have been generally accepted, although corporate cultural and multi-cultural problems have been difficult in some cases. For instance, the posting of a new document to the system is considerably easier than posting existing contracts. So the normal allowance of time and learning curve to accommodate existing or legacy systems must be allowed for in the planning stage.

The buying-in of the Domino solution was decided upon because of upgrade path security, as opposed to building a bespoke Extranet in-house – which the directors saw as being possibly less flexible for use as the business grew. The ability to configure the system to the customers' needs quickly, so that they have the right applications for their needs and can access the right information easily, was the key to this decision.

In all, business security is paramount, and the mere thought of letting other people into your inner sanctum of core systems makes this more pressing; so when looking at bespoke or boxed Extranets there is a lot of planning to do before taking one's first step along the implementation path.

GET STUCK IN TO HTML – THE BASICS </IF YOU HAVE TO!>

In This Chapter...

▶ The Web page language – it's all tags

▶ Helpful software you can use (if you really want to)

▶ A simple Web page: title, heading and paragraphs

▶ Formatting text with bold and italic type

▶ Inserting links to other pages and Web sites

The mechanics of creating a Web site in HTML are simple enough, and over the next three chapters we'll show you how to do it. Of course, whole books have been written on this subject so this isn't an exhaustive reference, but you'll find many more examples, tips and links to more information on the CD-ROM, plus a HTML quick reference glossary in Appendix E. For best results, treat these chapters as a tutorial – work through them and experiment with the examples yourself, and in a few days this will all seem very simple stuff.

At this point, in view of what we have written about whether you can afford the time to learn HTML, you might be asking yourself why we have included these details at all. Well, if you want to commission designers or have your Web site designed in-house, you need to know what developing a site involves, even if only to ensure that you are not going to have the wool pulled over your eyes by others who know a little bit more than you!

If you really don't want to learn HTML, then all is certainly not lost. As we saw in the last chapter, you can create a very successful e-commerce site with no knowledge of programming languages at all.

HTML – The Language Of The Web

As we've already noted, pages on the World Wide Web are written in a language called **HTML** (HyperText Markup Language). So what's that all about? Well, we've met hypertext already – those underlined, clickable links that make the Web so easy to navigate. A *markup language* is a set of codes or signs added to plain text to indicate how it should be presented to the reader, noting bold or italic text, typefaces to be used, paragraph breaks, and so on. When you type any document into your word processor, it adds these codes for you, but tactfully hides them from view: if you wanted bold text, for example, it *shows* you bold text instead of those codes. In HTML, however, you have to type in the codes yourself along with the text, and your browser puts the whole lot together before displaying it. Mind you, very few people write whole sites in raw HTML these days, because there are so many excellent Web authoring packages to do it all for you; but even these authoring packages give you the option of switching into HTML view to tweak the pages for some special effects.

The HTML codes are known as **tags**, and they consist of ordinary text placed between less-than and greater-than signs. Let's take an example:

```
<B>Welcome to my homepage.</B> Glad you could make it!
```

The first tag, <B>, means 'turn on bold type'. Halfway through the line, the same tag is used again, but with a forward-slash inserted straight after the less-than sign: this means 'turn off bold type'. If you displayed a page containing this line in your browser, it would look like this:

Welcome to our homepage. Glad you could make it!

Of course, there's more to a Web page than bold text, so clearly there must be many more of these tags. But don't let that worry you – you don't have to learn all of them! There's a small bundle that you'll use a lot, and you'll get to know those very quickly. Others will begin to sink in once you've used them a few times, but until they do, just turn to Appendix E to look them up!

Do We Need Special Software?

Believe it or not, creating a Web site is something you can do for free. Because HTML is entirely text-based, you can write your pages in Windows' Notepad, and throughout these chapters we're going to assume that's what you're doing. Indeed you can use any other word processor you want to, but you'll have to remember to save your files as plain text when you've finished. But there are other options, so let's quickly run through them.

JARGON BUSTER

WYSIWYG

A delightful acronym (pronounced 'wizzywig') for 'What you see is what you get'. This is used to describe many different types of software that can show you on the screen exactly what something will look like when you print it on paper or view it in your Web browser.

WYSIWYG Editors

In theory, WYSIWYG editors are the perfect way of working: instead of looking at plain text with HTML tags dotted around it, you see your Web page itself gradually taking shape, with images, colours and formatting displayed. They probably won't help you avoid learning something about HTML, though. Once in a while the editor won't do what you want it to do, and you'll have to switch to its text-editing mode to juggle the tags yourself. More often, you'll see something clever on someone else's page and want to find out how it was done: if you don't understand the language, you might remain envious forever!

GOOD QUESTION

How do I see how someone else's page was put together?

In Internet Explorer, either click on the **View** menu and choose **Source**, or right-click on the page and choose **View Source**. Notepad will open the HTML code for that page.

Here are two of the most popular software packages, but there are very many on the market:

▶ **Microsoft FrontPage.** You can find out more about this at **http://www. microsoft.com/frontpage**.

▶ **Adobe PageMill.** Visit **http://www.adobe.com/prodindex/pagemill/ main.html** for details, downloads and online payment.

Markup Editors

Using a markup editor is rather like using Notepad – you see all the HTML code on the page in front of you. But instead of having to type in tags yourself, a markup editor will insert them for you at the click of a button or the press of a hotkey, in the same way that you use your word processor. You might still choose to type in some of the simple tags yourself, such as the tag for bold text mentioned earlier, but for more complicated elements such as a table with a lot of cells, this automation is a great time and sanity saver.

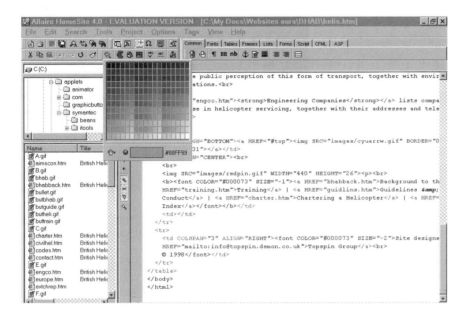

◀ Colour-coding
and one-click tag
insertion in
HomeSite.

Markup editors are also ideal for newcomers to HTML. If you don't know
one tag from another, just click the appropriate buttons on the toolbar to
insert them: once you've seen them appear on the page a few times, you'll
soon start to remember what's what!

Here are three of the most popular and feature-packed markup editors.
You'll need to register these if you want to use them beyond the trial period,
but they're a good place to begin.

▶ **HomeSite** from **http://www.allaire.com/products/homesite**

▶ **HTMLed** from **http://www.ist.ca**

▶ **WebEdit PRO** from **http://www.luckman.com**

Text Converters

Some of the latest word processors like Lotus WordPro and Microsoft Word
have begun to include features to turn your documents into Web pages. At
their simplest, they'll let you create an ordinary word processed document
and then choose a **Save as HTML** option from the **File** menu to convert it
into a Web page. The result won't be as effective as other pages on the Web,
but it's an ideal way to convert a long document when the only other option
is to add all the tags yourself!

Using Office on the Web

BY THE WAY

If you use Microsoft Office 97 onwards, the Web authoring features don't stop at Word. Excel allows you to save a worksheet in HTML format, and PowerPoint helps you create multimedia pages by converting slides to Web format. You'll also find a media library of pictures, sounds and animations that you can include in your pages, however you choose to create them.

You can also create Web pages from scratch in these programs. For example, Microsoft Word has its own Web Page Wizard that can set you up with a ready-to-edit template like the one shown in the next screenshot. To start it up, go to **File | New...**, then click the **Web Pages** tab and double-click **Web Page Wizard**. You can add and delete elements on the page, and use the standard drawing and editing toolbars to slot in anything else you need.

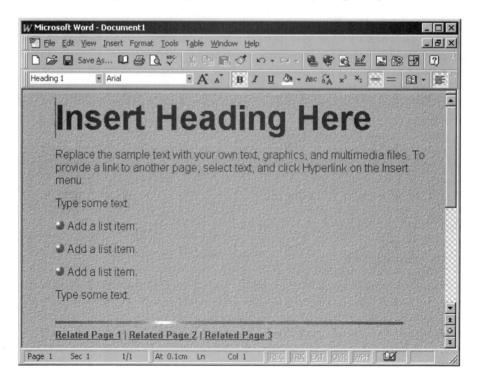

▶ Creating a Web page from a Microsoft Word template.

Let's Get Started

There are a few bits and pieces that will appear in almost every HTML document you write, so let's start by making a template file you can use every time you want to create a new page. Start Notepad, and type the text below (without worrying about the exact number of spaces or carriage returns). Save this file using any name you like, but make sure you give it the extension **.htm** or **.html**. Every Web page you write must be saved with one of these extensions – it doesn't matter which you choose, but you'll find life a lot easier if you stick to the same one each time!

```
<HTML>
<HEAD>
        <TITLE>Untitled</TITLE>
</HEAD>
<BODY>
</BODY>
</HTML>
```

None of those tags does anything exciting by itself, but it's worth knowing what they're for. The document is placed between the <HTML> and </HTML> tags, and falls into two separate chunks: the **head** (the section between <HEAD> and </HEAD>) and the **body** (between <BODY> and </BODY>).

The document's head is pretty dull: all it contains is the title of the document, inserted between the <TITLE> and </TITLE> tags. There are other bits and pieces that can be slotted in here, and you'll meet some of those in Chapter 23, but the title is the only element that must be there.

Do I have to type these tags in capitals?

GOOD QUESTION No, browsers don't care about the case of the tags. If you prefer <title>, or <Title>, or even <tItLe>, it's all the same to your browser. But typing tags in capitals makes them stand out from the rest of your text, which can be useful at times.

The body section is the one that matters. Between these two tags you'll type all the text that should appear on your page, and put in the tags you need to display images, set colours, insert hyperlinks to other pages and sites, and anything else you want your page to contain.

Now that you've created a basic template, let's start adding to it to build up a respectable-looking page. Make a copy of the file (so that you keep this template unchanged for creating more Web pages later) and open the copy in Notepad or your HTML editor.

Add A Title & Text

The first thing to do is to replace the word **Untitled** with a sensible title for the document, such as **Links to the Best News Sites**. Pick something that describes what the page will be about, but keep it fairly short: the text between the <TITLE> and </TITLE> tags will appear in the title-bar at the very top of most browsers, and if your entry is too long to fit, it'll just get chopped off!

Choose your title carefully

BY THE WAY

The title is more important than it might seem. First, some search engines will list the title of your page. Second, if someone likes your page enough to add it to their Favorites or Bookmarks list, this is the title they'll see in the list when they open it.

Now we'll add some text to the page. Either type the same as we've entered below, or replace the first and second paragraph entries with whole paragraphs if you prefer. When you've done that, save the file as **links.htm** or **links.html**, but don't close Notepad yet.

```
<HTML>
<HEAD>
        <TITLE>Test Page</TITLE>
</HEAD>
<BODY>
<H1>Welcome to my Test Page</H1>
Here's the first paragraph
<P>And here's the second paragraph
</BODY>
</HTML>
```

Now take a look at your masterpiece in your browser. There are several ways you can do this: find the file you just saved and double-click it, or open your browser and type the path to the file in the address bar, or choose **File | Open** in your browser and click on **Browse**. When your browser displays it, it should look just like the next screenshot.

Welcome to my Test Page

Here's the first paragraph

And here's the second paragraph

So what are those new tags all about? Let's take the <P> tag first. This tells your browser to present the following text as a new paragraph, which automatically inserts a blank line before it. And this raises an important point about HTML: you can't insert blank lines just by pressing Enter or Return. Although you can see blank lines in Notepad when you do that, your browser will just ignore them, which is why you need to start a new paragraph by entering <P>. (Notice that you don't have to put in a closing </P> at the end of a paragraph – the act of starting a new paragraph isn't an ongoing effect that has to be turned off again.)

GOOD QUESTION

How do I start a new line without starting a new paragraph?

Another tag, <BR>, will give you a 'line break'. In other words, the text that follows that tag will start at the beginning of the next line with no empty line inserted before it.

The other pair of tags that cropped up was <H1> and </H1> which format a line of text as a heading. You can choose from six sizes: H1 is the largest, followed by <H2> and </H2> down to the smallest, <H6> and </H6>. In one nifty little manoeuvre, these tags change the size of the text you place between them and make it bold. They also automatically start a new paragraph for the heading (so you don't need to place a <P> tag at the start of the line) and start a new paragraph for whatever follows the heading. Try changing the size of the heading by altering those tags to see the different effects, re-saving the file, and clicking your browser's **Refresh** button to update it.

Be Bold (Or Be Italic)

The tags for bold and italic text are easy to remember: <B> for bold and <I> for italic. As both of these are ongoing effects, you'll have to enter closing tags (</B> or </I>) when you want the effect to stop. And, just as in your word processor, you can combine these tags, so if your document contained this:

```
This is <I>italic</I>. This is <B>bold</B>. This is <B><I>bold &
italic</I></B>.
```

the result would look like this in your browser:

This is *italic*. This is **bold**. This is ***bold & italic***.

Lesser-used text formatting tags that might come in handy one day are superscript (^{and}) and subscript (_{and}). If you really feel the urge, you can underline text using another memorable pair of tags, <U> and </U>, but be careful how you use underlining: most people surfing the Web expect underlined text to be a hyperlink, and might find your gratuitous use of these tags confusing.

BY THE WAY

Spaces in HTML

Just as browsers ignore your use of the Enter or Return key when you create your Web pages, some have a similar attitude to the Spacebar. However many spaces you enter in a row, only the first will be recognised in some browsers – the rest are ignored. If you really need more than one space, either type in the code ** ** for each space you need (so **   ** would give you three spaces), or use the <PRE> tag explained on page 365.

Insert Links To Other Sites

The majority of Web sites contain links to other Web sites. After all, the entire Web works by being interconnected. So let's put in another <P> tag to start a new paragraph, and add a link as shown below:

<P>Visit <A REF="http://www.topspin-group.com"> Topspin's </A> Own Web Site.

Welcome to my Test Page

Here's the first paragraph

And here's the second paragraph

Visit Topspin's Own Web Site

This is a more complicated tag, so let's look at it bit-by-bit. Although we call these 'links', in HTML they're called **anchors**, and that's where the A comes from after the first < sign. An anchor usually begins with the <A HREF= tag. Following that comes the URL of the page you want to link to, always enclosed in double quotes, and the > sign to finish the opening anchor tag.

Immediately after the opening anchor tag, type the text you want visitors to your page to click on. This might be a single word, a sentence, or even a whole paragraph, but don't forget to put *something* here, or there'll be nothing to click on to reach that site! Finally, type the closing anchor tag, </A>.

BY THE WAY

Get it central

You can place elements centrally on the page by placing them between <CENTER> and </CENTER> tags (note the American spelling, though!). This applies to headings, paragraphs of text, images, and almost anything else you might want to include.

Links To Other Pages On Your Own Site

The link we just added used something called an **absolute URL**. In fact, that's the only type of URL you've seen so far: an absolute URL gives the whole path to the page you want to open, including the http:// bit and the name of the computer. When you want to create links to other pages on your own site you can use a different, simpler method.

Create a new HTML document and save it to the directory where the other is stored. Let's assume you've called it **morelinks.html**. Now, in your first document you can create a link to this new page by typing this anchor:

```
<A HREF="morelinks.html">Here's a few more links.</A>
```

Yes, it's just a filename. This is called a **relative URL**. It tells your browser to look for a file called **morelinks.html** and display it. Since a browser doesn't know where else to look, it searches the directory containing the document it's displaying at that moment. As long as **morelinks.html** really is in that same directory, the browser will find it and open it.

GOOD QUESTION

What's so great about relative URLs?

First, less typing. That also lessens the chances of mistakes. But best of all, you can click these links in your browser while you're designing your site to check that they work. If you click a link to an absolute URL, your browser will have to connect to your IAP first to find that computer, costing you money and time.

You can make a browser look somewhere different for a file in a similar way. Open the directory containing these two documents, create a subdirectory called **pages**, and move the **morelinks.html** file into it. The link we just added now needs to be changed to the following:

```
<A HREF="pages/morelinks.html">Here's a few more links.</A>
```

The browser now looks in the current directory for another directory called **pages**, and looks inside that for **morelinks.html**.

Finally, let's open **morelinks.html** and create a link back to our original document (which we called **links.html**) so that you can click your way to and fro between the two. To do this, we need to tell the browser to look in the parent directory of **pages** to find this file. If you're familiar with using MS-DOS, you'll recognise this straight away: to move up one level in the directory tree, just type two dots:

```
<A HREF="../links.html">Here's my first links page.</A>
```

Case sensitive filenames

BY THE WAY

When you refer to a page or file in your document, the case is vital. If you type in a link to **Index.html** and the file is actually called **index.html** or **Index.HTML**, the page won't be found. Most Web authors save all their files with lower-case names to remove any uncertainty. Similarly, although you can use long filenames, they mustn't include any spaces.

So far we've looked at linking to other Web pages, but a hyperlink needn't necessarily point to a **.html** document. If you have a movie file, a text file, a sound file, or whatever, create the link in exactly the same way entering the location and name of this file between the double quotes. If the file is particularly large, though, it's good practice to mention its size somewhere nearby so that people can choose whether or not to click that link.

E-mail Links

Another type of anchor allows a visitor to your page to click a link that opens their e-mail message window, with your e-mail address already inserted, ready for them to send you a message. This is a lot like any other anchor, with the URL replaced by your e-mail address. The only difference is that the word **mailto:** must be inserted immediately after that first quote sign. Here's an example – just replace the e-mail address with your own:

```
<A HREF="mailto:brian.salter@topspin-group.com">Click here to send
me an e-mail</A>
```

COLOURS, IMAGES & WEB PAGE LAYOUT

In This Chapter...

▶ **Choose page and text colours, and add a wallpaper image**

▶ **Select and change fonts, sizes and colours**

▶ **Divide the page into sections with horizontal rules**

▶ **Use images to add sparkle or act as links**

▶ **Create your own animations for your pages**

In the last chapter we created a basic Web page consisting of headlines, text (with a little style and paragraph formatting), and hyperlinks. As it stands it won't win any awards, but what matters most is that you've worked with a few HTML tags and seen the effect they have on a page when your browser displays it. Armed with this experience, let's improve the look of the page by adding colours, choosing images and fonts, and applying a few more formatting and design touches.

You Too Can Have A <BODY> Like Mine!

So far, in our example Web page, everything looks a bit dull. The background is white, the text is black, the hyperlinks are blue – these are the default colours set up by Internet Explorer, and it's using them because we haven't told it to use anything different. All of this is easily changed, though, by typing our preferences into that opening <BODY> tag.

This brings us to a new area of HTML. A tag like <B> is self-contained – it simply turns on bold text, with no complications. Other tags need to contain a little more information about what you want to do. A good example is the <FONT> tag, which we'll look at more closely later in this chapter. By itself, it isn't saying anything useful: which font? what size? what colour? You provide this information by adding **attributes** to the tag such as SIZE=3, FACE=Arial, and so on, so a complete font tag might be: <FONT SIZE=3 FACE=Arial>.

Attributes

JARGON BUSTER

These are additional pieces of information slotted into a tag. Each attribute is separated by a space, and needs an equals sign between the attribute itself and the setting to be used for it. It doesn't matter what order the attributes appear in, and you don't need to include a particular attribute if you don't want to change its setting.

The <BODY> tag doesn't have to contain attributes, but browsers will use their own default settings for anything you haven't specified, and different browsers use different defaults. Most Web authors like to keep as much control as possible over how their pages will be displayed, and make their own settings for the body attributes. There are six main attributes you can use in the <BODY> tag:

This attribute ...	... has this effect
BGCOLOR=	Sets the background colour of the Web page.
TEXT=	Sets the colour of text on the page.
LINK=	Sets the colour of the clickable hyperlinks.
VLINK=	Sets the colour of a link to a previously-visited page.
ALINK=	Sets the colour of a link between the time it's clicked and the new page opening.
BACKGROUND=	Specifies an image to use as the page's 'wallpaper'.

Without further ado, open the original **links.html** document you created in the last chapter, and change the <BODY> tag so that it looks like this:

```
<BODY BGCOLOR=MAROON TEXT=WHITE LINK=YELLOW VLINK=OLIVE ALINK=LIME>
```

Save the file, and take a look at it in your browser. Okay, the colour scheme may not be to your taste, but it's starting to resemble a 'real' Web page! Try swapping colours around to find a scheme you prefer. There are 140 colours to choose from, so skip ahead to Appendix F and pick a few from the list, or take a look at the Colour Chart on the CD-ROM that accompanies this book.

The other attribute is BACKGROUND=, which places a GIF or JPEG image on the Web page, and tiles it to fill the entire area. Let's assume you want to use an image file called **hoops.gif** which is in the same directory as the current document. Inside the body tag, add: BACKGROUND="hoops.gif" (not forgetting the double quotes). Your whole <BODY> tag might now look like this:

```
<BODY BACKGROUND="hoops.gif" BGCOLOR=MAROON TEXT=WHITE LINK=YELLOW
VLINK=OLIVE ALINK=LIME>
```

There are a few things worth bearing in mind if you choose to use a background image. First, make sure the image file isn't too large. If someone arrives at your page and sees a 50Kb background image starting to download, they'll probably rush away again without waiting to find out what else is on your page! Second, make sure you choose a text colour that will be easy to read over the background image (or an image that isn't too garish). Third, pick a BGCOLOR= colour that will allow your text to show up clearly – that way, if the background image is taking a while to download, visitors will still be able to read your page comfortably.

Set Up Your Font Options

At the moment you're also stuck with a single font (probably Times New Roman). Once again, this is set up by your browser by default and, of course, different browsers might use different default fonts. Fortunately, the <FONT> tag leaps to your rescue, allowing you to choose and change the font face, size and colour whenever you need to. Here's an example of a <FONT> tag using all three attributes:

```
<FONT FACE="Verdana,Arial,Helvetica" SIZE=4 COLOR=RED>...</FONT>
```

Let's take these one at a time. The FACE attribute is the name of the font you want to use. Obviously this must be a font on your own system, but the same font needs to be on the system of anyone visiting your page too: if it isn't, their browser will revert to their default font. You can keep a bit of extra control by listing more than one font (separated by commas) as in the example above. If the first font isn't available, the browser will try the second, and so on.

GOOD QUESTION

Which font faces should I use?

Most visitors to your site will have MS Serif, MS Sans Serif and Courier on their systems. TrueType fonts are better, and the safest are Arial and Times New Roman. Microsoft supplies a pack of fonts for the Web which many Web authors now use, including Comic Sans MS, Verdana, Impact and Georgia. You can download any of these you don't already have from **http://www.microsoft.com/truetype/fontpack/win.htm**.

Font sizes in HTML work differently from the way they do in your word processor. There are seven sizes numbered (unsurprisingly) from 1 to 7, where 1 is smallest. The default size for text is 3, so if you want to make your text slightly larger, use SIZE=4. The SIZE attribute doesn't affect the headings we covered in the previous chapter, so if you've used one of these somewhere between your <FONT> and </FONT> tags, it will still be formatted as a heading.

Big text, small text

BY THE WAY

If you find it hard to keep track of the font size you're currently using, don't bother trying! Instead, you can use `<BIG>` and `</BIG>` to make text one step larger, or `<SMALL>` and `</SMALL>` to make it one step smaller.

The colour of the text has already been set in the `<BODY>` tag, but you might want to slip in an occasional `<FONT COLOR=PURPLE>...` `</FONT>` to change the colour of a certain word, paragraph or heading. After the closing `</FONT>` tag, the colour will revert to that set in the `<BODY>` tag.

With the earlier changes to the `<BODY>` tag, and the addition of a couple of `</FONT>` tags, here's what the body of our document might look like now:

```
<BODY BGCOLOR=MAROON TEXT=WHITE LINK=YELLOW VLINK=OLIVE ALINK=LIME>

<FONT FACE="Arial" COLOR=YELLOW>
<H1>Welcome to my Test Page</H1>
</FONT>

<FONT FACE="Arial">

Here's the first paragraph
<P>And here's the second paragraph
<P>Visit <A REF="http://www.topspin-group.com"> Topspin's</A> Own
Web Site

</FONT>
</BODY>
</HTML>
```

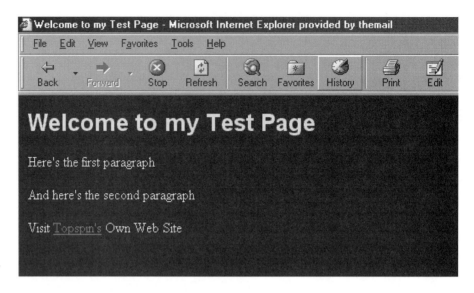

Horizontal Rules (Okay)

Horizontal rules are straight lines that divide a page into sections. For the simplest type of rule, the only tag you need is <HR>. This automatically puts a horizontal rule across the full width of the page on a new line, and any text that follows it will form a new paragraph. Because the rule isn't something that needs to be turned off again, there's no closing tag.

If you want to, you can get clever with rules by adding some (or all!) of the following attributes:

Use this attribute ...	... for this result
ALIGN=	Use LEFT or RIGHT to place the rule on the left or right of the page. If you leave this out, the rule will be centred.
SIZE=	Enter any number to set the height of the rule in pixels. The default setting is 2.
WIDTH=	Enter a number to specify the width of the line in pixels, or as a percentage of the page (such as WIDTH=70%).
NOSHADE	This removes the 3D effect from the rule. There's no equals sign, and nothing more to add.
COLOR=	Enter the name of a colour. The default setting depends upon the background colour. Only Internet Explorer supports this attribute – most other browsers will ignore it.

It's worth playing with the <HR> tag and its attributes to see what unusual effects you can create. For example, the following piece of code places a square bullet in the centre of the page which makes a 'minimalist' divider:

```
<HR SIZE=10 WIDTH=10 COLOR=LIME NOSHADE>
```

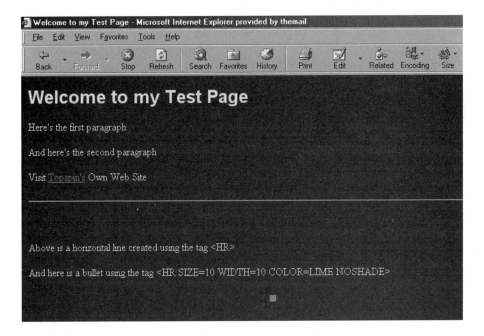

Add Spice With An Image

The horizontal rule is the simplest type of graphical content you can include on a page, but it's hardly exciting. To liven up a dull page, you can't go far wrong with a well-chosen image. Images on the Web are usually in one of two formats:

▶ **JPEG.** This format usually has a **.jpg** or **.jpeg** extension. The images are saved in 16 million colours, making them ideal for photographs but this format may create unnecessarily large files for pictures you create yourself.

Make your JPEGs smaller

When you create a JPEG image, you can use one of many image editing programs to increase the compression settings of the file itself. The higher the compression, the lower the quality of the picture; but it is usually quite safe to compress up to a setting of 70% without overly impacting on the visual quality of the picture. Experiment and find out for yourself!

▶ **GIF**. These images have a **.gif** extension, and save images in up to 256 colours. This gives pretty poor results for photographs, but it's often the ideal format for anything else. Using the latest version of the GIF format (GIF89a), you can opt to make one of the colours in the image **transparent**, so that when it appears on your page you'll be able to see the page's background colour (or BACKGROUND= image) in place of that colour.

Make your GIFs smaller

When you create a GIF image, try reducing its number of colours to 16 before you save it. In most cases you won't notice any difference in quality, but the size of the file will be much smaller, making it download a lot faster.

If you're unsure about which format to choose, create your images in 16 million colours and save them in JPEG format. Then reduce the number of colours to 256 and save again in GIF format. You can then compare the file sizes and picture qualities to decide which you want to stick with.

Once you've chosen the image you want to use, the <IMG> tag will slot it onto the page. This tag works rather like the <FONT> tag – by itself it's meaningless; all the information is supplied by adding attributes. Let's assume you want to insert an image called **splash.gif**, and the image file is in the same directory as your current HTML document:

```
<IMG SRC="splash.gif">
```

This is the `<IMG>` tag at its most basic: the SRC attribute (which is short for 'source') tells the browser where to find the image file you want to display, following exactly the same rules as those for relative URLs which we looked at in the previous chapter. Unless you preceded this tag with `<P>` or `<BR>`, the image will be placed immediately after the last piece of text you entered. If you enclose the entire tag between `<CENTER>` and `</CENTER>` tags, the image will be placed below the previous line of text, centred on the page. You do get a little more choice about where the image should be, though, by adding the `ALIGN` attribute:

This attribute...	Does this...
`ALIGN=TOP`	Aligns the top of the image with the top of the text on the same line.
`ALIGN=MIDDLE`	Aligns the middle of the image with the text on that line.
`ALIGN=BOTTOM`	Aligns the bottom of the image with the bottom of the line of text.
`ALIGN=LEFT`	Places the image on a new line, and against the left margin.
`ALIGN=RIGHT`	Places the image on a new line, and against the right margin.

Using these attributes, then, you can place the image roughly where you want it on the page. What's still needed is a bit of fine tuning: after all, if you use `ALIGN=MIDDLE`, the image will be butted right up against the text on the same line. The answer comes in the form of two more attributes which add some blank space around an image: `HSPACE=` inserts space either side of the image (horizontally), and `VSPACE=` adds space above and below it (vertically). Just enter a number in pixels after the equals sign. As usual with attributes, if you only need to use one of these there's no need to include the other. So far, then, an image might be inserted with a tag that looks like this:

`<IMG SRC="splash.gif" ALIGN=MIDDLE HSPACE=30 VSPACE=6>`

GOOD QUESTION

How do I create a GIF or JPEG image?

There are many good graphics programs around that can handle these formats, but the most popular by far is Paint Shop Pro. You can download a trial version from **http://www.jasc.com**. The latest versions also have built-in effects and filters that help the artistically challenged create some very arty images.

Enter The Image's Width & Height

Two of the most important <IMG> attributes are WIDTH= and HEIGHT=, with which you specify the size of the image. If you've experimented with the tags above, you'll have noticed that your browser displays the image properly without these tags, so you're probably wondering why on earth you'd bother to do this.

At the moment, you're looking at pages and images that are already on your own system – there's no downloading involved yet. When your page is on the Web and someone visits it, things work a little differently. When the browser arrives at an <IMG> tag with no width or height attributes, it has to download the image and display it before it can work out where to put the other parts of the page, such as text. However, if the browser already knows how much space is needed for the image, it can hold it in reserve and just display an empty box until the image downloads, with the text positioned correctly around it. Another reason is that some people surf the Web with the option to display images turned off: if you don't enter the dimensions of your images, they'll simply see a tiny placeholder icon instead of a full-size box, which might upset your carefully planned layout!

BY THE WAY

Enter an alternative

It's common practice to enter some alternative text in place of an image. This displays in the placeholder box until the image is downloaded and displayed, and also appears in a tooltip when the mouse moves onto the image. Add the attribute ALT="" and place a description of the image between the quotes, such as ALT="A picture of my cat".

You can find the image's dimensions easily by loading it into almost any graphics program. In Paint Shop Pro, for example, you'll find the width and height displayed in the bottom right-hand corner. Make a mental note of them, and add them to your tag like this:

```
<IMG SRC="splash.gif" ALIGN=MIDDLE HSPACE=30 VSPACE=6 WIDTH=84
HEIGHT=81>
```

Bear in mind that if you enter the dimensions of an image like this, the browser will take your word for it! In other words, the browser will scale the image to these proportions regardless of what the original image looked like. This can be useful to increase or decrease the size of an image without creating a new version of it (or to create weird effects), but it's also a prime opportunity to screw things up!

Reuse your images!

BY THE WAY

Try to reuse images on different pages if you can. After an image has been displayed once, it will be reloaded from the browser's cache rather than downloaded, making your site a more immediate and pleasing experience for your visitors.

Use An Image As An Anchor

In the last chapter you learnt how to create hypertext links, or anchors, to a Web page or file using the tag **<A HREF="*URL*"> *clickable text* </A>**. But the clickable section that appears on the page doesn't have to be text: you can use an image instead, or both image and text. For example, if you slot the whole image tag given above into the anchor tag, the image will appear exactly as it did before, but will now act as a clickable link:

```
<A HREF="morelinks.html"><IMG SRC="splash.gif" ALIGN=MIDDLE
HSPACE=30 VSPACE=6 WIDTH=84 HEIGHT=81 BORDER=0></A>Click this image
to open my other links page.
```

If you want to make both the text and the image clickable, add some text before or after the <IMG> tag like this:

```
<A HREF="morelinks.html">Click this image to open my other links
page.<IMG SRC="splash.gif" ALIGN=MIDDLE HSPACE=30 VSPACE=6 WIDTH=84
HEIGHT=81 BORDER=0></A>
```

Turn off the image border

BY THE WAY

When you use an image as a link, a border will appear around it. You can alter the thickness of the border by adding BORDER= to the <IMG> tag followed by a number in pixels. If you'd prefer to have no border, enter BORDER=0, but make sure it's obvious that the image is clickable to avoid confusing visitors to your page. The border attribute can be added to any image, whether it acts as a link or not.

How About A Little Animation?

The GIF image format has another little trick up its sleeve that can add sparkle to a page – you can use it to create animations. These are known by the simple enough name, **animated GIFs**, but you'll need special software to build the finished article. First, though, you need to create a series of images, each one slightly different from the others, like a cartoon, and save each with a different name and the **.gif** extension. Then you need to load these into the special software that can string them together in the order you choose, set the length of time that each frame of the animation should remain on the screen, and save them as a single animation (still with the extension **.gif**). The animation is placed on your page using exactly the same <IMG> tag and attributes as we looked at earlier. Two popular and easy-to-use animators are:

▶ **Microsoft GIF Animator** from **http://www.microsoft.com/ imagecomposer/gifanimator/gifanin.htm**.

▶ **Ulead GIF Animator** from **http://www.ulead.com**.

We obviously can't show you an animation on the printed page, but if we borrow one of Sidebottom's animated gifs from Chapter 19, it could be made up from the following two images:

Although the process is easy, try to keep the number of images in your animation to a minimum to prevent the file becoming too big – a five-frame animation will take almost as long to download as five separate images. Those Ulead people make a neat utility called SmartSaver (also on the CD-ROM) that can reduce an animation's size by up to 90 per cent: the trial version won't actually convert your images, but it will tell you how much smaller you can make them if you register your copy.

Useful HTML Extras

We haven't by any means exhausted the supply of HTML tags, but we have covered most of those you'll be using regularly, and you should have enough ammunition here to make a good start on your own site. You'll find more in Appendix E, and plenty of examples on the CD-ROM accompanying this book, but let's shift into 'quickfire' mode to look at a last little bundle of tags to keep handy.

Comments

You can enclose anything on your page between <!-- and --> tags, and your browser will ignore them. The intention of these comment tags is that you can put little notes in your document to help you edit it later, such as `<!--The next bit of code inserts the image-->`, but they can be usefully inserted around a piece of code that you want to remove from the page, but don't want to actually delete in case you need to reinstate it sometime.

Marquee

A marquee is a piece of text that scrolls across the page. Different browsers interpret this command in different ways, so it's best not to use it for any text that really matters, but it makes a neat effect. Begin by adding the following code:

```
<MARQUEE ALIGN=Middle HEIGHT=10 WIDTH=80% BGCOLOR=Maroon
SCROLLAMOUNT=3 BEHAVIOR=Scroll SCROLLDELAY=3 DIRECTION=Left HSPACE=0
VSPACE=0 LOOP=INFINITE>This text is scrolling</MARQUEE>
```

All the possible attributes are included above, and you'll recognise some of them, such as `HSPACE` and `VSPACE`. Height can be specified as a percentage of the page or (more usefully) as a number in pixels. Width is best set as a percentage. You can choose a `BGCOLOR` setting to blend the marquee into your page, or make it stand out, and the text will be displayed according to your last use of the `<FONT>` tag (or the `TEXT` attribute in the `<BODY>` tag). You can experiment with the `SCROLLAMOUNT` and `SCROLLDELAY` settings to achieve a comfortable speed, and change the `BEHAVIOR` setting to `Slide` or `Alternate`.

Paragraph Alignment

We met the `<P>` tag in the previous chapter. By itself, it inserts a blank line and places the following text on the next line. But the `<P>` tag also has an optional attribute, `ALIGN=`, that can be used with the settings `LEFT`, `CENTER` or `RIGHT`. The first two aren't particularly useful: by default, all paragraphs are left-aligned anyway, and it's easier to use the plain old `<CENTER>...</CENTER>` tags to centre elements on a page. But if you ever want to align a paragraph of text with the right margin, surround it with these tags:

```
<P ALIGN=RIGHT>This text is right-aligned.</P>
```

Note that you have to use a closing `</P>` tag if you add an attribute to this tag, otherwise all the remaining text on your page will be aligned the same way!

Lists

HTML gives you built-in ways of making bulleted or numbered lists easily with the addition of just a couple of tags. To create a list, just insert the tag `<LI>` at the beginning of each line. No paragraph or line-break tags are needed, so the following code would create a list containing three items, each on its own line:

```
<LI>Here's item one.<LI>Here's a second item.<LI>And here's a third.
```

Now decide whether you want a bulleted or a numbered list. For a numbered list, enclose the entire code between `<OL>` and `</OL>` tags (which stands for 'ordered list'); for a bulleted list, use `<UL>` and `</UL>` tags (meaning 'unordered list'), as shown in the next screenshot.

If you use a numbered list, you can add the `TYPE=` attribute to the `<OL>` tag to choose which numbering system you'd like to apply. The default is Arabic numbers. To use capital letters, enter `TYPE=A`. For small letters, `TYPE=a`. You can also use large Roman numerals (`TYPE=I`) or small Roman numerals (`TYPE=i`). So your complete tag might look like this:

```
<OL TYPE=I><LI>Here's item one.<LI>Here's a second item.<LI>And
here's a third.</OL>
```

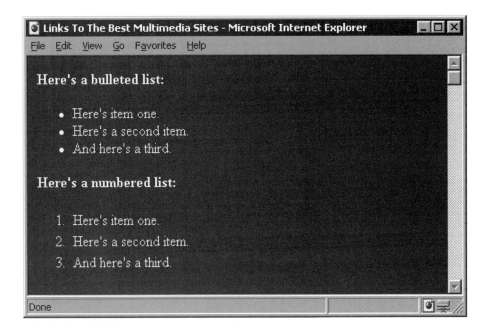

Make editing easier

Since browsers ignore the use of carriage returns, use them liberally to space out your code. For example, although you can enter list entries all on one line, your code will be easier to understand and edit later if you place each on its own line.

BY THE WAY

Preformatted Text

If you're having trouble laying out a piece of text exactly as you want it, enclose it between <PRE> and </PRE> tags. This way, all the spaces and carriage returns you type into that portion of your document will be displayed in exactly the same way in the browser with no need to muck about with <P> or <BR> tags. The ability to use the spacebar also gives you an easy way to indent a line of text.

Make This Your Internet Explorer Home Page

In Chapter 6 you learnt how to change your Home Page in Internet Explorer. Your choices were to use a blank document (so that Explorer didn't try to dial up every time you started it) or to use any other page on the Web. But now you know how to build your own pages, why not create your own start page instead, perhaps containing links to some of your favourite sites?

When the page looks okay loaded into Explorer, click your way to **View** | **Internet Options** | **General**. In the Home Page section at the top of the dialog box, click the button marked **Use Current**. Provided you don't move, rename or delete the HTML document you created (or any other files linked to it, such as images) this page will be displayed every time you run Internet Explorer, or click its **Home** toolbar button.

FROM DRAWING-BOARD TO WEB

In This Chapter...

▶ **Planning and preparing to build your site**

▶ **The quest for free Web space**

▶ **Find free graphics, animations and more**

▶ **Upload and test your Web site**

▶ **Publicise your site for maximum exposure**

▶ **Find out about visitor tracking**

Now that you know something about HTML, it's time to put on your hard hat and start building. But there's more to constructing a good Web site than a knowledge of HTML. How should the site be laid out? What about page design? Where do you find graphics files? How does your site get onto the Web? And how will everyone else know it's there? Looks like you've come to the right chapter …

Think First, Write Later!

A little planning never goes amiss, so try to do all your thinking before you start designing anything – especially graphics. It's no use spending ages designing a fabulous set of textual buttons for a page, if no-one but you will understand where they were linking to unless you put an explanatory paragraph beside each one! Remember that you'll know how to navigate your site, but your visitors won't, and they'll usually expect it to be obvious.

Decide what topics your site will cover, and how you can split them up into different pages rather than one long page. Make sure your first page contains links to all the others, and that those links really do explain what visitors will find there. On arrival at any other page, visitors should be able to switch back to the homepage with a single click and (if possible) to all your other pages too.

BY THE WAY

Ugh, I hate it when they do that!

When you plan your own site, consider what you like and dislike about other sites you've visited. For example, most people hate to find large graphics on a page before they know what the site is even about. Other pet hates are repetitive music, large unnecessary background WAV files, links that don't tell you what they're linking to, and text that's the wrong colour for the background.

Of course, if you're going to have a Web site, you want people to visit it. Consider why they'd visit your site and make sure you deliver what you promise. Popular sites are those that give something away (we all love freebies don't we?) – it may be software, useful information, or entertainment. Add a 'What's New' page to keep regular visitors informed about the latest changes and additions, and make sure it contains the dates of those changes and links to the relevant pages.

Finally, bear in mind that most visitors to your page are using a screen resolution of 800×600 on a 15-inch monitor. Although some sites ask visitors to switch screen resolutions to view their pages, no-one is likely to do that – they expect you to design a site that looks good at any screen size. Try adjusting your own resolution and the size of your browser window every so often to see your pages as others may see them.

BY THE WAY

Don't trust the download times!

If you use a program that tells you the download time (or 'weight') of a page as you build it, don't rely on it too much. Not everyone uses a 56Kbps modem, not everyone will have a good connection to your site, and a download time can't include the hugely variable connection times. Think in terms of at least doubling that figure.

Talk To Your Service Provider

Before you begin the creation process, check a few details with your service provider. First, of course, you want to know how much Web space is available to you. Here are three more things to find out:

▶ Ask if you can upload your files by FTP. A few IAPs have their own methods of handling this, but most will tell you the address to connect to using your FTP program. You'll log on using your normal username and password and start copying the files across.

▶ Find out if you can create your own directory structure. Most IAPs will let you upload whole directories, but a few insist that only files can be uploaded. If all your links refer to files in subdirectories and you later find out that everything has to be in the same directory, you'll have a lot of editing to do!

▶ If your site is addressed as a subsection of the IAP's domain, the URL to your site will normally be **http://www.serviceprovider/~companyname** or **http://www.companyname.serviceprovider/** with all the files (and subdirectories) in this directory making up your site. When somebody arrives at this directory an index file should be displayed automatically, and this would usually be your first welcoming page. In most cases this will be called **index.htm** or **index.html** or even **default.htm(l)**, but check this with your service provider in case their system uses something different.

The Quest For Free Web Space

As we mentioned earlier, there are companies out there that not only provide free Web access, but also free Web space – you don't have to pay, or buy anything else from them, you don't have to carry advertising , and you don't have to make any commitments. Just go there and check the details.

The down-side of this is that having your company site seen by your potential customers as being a subsection of one of these freebie Web site hosters is not going to put your own company in a very good light. What kind of image will it portray of your organisation? Do you really want to be regarded as cheapskate? Not just that, but if the company deletes all your files, or their computers go down for six months, you're not in a strong position to complain about it.

Nevertheless, if you want to try out some free Web space as an experiment, point your browser at one of these:

▶ Freeserve at **http://www.freeserve.co.uk**

▶ Freenet at **http://www.freenet.co.uk**

▶ ConnectFree at **http://www.connectfree.co.uk**

▶ Free-Online at **http://www.free-online.net**

▶ Callnet at **http://www.callnetuk.com**

Of course it's under construction!

There's a trend on the Web to add 'Under Construction' graphics to indicate that a Web site isn't finished. Don't fall into that trap! The entire Web is under construction, and a good site should always be evolving. If by 'Under Construction' you mean that the links don't work, either remove them or fix them!

You Need Buttons, Backgrounds, Bullets, Applets...

Armed with a good graphics program, there's not much you can't do, however limited your artistic talents. But why bother? You can find everything you need on the Web and download it for your own use. There are many sites handing out the many bits and pieces you might like to add to your pages, but for starters why not look up the Microsoft Site Builder Gallery at **http://www.microsoft.com/gallery/default.asp** which will provide you with a bit of everything, including complete 'theme' sets of backgrounds, images and icons. For a little help on the art of page design itself, visit one of these:

▶ Creating Killer Sites at **http://www.killersites.com**

▶ Jeffrey Zeldman Presents... at **http://www.zeldman.com**

▶ HTML Authoring at **http://www.asiweb.com/htmlauth.htm**

▶ The Web Developer's Virtual Library at **http://www.stars.com**

Or, if you learn more easily by discovering how not to do it, visit Web Pages That Suck at **http://www.webpagesthatsuck.com**.

You're Ready To Upload

Or are you? Before you do so, load all your pages into your browser one by one and check them. Test all your internal links (links to other pages from your own site) by clicking them to make sure they work. If your HTML software has a built-in spell-checker, use it.

Now follow the instructions you were given by your service provider to upload the files to the Web server. At the risk of being obvious (not everyone realises this straight off), every file that forms a part of your site must be uploaded – images, documents, ZIP files, sound files ... If it's supposed to be a part of your Web site, it must be on the Web server where everyone else can see it and not just on your own computer. As you upload, make sure you keep the directory structure the same. For instance, if all your graphics files are in a subdirectory called **images** (and your links to them look something like `<IMG SRC="images/mypicture.gif">`), you must have a directory on the Web server called **images**, in the same relative location to your HTML documents, that contains the same graphics files.

Easy site upload with FTP

BY THE WAY

When you upload using an FTP program such as FTP Explorer, you don't have to transfer the files one-by-one. Once you've connected to your online directory, following the instructions given by your service provider, just select all the files and directories that make up your site in Windows Explorer and drag them into FTP Explorer's main window to transfer the lot in one go.

When your site is uploaded to the server, start your browser, type your URL into the address-bar and check each page to make sure that everything is as it should be (including all your links to other Web sites). If you need to change a file, make the change on your own system and then upload the file again – provided you don't change its name, it should replace the original. Depending upon your service provider's system, you should be able to see all your files and subdirectories in your FTP program and delete or rename them as needed.

Hit The Publicity Trail

So you have a Web site, and it works. Now you want people to come and visit it, so you need to let them know it exists. One method is to contact other business sites covering similar subjects and ask if they'd like to exchange links – you add a link to their sites in return for links to yours. The other, more useful, way to publicise your site is to get it listed with as many search engines as you can. There are two ways to do this which should capture almost every search engine going.

Feed The Robots

The first thing to do is to adjust your homepage in such a way that the search engines using roving robot-programs will find your site and describe it correctly. First, make sure that the title of your page (which appears between the <TITLE></TITLE> tags) is as meaningful as possible. Second, add the <META> tag to the header of your page. This tag has two attributes: NAME= (which can be "keywords" or "description") and CONTENT=. Let's say your site is about camels:

```
<HTML>
<HEAD>

<TITLE>The Ultimate Camel Reference</TITLE>

<META NAME="keywords" CONTENT="camels, dromedaries, quadrupeds">

<META NAME="description" CONTENT="The ultimate database of camel
information, plus our fabulous Spot The Hump competition!">

</HEAD>
<BODY>
</BODY>
</HTML>
```

In the keywords tag, list the words that people might type into a search engine to find sites like yours. In the description tag, type a short paragraph that explains what your page is about, to whet the appetite of intrepid Web-surfers. Most search engines will display this description below the link to your site. It also helps if the first paragraph of text on your page sounds reasonably descriptive and appetising: some search engines will quote from this instead of using your meta description.

What happens if I don't add a META tag?

GOOD QUESTION

Either a large bundle of search engines won't be able to add your site to their database, or they'll index it wrongly. For example, if you leave out the description, the index will probably consist of the first few lines from your page which may contain no useful information at all.

Submit To The Directories

Some search engines and directories don't use robots, so you'll need to submit details of your site to them manually. One way to do this is to visit each search site, one-by-one, and look for a link marked **Add Your Site** or something similar, and then follow the instructions.

A better method is to visit a service that can submit your details to many search sites at once. There are hundreds of different search sites, and these services will want money from you to submit to the whole lot, but their free services cover several dozen of the major search engines and directories. Choose one of these services and nip along to fill in the details:

▶ Add Me! at **http://www.addme.com**

▶ Submit It! at **http://www.submit-it.com**

▶ WebPromote at **http://www.webpromote.com**

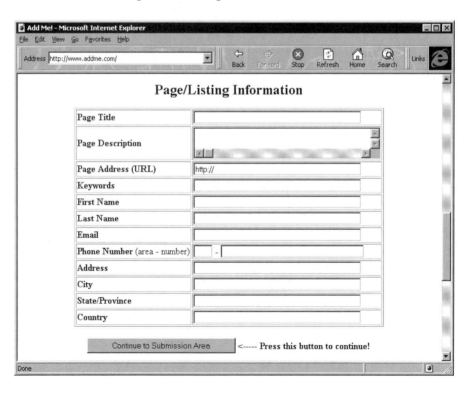

You might even choose to visit all three – keep a note of the search engines your details were submitted to using the first service, and then see if the remaining services cover any others. Take your time filling in the information, and make sure it's correct. When the form appears on the screen, you might want to disconnect from the Internet while you fill it in so that you don't feel rushed.

Gauge Audience Reaction

The only way to get true feedback about your site is to include e-mail links on your pages, as we covered in Chapter 19, and to encourage visitors to tell you what they liked, what they didn't like, and what they were hoping to see.

Another device that appeals to some people is to place a counter on your page that tells you (roughly) how many visits (or 'hits') your site has received. You might even want to put a counter on every page to get a rough idea of which links most visitors find tempting from your homepage.

But if you put a counter on these pages they will be visible to everyone, and why would you want to do that on a business site? We'd suggest that you ignore such gimmicks and leave them to those who have personal Web sites and egos to boot!

If you are determined to have a counter however, one of the most informative and reliable counter-services can be found at ICount (**http://www.icount.com/register.html**). Fill in the simple details, choose a password if you don't want anyone else to see your page statistics, and the service will then display some HTML code. Swipe it with the mouse, copy it to the clipboard, and then paste it into one of your pages. You'll need to repeat this for each counter you want.

But why have a page counter at all? If you have signed up to a proper business Web account, you will almost certainly be offered this facility by your IAP. Ask them what type of tracking they can offer you, and if they don't have anything to help you gauge the success of your site, consider whether you really want to keep your Web site with them.

25

EPILOGUE

An ambitious yuppie finally decided to take a vacation. He booked himself on a Caribbean cruise and proceeded to have the time of his life – until the boat sank. The man found himself swept up onto the shore of an island with no other people, no supplies, nothing. Only bananas and coconuts.
After about four months he was lying on the beach one day when the most gorgeous woman he had ever seen rowed up to him.

In disbelief he asked her, "Where did you come from? How did you get here?"

"I rowed from the other side of the island," she replied. "I landed here when my cruise ship sank."

"Amazing," he said. "You were really lucky to have had a rowing boat wash up with you."

"Oh, this?" replied the woman. "I made the boat out of raw material that I found on the island; the oars were whittled from gumtree branches; I wove the bottom from palm branches and the sides and stern came from a eucalyptus tree."

"But ... but that's impossible," stuttered the man. "You had no tools or hardware. How on earth did you manage?"

"Oh, that was no problem," replied the woman. "On the south side of the island there is a very unusual strata of alluvial rock exposed. I found that if I fired it to a certain temperature in my kiln, it melted into forgeable ductile iron. I used that for the tools, and used the tools to make the hardware." The man was stunned.

"Let's row over to my place," she said. After an hour of rowing she docked the boat at a small wharf. As the man looked onto shore he nearly fell out of the boat. Before him was a stone walk leading to an exquisite bungalow painted in blue and white. While the woman tied up the rowing boat with an expertly woven hemp rope, the man could only stare straight ahead, dumbstruck. As they walked into the house, she said casually, "It's not much, but I call it home. Sit down please; would you like a drink?"

"No, no thank you," he said, still dazed. "Can't take any more coconut juice."

"It's not coconut juice," the woman replied. "I have a still. How about a Piña Colada?"

Trying to hide his continued amazement, the man accepted, and they sat down on her couch to talk. After they had exchanged their stories, the woman announced, "I'm going to slip into something more comfortable. Would you like to take a shower and shave? There is a razor upstairs in the cabinet in the bathroom."

No longer questioning anything, the man went into the bathroom. There in the cabinet was a razor made from a bone handle. Two shells honed to a hollow ground edge were fastened on to its end inside a swivel mechanism. "This woman is amazing," he mused. "Whatever next?"

When he returned she greeted him wearing nothing but vines – strategically positioned – and smelling faintly of gardenias. She beckoned for him to sit down next to her.

"Tell me," she began, suggestively, slithering closer to him. "We've been out here for a very long time. You've been lonely. There's something I'm sure you really feel like doing right now; something you've been longing for all these months? You know ..." She stared into his eyes.

He couldn't believe what he was hearing. "You mean ..." he replied, "I can check my e-mail from here?"

APPENDICES

In These Appendices...

GETTING CONNECTED WITH WINDOWS 95/98

Windows 95 and 98 both include support for Internet connections that Windows 3.x didn't, making it easier to set up and a lot cleaner to use. There are three tasks to take care of: first you'll need to install the **TCP/IP** protocols that let your computer talk in 'Internet language'; second you'll install the **Dial-Up Adapter** that lets your computer make calls through your modem; and finally you'll create a **Dial-Up Networking connection** that you can double-click when you want to go online.

Installing TCP/IP

1   Open Control Panel and double-click the **Network** icon.

2   Click the **Add...** button.

3   In the left pane of the next dialog choose **Microsoft**, and in the right pane choose **TCP/IP**.

4   Click **OK**. You'll be prompted to restart your computer, but you might prefer to delay doing that until you've finished all the installations.

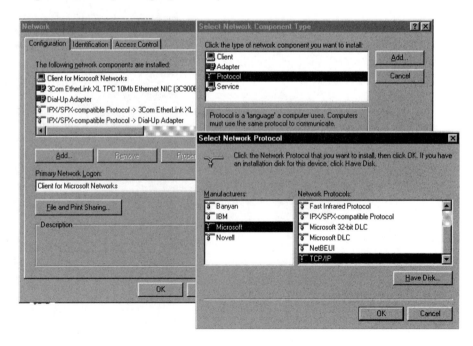

▶ The sequence of dialogs you'll see when installing the TCP/IP protocols.

Installing The Dial-Up Adapter

1   Check to see if you have **Dial-Up Networking** installed already. Double-click the **My Computer** icon and look for a folder-like icon labelled **Dial-Up Networking**. If it's there, skip straight to step 5. If you don't have that icon, you'll need to install it as follows (making sure you've got your Windows installation disks at the ready).

2   Open **Control Panel** and double-click **Add/Remove Programs**.

3   Click the **Windows Setup** tab, then select **Communications** and click the **Details...** button.

4   Check the box beside **Dial-Up Networking**, click **OK**, then click **OK** again to install it.

5   With Dial-Up Networking installed, go back to Control Panel, double-click **Network**, and then double-click on **Dial-Up Adapter**.

6   Click the tab marked **Bindings** and make sure there's a checkmark in the box beside **TCP/IP**. (If there isn't, click the box until the checkmark appears.) Click **OK**.

Creating A Dial-Up Networking Connection

1   Open **My Computer** and double-click the **Dial-Up Networking** icon.

2   Double-click the **Make New Connection** icon.

3   On the first page enter a name for your connection (any name you like). Click **Next**, and type the area code and phone number you were given to dial in to your provider's computer. Select the **United Kingdom** entry from the drop-down list of country codes. Click **Next**, then click **Finish**.

4   Now right-click this new connection's icon and select **Properties**. If you're dialling a local number to your access provider, remove the checkmark beside **Use country code and area code**. (If you were given an 0345, 0645 or 0845 number, which is charged at local rate, you'll need to leave this box checked.)

5   Click the **Server Type** button or tabbed page. Select **PPP: Windows 95, Windows NT 3.5, Internet** from the drop-down list, and make sure the only boxes that are checked on this page are **Enable software compression** and **TCP/IP**, as shown in the next screenshot.

6 Next, click the **TCP/IP Settings...** button and grab the list of details your service provider gave you.

7 If your service provider gave you your own IP address, select the **Specify an IP address** button and then enter the address in the box beneath. Otherwise make sure **Server assigned IP address** is selected.

8 Make sure **Specify name server addresses** is selected, and type the DNS address you were given into the **Primary DNS** box. If you were also given an alternative DNS address, type this into the **Secondary DNS** box.

9 Click **OK**, and **OK** again, and your connection is ready to roll!

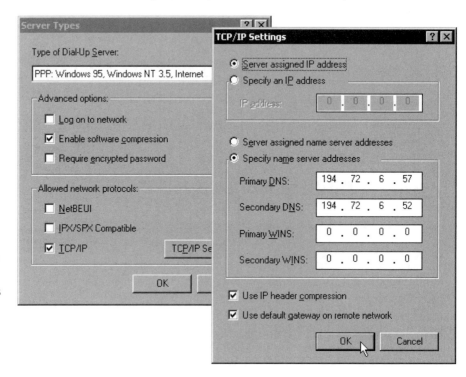

▶ Following steps 7 and 8, this is how those dialogs should look once you've entered your settings into them.

Using Your Connection

To start your connection, open your Dial-Up Networking folder and double-click the icon you just created. A dialog will appear into which you'll need to enter your username and the logon password you were given. To save you doing this every time, check the box marked **Save password**, then click **OK**.

Get a fast connection

To get to that connection icon more quickly, drag it onto your desktop or Start menu to create a shortcut within easy reach. By editing the shortcut's properties, you could even add a shortcut-key for ultra-quick access when you need it.

This box will be replaced by a smaller one that will keep you informed about what's happening with messages like **Dialling** and **Verifying username and password**. Soon you should see the magic word **Connected**. If so, you can now turn to Part Two of this book, start one of your client programs, and get well and truly Netted!

When you've finished surfing and you're ready to log off, you need to click the **Disconnect** button. Where you find this will depend on your version of Windows 95. If the connection dialog minimised to a button on the Taskbar when you connected successfully, click that Taskbar button and you'll see the Disconnect button and the length of time you've been online. If the dialog vanished entirely when you connected, double-click the little icon in the tray that shows two tiny green computers: as well as the Disconnect button, you'll see your total online time together with the amount of data sent and received so far.

Automatic Dial-Up On Demand

The first time you run Internet Explorer it should display the Connection Wizard, a small program that prompts you for details about how you want to connect to the Internet. Armed with this information, Explorer can dial up automatically when you select an Internet shortcut or type an URL into its address bar, saving you the need to find and start your DUN connection manually.

If the wizard doesn't appear, and you like the 'wizardly' approach to entering details, you can start it yourself by clicking the appropriate entry in the **Internet Tools** folder on the Start menu. Alternatively, open Control Panel, double-click **Internet** and choose the **Connection** tab, then follow these steps:

1 Make sure the option button labelled **Connect to the Internet using a modem** is selected.

2 Click the **Settings** button beside that option.

3 In the dialog that appears, select your Dial-Up Networking connection by name from the drop-down list box (or the connection that you want to use as the default, if you have more than one).

4 Enter your username and password in the appropriate fields lower down the page.

5 The remaining options are set at sensible values, so just click **OK** to confirm.

B

GETTING CONNECTED WITH WINDOWS 3.1

Although later versions of Windows have built-in support for Internet connections, Windows 3.x can also be configured for the Internet – if you have a mind to. When you subscribed to your access provider you probably received a disk that includes a program called **Trumpet Winsock**. If you didn't, phone up and ask for it!

There are two steps to connecting: the first task is to install Trumpet Winsock and to edit your AUTOEXEC.BAT file so that Windows knows where to find this program. The second is to configure the program itself using the list of technical details you were given. (If you get into difficulties, Trumpet includes plenty of useful documentation to help you on your way.)

Installing Trumpet Winsock

1   Create a directory on your hard disk called C:\TRUMPET.

2   Copy all the Trumpet Winsock files from your IAP's disk into this directory (unzipping them if they were supplied in a ZIP archive).

3   Create a new program item in Program Manager with the command line **C:\TRUMPET\TCPMAN.EXE** so that you can start this program easily when you're ready to connect.

4   Now you need to edit your AUTOEXEC.BAT file using System Editor or Notepad to add this new directory to your path statement. After you've done so, it might look like this:

SET PATH=C:\;C:\DOS;C:\WINDOWS;C:\TRUMPET;

5   Shut down Windows and reboot your computer to force Windows to read this newly edited AUTOEXEC.BAT file.

GOOD QUESTION

What is a Winsock anyway?

Winsock stands for Windows Sockets, and it's the software that Windows needs to be able to talk 'Internet language', using the TCP/IP protocols we met earlier. It doesn't do anything exciting, but it's the vital link that lets all your Internet programs talk to your IAP's computer.

Configuring Trumpet Winsock

1 Start Trumpet Winsock by double-clicking TCPMAN.EXE in your new TRUMPET directory (or by double-clicking its Program Manager icon if you created one).

2 As the program opens you'll see a dialog containing several fields into which you'll need to enter the details you were given by your IAP. (This dialog appears only the first time you run the program, and these settings will be saved the first time you close it.)

3 Type the **IP address**, **Netmask**, **Name server** (DNS) and **Default Gateway** IP addresses and the **Domain Suffix** into the correct fields (remembering to type the dots between each number). If you were given two DNS addresses, type both into the **Name server** field leaving a single space between them.

4 Check the **Internet SLIP** or **Internal PPP** box according to the type of connection you were given by your IAP, and make sure that the port setting matches the port to which your modem is connected and its correct speed is entered.

5 Click **OK** and you'll see the main Trumpet window – you're now ready to dial up and connect.

6 Open the **Dialer** menu and click **Login**. In the three dialogs that appear one at a time, enter the phone number you were given to dial in, your username, and your password.

7 If all goes according to plan, Trumpet will connect to your IAP and you'll see a message like **CONNECT 38400** appear (it's the word 'Connect' that matters – the speed will depend upon your own modem). Press the ESC key on your keyboard, and you're ready to start one of your Internet programs, turn back to Part 2 and start surfing!

If instead you see a message like **Script Aborted**, you have two options:

▶ Go back to the **Dialer** menu and choose **Manual Login**. Type **ATDT** followed by the phone number of your IAP's computer. As Trumpet tries to connect you, prompts will appear on the screen such as **Username:** and **Password:**. Type these details as you're prompted for them, pressing Enter after each. When you see the **CONNECT** message press ESC and you're officially online.

▶ Contact your IAP's support line to ask for a login script – the chances are that they'll have been asked for this many times before. Failing that, try editing the file LOGIN.CMD in your TRUMPET directory, according to the details included in Trumpet's own documentation.

USING NETSCAPE NAVIGATOR

In the sections of this book that deal with the World Wide Web and browsers, we've assumed that you're using Microsoft's Internet Explorer. If you're not, you're probably using the other contender for the crown, Netscape Navigator. Most of the facilities available in Explorer are also available in Navigator, and many of them can be accessed by similar toolbar buttons, menu options, or keystrokes, so you'll probably find it easy to steer Navigator around the Web from reading the earlier chapters.

Nevertheless, to prevent confusion, the following table lists the main browser features that are found in different places or have different names to the Explorer counterparts.

To do this ...	... select this Netscape option
Reload the current page	Click the **Reload** button, or press Ctrl+R.
View the document's HTML source	Go to **View I Page Source**.
Open a second browser window	Press Ctrl+N, or select **File I New Window**. The new window will display your Home Page.
View the History list	Press Ctrl+H, or select **Window I History**.
Save a link to a site to visit again	Select **Bookmarks I Add Bookmark**, or press Ctrl+D. Bookmarks are the equivalent of Explorer's 'Favorites'.
Organise your bookmarks	Press Ctrl+B, or select **Window I Go to Bookmarks**.
Visit a bookmarked site	Select **Bookmarks** and click the desired site on the menu.
Switch off automatic display of images	Open the **View** menu and click on **Show Images**.
Switch off Navigator's toolbar	Click on **View I Show Navigation Toolbar**.
Switch off the address bar	Click on **View I Show Location Toolbar**.
Switch off the lower button bar	Click on **View I Show Personal Toolbar**.
View a list of installed plug-ins	Go to **Help I About Plug-ins**.
Open the default search engine site	Click the **Search** button on the main toolbar.
Choose a different Home page	Go to **Edit I Preferences...** and choose the **Navigator** in the left panel. You can set different pages to be shown when Navigator is starting and when you click the Home button.
Edit settings for plug-ins and viewers	Go to **Edit I Preferences...** and click the **Applications** in the left panel.
Turn on/off support for active content	Go to **Window I Security Info** and select from a list of content types to choose settings for each.

To do this ...	... select this Netscape option
Change the size of the cache	Go to **Edit I Preferences...**, click on **Advanced** followed by **Cache** and type a new figure into the **Disk Cach**e box.
Empty the cache directory	Go to **Edit I Preferences...**, click on **Advanced** and then **Cache**, and click the **Clear Disk Cache** button.
Find cool sites to visit	Click the **New & Cool** button on the lower button bar and choose **What's New** or **What's Cool**.

JARGONBUSTER SUPER REFERENCE

Arriving on the Internet is a bit like arriving in a foreign country – suddenly everyone around you seems to be talking a different language. This is the part of the book that helps you to find out what they're going on about, or even helps you to learn to speak like a native yourself. Yes, it's all the technical stuff, but we'll keep it as painless as possible.

Keep a look out for words and phrases in *italic* text – they indicate a related entry. The figures you'll find in square brackets (such as [252]) at the end of some of the definitions are the page numbers on which you'll find the subject covered in more depth.

access provider A general term for a company that lets you connect to the *Internet* by dialling in to their computer in return for money. This may be an *Internet Access Provider* or an *online service*. [17]

ActiveX A new multimedia programming system developed by Microsoft for use on the *World Wide Web*. [195]

alias A nifty short name for something whose real name is much longer. For example, your *e-mail* software will usually let you refer to yourself as Joe Bloggs instead of **joe_bloggs@somewhere.co.uk**.

animated GIF A type of animation created by loading two or more *GIF* images into an animation program, setting an order and delay times, and re-saving as a single file. [322]

anonymous FTP A method of getting access to files on an *FTP* site without needing special permission or a *logon* name. Instead you enter **anonymous** as your logon name, and your e-mail address as your password. [152]

anonymous re-mailers Services that will forward your *e-mail* messages or newsgroup *articles* after stripping out your personal details, so that no-one can tell who sent them.

Archie A system that lets you track down files on *FTP* sites by entering the name of the file (or part of it) into a program that can search through indexes of files on these computers.

article For no particularly good reason, the name for a message sent to a *newsgroup*. [125]

archive A single file which usually contains several (or many) other files to make for quicker and easier *downloading*. Most archives also compress these files into a smaller space than they'd ordinarily take up, speeding up downloads still further.

ASCII Pronounced 'ass-key', and often referred to as **plain text**. This is a text system that allows ordinary numbers and letters, punctuation marks such as spaces, tabs and carriage-returns, plus a few special characters, but no formatting or font information. ASCII text can be recognised by almost any type of computer and read in any word processor. [103]

attachments Files included with a message to be sent by *e-mail* or to a *newsgroup*. Messages that contain attachments are indicated by a paper-clip icon in most software. [99]

attributes In *HTML*, these are additions to *tags* that let you specify or change what the tag should do. For example, <HR> creates a rule across the page. Adding the WIDTH= and ALIGN= attributes lets you create a short rule placed on the left side of the page. [312]

bandwidth A general term for the amount of information that can be transferred over an Internet connection. Often used in terms of 'wasting bandwidth' by, for example, sending the same *article* to 30 different *newsgroups* when it was only relevant to one. [16]

BBS (Bulletin Board System) A computer which provides an *e-mail* service and file archives (and perhaps more) which members can connect to via a modem. Some online services such as CompuServe started life as BBSs before becoming connected to the *Internet*.

binaries or binary files The term for a file that contains anything but plain *ASCII* text (such as a program, movie or formatted document). Also appears in *newsgroup* names to indicate that non-text files can be attached to *articles* in the group. [104]

Bookmarks The Netscape Navigator name for *Favorites*. [52]

bounced e-mail *E-mail* messages that come back to you instead of being delivered, usually because you typed the *e-mail address* wrongly. [109]

browser The vital piece of *Internet* software, ostensibly designed for viewing pages from the *World Wide Web*, but capable of handling almost all of your Internet activities. The two most popular browsers are Microsoft's Internet Explorer, and Netscape's Navigator. [48]

cache A directory on your own system into which your *browser* stores all the files it *downloads* from the *World Wide Web* in case you want to view those pages again – it can then load them quickly from this directory instead of downloading them all over again. [72]

chat A type of conversation which takes place by typing messages back and forth instead of speaking (other than to swear at the chat software). A popular chat system is *IRC*, but online services have their own chat rooms, and other software allows one-to-one chatting by 'dialling-up' an *e-mail address* rather like using a telephone. [134]

client The name for something (usually a software program) that makes use of a service. For example, your *e-mail* program is a client that makes use of the e-mail service. The opposite term is server. [11]

compressed files see *archive.*

containers The name for the type of *tags* used in *HTML* that must have a closing tag (such as `<B>...</B>` for bold text). The text to which the tags are being applied is contained within them. [312]

cookies Small text files that some Web *sites* store on your computer so that they know who you are next time you visit. [179]

cyberspace A word coined by William Gibson in his novel 'Necromancer'. It's used as a very generalised term for the Internet and everything that comes with it.

Dial-Up Networking The *TCP/IP stack* built into Microsoft Windows 95, Windows NT 4.0, and later operating systems, that makes setting up an Internet connection a relatively pain-free task.

DNS see *Domain Name System.* [30]

domain name The name given to a computer on the *Internet* that's (vaguely) recognisable to human beings, such as **www.royalnetwork.com**. Every computer on the Net has its own unique name. [8]

Domain Name System (DNS) Also defined as Domain Name Server. This system translates the friendly *domain names* that we humans like to work with into *IP addresses* that computers like to work with. [30]

dot address Another name for *IP address*. [29]

downloading The act of copying files (of any type) to your own computer from some other computer. The opposite term is *uploading*.

Dynamic HTML A formal name for the combination of ordinary *HTML* and scripting in languages such as *JavaScript* that can be used to create feature-rich interactive Web *pages*. [195]

e-mail or email Short for 'electronic mail', a system that lets you send text messages over a *network* from one computer to another.

e-mail address An address consisting of your *username* and the *host* name of your service provider's computer, in the form **username@host**. Because this host name is unique, and you're the only subscriber with that username, the e-mail address is as personal to you as your phone number. [106]

emoticons Little pictures (usually faces) made out of typed characters and viewed sideways-on, such as :-) meaning happy. [107]

encryption The term for altering data or text to turn it into meaningless gobbledegook. Only someone with the correct decoding information (or 'key') can read and use it. [182]

Extranet A new buzzword that refers to an Intranet that is partially accessible to authorized outsiders. Whereas an Intranet resides behind a *firewall* and is accessible only to people who are members of the same company or organisation, an Extranet provides various levels of accessibility to outsiders. You can access an Extranet only if you have a valid username and password, and your identity determines which parts of the extranet you can view. Extranets are becoming a very popular means for business partners to exchange information. [285]

FAQ (Frequently Asked Questions) A list of questions and answers on a particular subject. These are frequently placed in *newsgroups* so that the group doesn't become bogged down with new users asking the same questions all the time. You'll also find FAQs on *Web sites*, and almost everywhere else in the computing world. [186]

Favorites A menu in Microsoft's Internet Explorer *browser* (and a corresponding directory on your hard disk) containing shortcuts to sites that you visit regularly. You can revisit a site easily by clicking its name on the menu, and add new sites to the menu with a couple of clicks. [52]

FTP (File Transfer Protocol) One of the many *protocols* used to copy files from one computer to another on the Internet. Also used in terms like 'an FTP site' (a site that lets you grab files from it using this protocol), and as a verb, as in 'You can ftp to this site'. [150]

Finger A command (or a software program that sends the command) that returns information about someone whose *e-mail address* you entered. Also used as a verb, so this is one instance in which you can 'finger' someone and get away with it.

Firewall A system designed to prevent unauthorised access to or from a private *network*. Firewalls can be implemented in both hardware and software, or a combination of both. Firewalls are frequently used to prevent unauthorised *Internet* users from accessing private networks connected to the *Internet*, especially *Intranets*. All messages entering or leaving the *Intranet* pass through the firewall, which examines each message and blocks those that do not meet the specified security criteria. [134]

flame A negative or abusive response to a *newsgroup article* or an *e-mail* message.

follow-up A reply to an *e-mail* or *newsgroup* message that contains the same subject line (prefixed with RE) and continues the same *thread*.

freeware Software that you don't have to pay for. [162]

gateway A program or device that acts as a kind of translator between two *networks* that wouldn't otherwise be able to communicate with each other.

GIF One of the two major graphics formats used on the *Internet* (along with *JPEG*). GIF images can be saved with between 2 and 256 colours, so they contain less information than the 16-million-colour JPEG format, and therefore make smaller files. They're suitable for anything but photographs and the most lifelike art. See also *animated GIFs*. [322]

Gopher A menu-based system for storing, searching for, and retrieving documents, which was the precursor to the *World Wide Web*. [58]

history list A list of recently-visited sites stored by your *browser* so that you can see where you've been, get back there easily, or find out what someone else has been using your browser for. [53]

homepage Two definitions for this one. 1. The page displayed in your *browser* when you first run it, or when you click the Home button. 2. The first page (or main contents page) of a *Web site*. [62]

host A computer connected directly (and usually permanently) to the *Internet* that allows other computers to connect to it (like your service provider's computer). This also leads to the expression 'host name' which means the same as *domain name*.

HTML see *Hypertext Markup Language*. [48]

HTTP (HyperText Transfer Protocol) The *protocol* used to transfer Web pages around the *Internet*, along with the images and other ingredients that go with them.

hypertext A system of clickable text used on the *World Wide Web*, as well as in older Windows help files and CD-ROM-based encyclopaedias. A hypertext *link* can be inserted wherever a cross-reference to another part of the document (or an entirely different document) is needed. [47]

Hypertext Markup Language (HTML) A fairly simple system of textual codes that can be added to an *ASCII* text file to turn it into a *Web page*. [48]

IAP see *Internet Access Provider*. [17]

IMAP A protocol for retrieving *e-mail* messages. The latest version, IMAP4, is similar to *POP3* but supports some additional features. For example, with IMAP4 you can search through your e-mail messages for keywords while the messages are still on mail server. You can then choose which messages to download to your machine.

Internet Often shortened to just 'the Net', the Internet is a gigantic *network* of computers, all linked together and able to exchange information. No-one owns or controls it, and anyone can connect to it. Without the capital 'I', an internet is a more general term for networks connected to each other.

Internet Access Provider (IAP) A company that allows anyone to connect to the *Internet* by dialling into their *host* computer. All they ask in return is that you give them money. Also sometimes referred to as an Internet Service Provider, or ISP. [17]

Internet Protocol (IP) see *TCP/IP*. [11]

Intranet An Intranet is a *network* based on TCP/IP protocols belonging to an organisation, usually a corporation, accessible only by the organisation's members, employees, or others with authorisation. An Intranet's Web site looks just like any other *Web site*, but the firewall surrounding an Intranet fends off unauthorised access. Like the Internet itself, Intranets are used to share information. Secure Intranets are now the fastest-growing segment of the Internet because they are much less expensive to build and to manage than a private network based on proprietary protocols. [134]

IP address (Internet Protocol Address) Every computer on the *Internet* has its own unique address, which can appear in two forms: the friendlier *domain name*, or as an IP address that computers themselves use. This consists of four numbers separated by dots, such as 148.159.6.26. Also known as a 'dot address'. [29]

IRC (Internet Relay Chat) An *Internet* service that provides one of the most popular *chat* systems which can be accessed using many different IRC programs. Chat rooms in IRC are referred to as 'channels'. [134]

ISDN An abbreviation for Integrated Services Digital Network. An ISDN line allows faster access to the *Internet* than current modems allow, and can simultaneously handle voice and data. [22]

ISP (Internet Service Provider) see *Internet Access Provider.* [17]

Java A software-programming language developed by Sun MicroSystems Inc. The language is often used to write small programs called 'applets' that can be inserted in a *Web page.* [195]

JavaScript A similar language to *Java*, except that it's written in plain text and can be inserted 'as is' into an *HTML* document to place effects or small programs on a *Web page.* [195]

JPEG Along with *GIF*, this is one of the two most-used formats for images on the Net. This format saves information for 16.7 million colours, making it ideal for photographs but creating unnecessarily large files for most forms of artwork. [171]

leased line A line leased from the telephone company that provides a permanent, dedicated connection to an *Internet Access Provider*. Leased lines are lightning fast and cost a small fortune. (Also known as a 'T1 connection'.) [23]

link As a noun, a link is a piece of clickable *hypertext*, identifiable by being underlined and a different colour from the ordinary text around it. As a verb, to link to a site or page means the same as to open or *download* it.

log off A synonym for 'disconnect' – logging off means telling the computer you're connected to that you've finished for this session.

log on/logon Either of these can be used as a noun or a verb. When you log on to a service or computer you are identifying yourself, usually by entering a *username* and password. This act may be referred to as 'a logon', or 'logging on'. Your username may be termed a 'logon name'.

lurking A cute term for observing something without taking an active rôle. This may refer to visiting *chat* rooms and just following conversations rather than chatting, or reading *newsgroups* without *posting* any *articles* yourself.

mailing list This can mean two things. 1. A list of *e-mail addresses* to which you can send the same message without making endless copies of it, all with different addresses inserted. 2. A discussion group similar to a *newsgroup*, but all the messages sent to the group are forwarded to its members by e-mail. [130]

mail server A computer (or program) dedicated to transferring *e-mail* messages around the *Internet*. This might be referred to as an *SMTP* server or a *POP3* server. [30]

Meta tag A special *HTML* tag that provides information about a *Web page*. Unlike normal HTML tags, meta tags do not affect how the page is displayed. Instead, they provide information such as who created the page, how often it is updated, what the page is about, and which keywords represent the page's content. Many *search engines* use this information when building their indices. [333]

MIME (Multipurpose Internet Mail Extensions) A method of organising different types of file by assigning each its own 'MIME type'. Most of the *Internet* software you use can recognise these types and determine what to do with a file it receives (or ask you how you want to treat it). MIME is used to handle *attachments* in *e-mail* and *newsgroup* messages, as well as files found on *Web pages*. [103]

mirror site An exact copy of a site located on a different computer. Many popular sites have one or more mirrors around the world so that users can connect to the site nearest to them, thus easing the load on the main computer. [164]

modem An acronym formed from the words 'modulator' and 'demodulator'. A modem converts data back and forth between the format recognised by computers and the format needed to send it down telephone lines. [16]

MPEG Along with *QuickTime*, one of the two most popular formats for movie files on the *Internet*, requiring an MPEG player and (ideally) special hardware for playback.

MUD (Multi User Dungeon) A type of text-based adventure game that might be played by a single user, or by multiple users adopting characters and 'chatting' by typing messages.

netiquette An amalgamation of the words 'Internet' and 'etiquette' that refers to good behaviour on the Net. Netiquette essentially boils down to two rules: avoid offensive comments and actions, and don't waste Internet resources (or *bandwidth*). [110]

network Two or more computers that are connected to each other (or can be connected via telephone lines and *modems*) and can pass information back and forth.

newbie A colloquial name for someone new to the *Internet*, or to a particular area of it, and is perhaps prone to a bit of fumbling around. Although a slightly derogatory term, it's not meant to be offensive – you might describe yourself as a newbie when appealing for help. [93]

newsgroups A discussion group with a particular topic in which users leave messages for others to read and reply to. There are almost 30 000 such groups, and many more *mailing lists* which follow similar methods. Newsgroups are sometimes referred to as *Usenet* groups. [114]

newsreader The software program you use to access *newsgroups*, and to read, send and reply to *articles*. [116]

news server A computer (or program) dedicated to transferring the contents of *newsgroups* around the Net, and to and from your computer. This might be referred to as an *NNTP* server. [116]

NNTP (Network News Transfer Protocol) One of many *protocols* used on the Net to transfer information around. This particular protocol handles messages from *newsgroups*.

offline A synonym for 'not connected'. In Net terms, being offline is generally a good thing (unless you're trying and failing to get *online*): the ability to compose messages offline and send them all in a bunch later, or view *downloaded* files offline, can save you money in connection charges.

online A synonym for 'connected'. Anything connected to your computer and ready for action can be said to be online. In *Internet* terms, it means that you've successfully dialled in to your service provider's computer and are now connected to the Net. The opposite term is *offline*.

online service A members-only service that allows users to join discussion groups (or 'forums'), exchange *e-mail* messages with other members, download files, and a fair bit more besides. Most popular online services (such as America Online and CompuServe) are now connected to the *Internet* as well. [17]

packet The name for a unit of data being sent across the Net. A system called 'packet switching' breaks a file up into packets, marks each with the addresses of the sending and receiving computers, and sends each packet off individually. These packets may arrive at your computer via different routes and in the wrong order, but your computer uses the extra information they contain to piece the file back together.

PING (Packet Internet Groper) The name of a command (or a program that sends a command) that tests a connection between two computers. It does this by sending a tiny amount of data to a specified computer and noting how long it takes to reply. (The reply, incidentally, is called a PONG.)

plug-in An add-on program for a *browser* that can play or display a particular type of file in the browser's own window.

PoP (Point of Presence) An unnecessarily technical name for a phone number you can dial to connect to your service provider's computer. Many service providers have PoPs all over the country; others cater just for the major cities or a single small area. [21]

POP3 (Post Office Protocol) One of two *protocols* (along with *SMTP*) used to transfer *e-mail* messages around the Net. POP is used for receiving e-mail, and lets you collect your messages from any computer you happen to be using. The '3' refers to the latest version of the protocol. [95]

Portal A *Web* site or service that offers a broad array of resources and services, such as *e-mail*, forums, *search engines*, and online shopping malls. The first Web portals were online services such as AOL, that provided access to the Web, but now most of the traditional search engines have transformed themselves into Web portals to attract and keep a larger audience. [88]

posting When you send an *e-mail* message, the word 'sending' is quite good enough. When you send a message to a *newsgroup*, it isn't. Instead, for no adequately explained reason, the word 'posting' is used. [123]

PGP (Pretty Good Privacy) A popular, but complicated, system of *encryption*. [182]

PPP (Point to Point Protocol) A *protocol* used to connect computers to the Internet via a telephone line and a *modem*. It's similar to *SLIP*, but more recent and easier to set up.

protocol A type of 'language' that two computers agree to speak when they need to communicate and don't speak each other's native language. In other words, a sort of Esperanto for computers, but networking and *Internet* connections use a great many different protocols to do different things. [11]

proxy server A *server* that sits between a client application, such as a Web browser and a real server. It intercepts all requests to the real server to see if it can fulfill the requests itself. If not, it forwards the request to the real server.

QuickTime Along with *MPEG*, this is one of the most popular movie file formats on the Net, developed by Apple. To view these files you'll need the QuickTime Viewer. There is also a virtual reality version (QuickTime VR) which is gaining popularity.

RealAudio The most popular format for *streaming* audio on the Net, requiring the RealAudio Player (included with Internet Explorer) for playback.

refresh (or **reload**) Forcing the *browser* to *download* a Web page again by clicking a toolbar button labelled Refresh (in Internet Explorer) or Reload (in Netscape Navigator). You might do this to make sure you're looking at the latest version of a page, or as an attempt to get things moving again if the page began to download and everything ground to a halt.

rot13 (rotated 13) A simple method used to *encrypt e-mail* and *newsgroup* messages so that you won't accidentally read something that might offend you.

router Device that connects two LANs (Local Area Networks), but provide additional functionality, such as the ability to filter messages and forward them to different places based on various criteria. The Internet uses routers extensively to forward packets from one host to another.

search engine A *Web site* that maintains an index of other Web pages and sites, allowing you to search for pages on a particular subject by entering keywords. Because these engines gather their information in different ways, you can get markedly varying results from using different search sites. [78]

server A computer or program that provides a service to a *client*. For example, your *e-mail* client (the program that lets you work with e-mail messages) connects to your service provider's mail server when you decide to send or receive your e-mail. [11]

service provider A general term for a company that gives you access to the *Internet* by letting you dial in to their computer. This may be an *Internet Access Provider* or an *online service*. [17]

shareware A system for selling software that lets you try before you buy. If you like the program, you pay for it. If you don't, you stop using it and delete it from your system. [162]

signature A short piece of text you can create that gets appended to your *e-mail* and *newsgroup* messages when you send them. This might give contact information (perhaps your name, e-mail address, company name, etc), a neat little phrase or quote, or perhaps an elaborate piece of *ASCII* art (rather like an *emoticon*, but bigger). [106]

SLIP (Serial Line Internet Protocol) A similar *protocol* to PPP, but older and best avoided (especially if you use Windows 95, Windows NT 4.0, or later).

smiley see *emoticon*. [107]

SMTP (Simple Mail Transfer Protocol) Along with *POP3*, one of the two *protocols* that are used to transfer *e-mail* messages around the Net. SMTP can be used to both send and receive messages, but POP3 has more flexibility for receiving. When POP3 is being used, SMTP simply handles the sending of messages. [95]

source The name for the *HTML* document that forms a *Web page*, containing all the *tags* that determine what your *browser* should display, and how. You can look at the source for a Web page in Internet Explorer by clicking the View menu and selecting Source.

spamming A Net jargon term for sending the same message to multiple *newsgroups* or *e-mail* recipients regardless of their interest (or lack of it). Most spamming consists of unsolicited advertisements. Apart from the personal aggravation it causes, spamming is also a massive waste of *bandwidth*. [189]

streaming Some of the latest formats for video and audio on the Net allow the file to play while it's being *downloaded*, rather than forcing you to wait for the entire file to download first. [173]

tags The name for the *HTML* codes added to a plain *ASCII* document which turn it into a *Web page* with full formatting and *links* to other files and pages. [312]

talk A talk program lets you speak to someone elsewhere in the world using your *modem* and Internet connection instead of your telephone. You need a soundcard and microphone, and the other person must be using the same program you are. Also known as Voice On the Net (VON). The term 'talk' is also used to describe the kind of typed *chat* that takes place between two people rather than a group in a chat room. [134]

TCP/IP (Transmission Control Protocol/Internet Protocol) Two vital *protocols* that work together to handle communications between your computer and the rest of the *Internet*. [11]

TCP/IP Stack For a computer to connect to the *Internet*, it must have a TCP/IP stack, which consists of *TCP/IP software*, *packet* driver software, and sockets software. Windows 95 and later Windows operating systems come with their own TCP/IP stack called *Dial-Up Networking*. In Windows 3x, the TCP/IP stack has to be installed separately: one of the best stacks is Trumpet Winsock. (See also *Winsock*.) [350]

Telnet A program that allows *Internet* users to connect to a distant computer and control it through their own computer. Nowadays the main use of Telnet is in playing games like *MUDs*.

thread An ongoing topic of conversation in a *newsgroup* or *mailing list*. When someone posts a message with a new subject line they're starting a new thread. Any replies to this message (and replies to replies, and so on) will have the same subject line and continue the thread. [121]

TLAs (Three Letter Acronyms) Not necessarily acronyms, and not necessarily three letters either, but TLAs are a type of shorthand for common phrases used in conversation and messages on the Net, such as BTW for 'By the way'. [106]

Transmission Control Protocol (TCP) see *TCP/IP*.

uploading The term for copying files from your own computer to a distant computer, usually by using *FTP*. The opposite term in *downloading*.

URL (Uniform Resource Locator) (Pronounced 'earl'.) The unique 'address' of a file on the *Internet* consisting of a *protocol* (such as http://), a computer name (such as www.computer.co.uk) and a path to the file on that computer (such as /public/files/program.zip). [56]

Usenet A large *network* that distributes many of the Net's *newsgroups*. [114]

username A unique name you're assigned by a service that enables you to *log on* to it and identify yourself, demonstrating that you're entitled to access it. When you set up your *Internet* access account, your username will usually form part of your *e-mail address* too. [27]

UUencode/UUdecode To send computer files in *e-mail* or *newsgroup* messages, they have to be converted to plain *ASCII* text first. Uuencoding is a system for converting files this way; uudecoding converts the text back into a file at the other end. Special software may be needed to do this, but many e-mail and newsgroup programs have built-in automatic uuencode/uudecode facilities. [103]

VBScript A scripting language developed by Microsoft, similar to *JavaScript*. [195]

Veronica An acronym for 'Very Easy Rodent-Oriented Net-wide Index to Computerized Archives'. Veronica is a facility built into *Gopher* that allows searching for files on gopher sites.

viewer A program used to view, play or display files that you find on the Net. Unlike a *plug-in*, a viewer will open the file in its own separate window. Because it's a stand-alone program, you can also use it *offline* to view files already on your own system.

virus A small program created by a warped mind that can use various methods to attach itself to programs. When the program is run, so is the virus. A virus might do no more harm to your system than making it go beep occasionally, or it might trash all your data and even make your computer unusable. The main risk of 'catching' a virus comes from using programs on a floppy disk of unknown origin or *downloaded* from the *Internet* without first running them through virus-checker software. [70]

Voice On the Net (VON) see *talk*. [135]

VRML (Virtual Reality Modelling Language) A language used to build 3-dimensional models and 'worlds' that you can view using special software. [193]

WAIS (Wide Area Information Server) A little-used service for searching databases of information on the Net.

Web see *World Wide Web*.

Web page A single document (usually with the extension .htm or .html) forming a tiny part of the *World Wide Web*, often containing text, images, and links to other pages and files on the Web. To view Web pages you need a *browser*. [47]

Web server A computer or program dedicated to storing Web *pages* and transmitting them to your computer to be viewed in your *browser*. [11]

Web site A collection of related Web *pages* and files, usually created by or belonging to a single individual or company, and located on the same *Web server*. [11]

Web space Usually refers to space on a *Web server* provided to *Internet* users so that they can create and publish their own *Web sites*. This space may be provided free, or for a monthly charge. [11]

Whois A command (or a program which can send the command) that can find someone's *e-mail address* and other information about them based on the name you enter.

Winsock An abbreviation of Windows Sockets, the sockets software program for Windows operating systems called Winsock.dll that forms the basis of a *TCP/IP stack*. [340]

World Wide Web A vast collection of documents and files stored on *Web servers*. The documents are known as *Web pages* and are created using a language called *HTML*. All these pages and files are linked together using a system of *hypertext*.

HTML TAG GLOSSARY

The following is a quick reference guide to the most useful HTML tags together with their attributes. You'll find examples of these and more on the CD-ROM if you'd like to see what they look like in use (and, perhaps, just copy the code instead of trying to understand it!).

The list below has been set out as follows:

▶ For HTML elements that must have a closing tag, both the opening and closing tags are included, separated by an ellipsis which is where your own text will go.

▶ Where information must be placed between double quotes, they have been included.

▶ As usual, any text in **_bold italics_** will be substituted with your own settings.

▶ Where only fixed alternatives are available (as in the case of alignment options) they are separated by pipe symbols, such as **left | right | center**.

Comments

`<!--...-->`
Turns all the text between these elements into a comment ignored by browsers.

Document Structure

`<HTML>...</HTML>`
Encloses the whole document, containing the `<HEAD>` and `<BODY>` sections.

`<HEAD>...</HEAD>`
The header portion of the document, containing the `<TITLE>` and, optionally, the `<META>` elements.

`<BODY>...</BODY>`
Encloses the body portion of the document, including all text to be displayed and tags used for formatting, links, images etc. Optional attributes are:

BGCOLOR=_colour_	Colour of the page background.
TEXT=_colour_	Default colour of the page's text.
LINK=_colour_	Colour of hypertext links.
VLINK=_colour_	Colour of visited links.
ALINK=_colour_	Colour of active (just-clicked) links.
BACKGROUND=_"file"_	Image file to be tiled as page wallpaper.

\<BASE\>

Specifies a URL from which all relative links in a document will be resolved, or a default frame- or window-name into which all links will be opened. One or both of these attributes must be used:

HREF=_"url"_	The base URL to resolve links.
TARGET=_"frame"_	The default frame- or window-name.

\<META\>

Provides information about the document itself, such as providing descriptions and keywords for use by search engines, or author and expiry details. Either or both of the first two attributes may be used; the CONTENT attribute must be present.

HTTP-EQUIV=_http header_	Recognised HTTP header such as **Expires**.
NAME=_meta name_	Name of META information, such as **Author**.
CONTENT=_value_	The value to be associated with the given name.

Title & Headings

\<TITLE\>...**\</TITLE\>**

Encloses the title of the document. This must be included in the header.

\<H1\>...**\</H1\>**

Encloses text to be formatted as a heading. \<H1\> defines the largest possible heading, \<H2\> is slightly smaller, and so on down to \<H6\>, the smallest. Any of these can take the optional attribute:

ALIGN=center|left|right	Aligns the heading on the page. The default is **left**.

Character Formatting

<FONT>...</FONT>
Specifies or alters the type and style of font to be used for the enclosed text. Takes one or more of these attributes:

FACE="*font1, font2,* ..."	Name of font to be used, plus alternatives.
SIZE=1|2|3|4|5|6|7	Size of the font to use. The default size is 3.
COLOR=*colour*	Colour in which the text should be displayed.

<B>...</B>
Formats the enclosed text in bold type.

<I>...</I>
Formats the enclosed text in italic type.

<U>...</U>
Underlines the enclosed text.

<S>...</S>
Strikes through (crosses out) the enclosed text.

<EM>...</EM>
Emphasises the enclosed text; most browsers will format this as italic type.

<STRONG>...</STRONG>
Strong emphasis of the enclosed text; most browsers will format this as bold type.

<TT>...</TT>
Formats the enclosed text using a typewriter-style font.

<BIG>...</BIG>
Makes the enclosed text one size larger.

<SMALL>...</SMALL>
Makes the enclosed text one size smaller.

\^{...\}

Formats the enclosed text as superscript.

_{...\}

Formats the enclosed text as subscript.

\<BLOCKQUOTE>...\</BLOCKQUOTE>

Formats the enclosed text as a quotation, usually by indenting it left and right.

\<PRE>...\</PRE>

Displays the enclosed text exactly as typed, observing carriage returns, styles, spaces etc.

Paragraphs & Layout

\<P>

Indicates the start of a new paragraph, inserting a blank line before the text that follows this tag, and aligning it with the left margin by default.

\<P ALIGN=center|left|right>...\</P>

Works in the same way as \<P> by itself, but aligns the enclosed text centrally or with the left or right margins.

**\
**

Inserts a line break at the point where the tag appears. You can use this repeatedly to insert blank lines as well. Optionally takes the following attribute:

> **CLEAR=left|right|all**   The following text will be placed at the next point where there is a clear position at the left or right margin, or a clear position at both margins.

\<NOBR>...\</NOBR>

Prevents the enclosed text from breaking at the right margin.

\<WBR>

Marks a point where the text may be wrapped to the next line if a break is necessary in a line. Usually used within \<NOBR> tags.

<HR>
Places a horizontal rule across the width of the page with a blank line above
and below it. Optional attributes are:

WIDTH=*number*(%)	Width of the line in pixels or as a percentage of page width.
SIZE=*number*	Height of the line in pixels. The default is 2.
COLOR=*colour*	Colour of the line (automatically made solid).
NOSHADE	Removes 3D shading to make a solid line.
ALIGN=center|left|right	Sets alignment of the line. The default is **center**.

<CENTER>...</CENTER>
Places all the enclosed text, images and other content centrally on the page.

Lists

<LI>
Creates a list entry when used with <UL>, <OL> or <DIR>. Automatically
places the entry on a new line. <LI> can also be used by itself to place a
bullet at the start of a new line.

<UL>...</UL>
Creates an unordered (or bulleted) list, using entries placed after <LI> tags.

<OL>...</OL>
Creates an ordered (numbered) list, using entries placed after <LI> tags, and
taking the following optional attributes:

START=*number*	The number from which the list should count.
TYPE=1|A|a|I|i	The numbering system to use: numerical | capital letters | small letters | roman numerals | small roman numerals. The default is numerical.

<DIR>...</DIR>
Creates a directory list of entries by indenting the <LI> entries that follow.

<DL>...</DL>
Creates a definition list, using <DT> and <DD> to create the list entries within the <DL> tags.

<DT>
Creates an entry in a definition list. The entry is automatically placed on a new line and aligned with the left margin.

<DD>
Creates a definition for a <DT> entry. The text following the <DD> tag is automatically placed on a new line and indented.

Images & Multimedia

<IMG>
Inserts an image at that point on the Web page. The SRC= attribute is required, the others are optional.

SRC="*filename*"	The URL, or name and location, of the image file.
ALIGN=top|middle|bottom |left|right	Alignment of the image. The default is **left**.
WIDTH=*number*	The width of the image.
HEIGHT=*number*	The height of the image.
VSPACE=*number*	The space in pixels to leave clear above and below.
HSPACE=*number*	The space in pixels to leave clear to either side.
ALT="*text*"	Alternative text to be displayed.
BORDER=*number*	0 means no border. Higher numbers give thicker borders.
USEMAP=*map name*	Indicates that this is an image map, and gives the name of the map to be used.

<MAP>
Used with client-side image maps to specify the name of the map, and to plot the co-ordinates of areas of the image and assign URLs to them. Takes the attribute:

NAME=*map name*   Specifies the name of the map.

<SCRIPT>...</SCRIPT>
Inserts a script into an HTML document, usually in the header. Needs the attribute:

LANGUAGE=JavaScript|
VBScript   The name of the scripting language used.

<MARQUEE>...</MARQUEE>
Places a scrolling marquee on the Web page using the text enclosed within these tags. The text will be the colour last specified (either in the <BODY> tag or by enclosing the entire marquee code within <FONT> tags.) The available attributes are:

WIDTH=*number (%)*	Width of the marquee in pixels or as a percentage of page width.
HEIGHT=*number*	The height of the marquee.
VSPACE=*number*	The space in pixels to leave clear above and below.
HSPACE=*number*	The space in pixels to leave clear to either side.
ALIGN=top|middle|bottom	Aligns the marquee with any text on the same line.
BGCOLOR=*colour*	The colour of the marquee's background.
DIRECTION=left|right	The direction in which the text should move. The default is **left**.
BEHAVIOR=scroll|slide| alternate	Determines how the text should movE The default is **scroll.**
LOOP=*number*|infinite	The number of times the marquee should repeat, or an endless repetition.
SCROLLAMOUNT=*number*	How many pixels the text should scroll at a time.
SCROLLDELAY=*number*	Length of pause between each movement of the text.

\<APPLET\>...\</APPLET\>

Inserts a Java applet on the Web page, taking these attributes:

CODE="*class file*"	The name of the Java class to be run.
CODEBASE=*location*	The location of the class file if not in the same directory as the HTML document.
WIDTH=*number*	The required width of the applet.
HEIGHT=*number*	The required height of the applet.
VSPACE=*number*	The space in pixels to leave clear above and below.
HSPACE=*number*	The space in pixels to leave clear to either side.
ALIGN=center|left|right| **middle|texttop|textbottom|** **textmiddle|baseline**	The alignment of the applet.
ALT="*text*"	Alternative text to be displayed if the browser doesn't support Java applets.
NAME=*name*	Assigns a name to the applet.

\<PARAM\>

A tag used with Java applets to specify optional settings that might have been built into the applet by its author. Takes the following two attributes:

NAME=*name*	The specified parameter name.
VALUE="*value*"	The chosen value for that parameter.

Links

\<A\>...\</A\>

Creates a link to the Web document or file named in the HREF= attribute, or creates an anchor that can be linked to by using the NAME= attribute.

HREF="*url*|*name*"	Formats the enclosed text as a link to the URL or named anchor. The value may also be "**mailto:***e-mailaddress*".
TARGET="*frame*"	Specifies the name of a frame or window in which the linked document should be opened.
NAME="*name*"	Creates an anchor at the point where the enclosed text occurs that can be linked to by adding *#name* to the end of the HREF= value.

383

Tables

<TABLE>...</TABLE>
Formats the enclosed text (including the rest of the tags in this category) as a table. The following optional attributes can be added:

ALIGN=center|left|right	Sets the alignment of the table. The default is **left**.
BORDER=number	Thickness of border. The default is no border.
WIDTH=number(%)	Width of the table in pixels or as a percentage of page width.
CELLPADDING=number	Space between the sides of a cell and its contents, in pixels.
CELLSPACING=number	Space between the table's border and its cells, in pixels.
BGCOLOR=colour	Background colour of the table (recognised only by Internet Explorer).
BACKGROUND="file"	Image file to be used as a table's background (Explorer only).
BORDERCOLOR=colour	The colour of the table border (Explorer only).

<TR>...</TR>
Short for 'table row'. The enclosed text and <TD> tags will form a new row of cells in a table. (The closing </TR> tag can be left out with no harmful effects.) This tag can take the ALIGN, BGCOLOR, BACKGROUND and BORDERCOLOR attributes exactly as used by the <TABLE> tag, plus the following:

VALIGN=top|middle| **bottom|baseline**	Sets the vertical alignment of all text in this row.
CHAR="character"	Sets a particular character that will be aligned according to the ALIGN= setting.
CHAROFF="number%"	Sets a percentage offset for the first alignment character.

<TD>...</TD>
Short for 'table data'. This tag creates a new cell in the current row and encloses the text (or other content) to be placed in that cell, although the closing tag may be left out. <TD> can take the ALIGN, BGCOLOR,

BACKGROUND, BORDERCOLOR, VALIGN, CHAR and CHAROFF attributes
mentioned above, as well as the following:

COLSPAN=*number*   The number of columns that this cell will span.

ROWSPAN=*number*   The number of rows that this cell will span.

NOWRAP   Prevents the text from wrapping in a cell.

<CAPTION>...</CAPTION>
Can be used within the <TABLE> element to create a caption above the table
using the enclosed text. The available attribute is:

ALIGN=top|bottom|left
     |right   Sets the alignment of the caption.

HTML COLOUR NAMES

Colours in HTML come in two flavours: *named colours* and *hex numbers representing colours*. The hex system is explained in greater detail on the CD-ROM but, in brief, any colour you want to use is made up of varying proportions of red, green and blue. Each of these three colours can have a value of anything from 0 to 255, which gives a total of 16.7 million possible shades.

However, there are still some browsers that can't display all these colours. To ensure that your pages look the way they're supposed to on almost any system, it's preferable to stick with the 140 colours listed below. The corresponding hex numbers are given here too, and you can enter either into your HTML documents – the tag <FONT COLOR=FF0000> means just the same as <FONT COLOR=RED>. For want of a better system, the colours are simply presented in alphabetical order by name. You'll also find a colour chart with swatches on the free CD-ROM accompanying this book.

Name	Hex	Name	Hex
AliceBlue	F0F8FF	Cyan	00FFFF
AntiqueWhite	FAEBD7	DarkBlue	00008B
Aqua	00FFFF	DarkCyan	008B8B
Aquamarine	7FFFD4	DarkGoldenrod	B8860B
Azure	F0FFFF	DarkGray	A9A9A9
Beige	F5F5DC	DarkGreen	006400
Bisque	FFE4C4	DarkKhaki	BDB76B
Black	000000	DarkMagenta	8B008B
BlanchedAlmond	FFEBCD	DarkOliveGreen	556B2F
Blue	0000FF	DarkOrange	FF8C00
BlueViolet	8A2BE2	DarkOrchid	9932CC
Brown	A52A2A	DarkRed	8B0000
Burlywood	DEB887	DarkSalmon	E9967A
CadetBlue	5F9EA0	DarkSeaGreen	8FBC8F
Chartreuse	7FFF00	DarkSlateBlue	483D8B
Chocolate	D2691E	DarkSlateGray	2F4F4F
Coral	FF7F50	DarkTurquoise	00CED1
CornflowerBlue	6495ED	DarkViolet	9400D3
Cornsilk	FFF8DC	DeepPink	FF1493
Crimson	DC143C	DeepSkyBlue	00BFBF

Name	Hex	Name	Hex
DimGray	696969	LightYellow	FFFFE0
DodgerBlue	1E90FF	Lime	00FF00
Firebrick	B22222	LimeGreen	32CD32
FloralWhite	FFFAF0	Linen	FAF0E6
ForestGreen	228B22	Magenta	FF00FF
Fuchsia	FF00FF	Maroon	800000
Gainsboro	DCDCDC	MediumAquamarine	66CDAA
GhostWhite	F8F8FF	MediumBlue	0000CD
Gold	FFD700	MediumOrchid	BA55D3
Goldenrod	DAA520	MediumPurple	9370DB
Gray	808080	MediumSeaGreen	3CB371
Green	008000	MediumSlateBlue	7B68EE
GreenYellow	ADFF2F	MediumSpringGreen	00FA9A
Honeydew	F0FFF0	MediumTurquoise	48D1CC
HotPink	FF69B4	MediumVioletRed	C71585
IndianRed	CD5C5C	MidnightBlue	191970
Indigo	4B0082	MintCream	F5FFFA
Ivory	FFFFF0	MistyRose	FFE4E1
Khaki	F0E68C	Moccasin	FFE4B5
Lavender	E6E6FA	NavajoWhite	FFDEAD
LavenderBlush	FFF0F5	Navy	000080
LawnGreen	7CFC00	OldLace	FDF5E6
LemonChiffon	FFFACD	Olive	808000
LightBlue	ADD8E6	OliveDrab	6B8E23
LightCoral	F08080	Orange	FFA500
LightCyan	E0FFFF	OrangeRed	FF4500
LightGoldenrodYellow	FAFAD2	Orchid	DA70D6
LightGreen	90EE90	PaleGoldenrod	EEE8AA
LightGray	D3D3D3	PaleGreen	98FB98
LightPink	FFB6C1	PaleTurquoise	AFEEEE
LightSalmon	FFA07A	PaleVioletRed	DB7093
LightSeaGreen	20B2AA	PapayaWhip	FFEFD5
LightSkyBlue	87CEFA	PeachPuff	FFDAB9
LightSlateGray	778899	Peru	CD853F
LightSteelBlue	B0C4DE	Pink	FFC0CB

Name	Hex
Plum	DDA0DD
PowderBlue	B0E0E6
Purple	800080
Red	FF0000
RosyBrown	BC8F8F
RoyalBlue	4169E1
SaddleBrown	8B4513
Salmon	FA8072
SandyBrown	F4A460
SeaGreen	2E8B57
Seashell	FFF5EE
Sienna	A0522D
Silver	C0C0C0
SkyBlue	87CEEB
SlateBlue	6A5ACD

Name	Hex
SlateGray	708090
Snow	FFFAFA
SpringGreen	00FF7F
SteelBlue	4682B4
Tan	D2B48C
Teal	008080
Thistle	D8BFD8
Tomato	FF6347
Turquoise	40E0D0
Violet	EE82EE
Wheat	F5DEB3
White	FFFFFF
WhiteSmoke	F5F5F5
Yellow	FFFF00
YellowGreen	9ACD32

DIRECTORY

UK Internet Access Providers

Use the list below to find an IAP with a local POP and the services you're looking for, then give them a ring, ask about pricing, and check some of the other details mentioned in Chapter 3. All the IAPs noted here offer the basic services of e-mail, World Wide Web, FTP, Telnet, Gopher, IRC and newsgroup access.

Bear in mind that this isn't an exhaustive list, and these details change regularly – for example, more and more IAPs are starting to offer free Web-space and allocations are gradually increasing – so it doesn't hurt to ask if the details don't exactly match what you want. Most IAPs have special packages for business users and other connection options available.

Provider name	Telephone	Web site	E-mail address
1st Solution Internet	01344 761350	www.1st-solution.co.uk	sales@1st-solution.co.uk
1Way	0117 9414141	www.1way.co.uk	sales@1way.co.uk
AAP InterNet	0181 4271166	www.aapi.co.uk	sales@aapi.co.uk
Abbotsbury Software Ltd	01305 871543	www.wdi.co.uk	karl@wdi.co.uk
Abel Internet	0131 4455555	www.abel.net.uk	sales@abel.net.uk
Abling Ltd	01823 353771	www.abling.co.uk	info@abling.co.uk
ACE Ltd	01670 528204	www.ace.co.uk	info@ace.co.uk
ACGNET	0171 3779114	www.acgnet.co.uk	sales@acgnet.co.uk
Adept	01843 850444	www.adept.co.uk	sales@adept.co.uk
AIC-Entanet	01279 865290	www.aic.co.uk/entanet	entanet@aic.co.uk
Airtime Internet Resources	01254 676921	www.airtime.co.uk	sales@airtime.co.uk
Amity Internet	0500 200171	www.amity.co.uk	info@amity.co.uk
Andover Online	01264 334822	www.andover.co.uk	sales@andover.co.uk
AngliaNet Limited	01473 211922	www.anglianet.co.uk	sales@anglianet.co.uk
AOL	0800 2791234	www.aol.com	queryuk@aol.com
Argonet	0500 585586	www.argonet.co.uk	info@argonet.co.uk
Intensive Networks Ltd	01672 511054	www.intensive.net	sales@intensive.net
Astra Internet	0800 0182001	www.astra.co.uk	sales@astra.co.uk
Atlas Internet	0171 3120400	www.atlas.co.uk	info@atlas.co.uk

Provider name	Telephone	Web site	E-mail address
Aviators Network	01727 868468	www.avnet.co.uk	info@avnet.co.uk
Baynet Internet Services	01222 256401	www.baynet.co.uk	enq@baynet.co.uk
Beacon Internet Services	01749 831056	www.thebeacon.co.uk	sales@thebeacon.co.uk
BOGOMIP	0800 137536	www.bogo.co.uk	info@bogo.co.uk
BOOTS Internet	01462 743112	www.boots.com	support@boots.com
Bournemouth Internet	01202 292900	www.bournemouth-net.co.uk	sales@bournemouth-net.co.uk
Brunel Internet	01922 59890	www.brunel.co.uk	sales@brunel.co.uk
BT Internet	0800 800001	www.btinternet.com	support@btinternet.com
BusinessNet	0171 3909933	www.business.net.uk	sales@business.net.uk
Cable & Wireless Communications	0500 200980	www.cwcom.net	sales@mcmail.com
Cable Internet	0500 541542	www.cableinet.co.uk	sales@cableinet.co.uk
Cable Online	0800 506506	www.cableol.net	custops@cableol.net
CableNet	01424 830900	www.cablenet.net	info@cablenet.net
Capethorn	0990 168160	www.pobox.co.uk	andrew@pobox.co.uk
Cerbernet	0171 3608000	www.cerbernet.co.uk	sales@cerbernet.co.uk
Charis Internet Services	0121 2485800	www.charis.net	enquiries@charis.net
City NetGates Ltd	0117 9074000	www.netgates.co.uk	sales@netgates.co.uk
CityScape	01223 566950	www.cityscape.co.uk	sales@cityscape.co.uk
Cityway Internet	0181 9306666	www.cityway.com	info@cityway.com
CIX	0845 3555050	www.cix.co.uk	sales@cix.co.uk
ClaraNET Ltd	0800 3582828	www.clara.net	info@clara.net
Cocoon Internet Services	0171 3738461	www.cocoon.co.uk	admin@cocoon.co.uk
Colloquium	0500 008543	www.colloquium.co.uk	sales@colloquium.co.uk
ComeNet Technology Ltd	0181 3579111	www.come.net.uk	sales@come.net.uk
CompuServe Information Services (UK) Ltd	0990 000200	world.compuserve.com	70006.101@compuserve.com
Connect 2 Internet	0800 4960777	www.connect-2.net	penny@connect-2.net
Creative Online Media	01232 370124	www.globalgateway.com	john@globalgateway.com
Cybase Ltd	0151 2274244	www.cybase.co.uk	sales@cybase.co.uk

Provider name	Telephone	Web site	E-mail address
Cyber Ware Ltd.	01733 765050	www.cyberware.co.uk	mail@cyberware.co.uk
CYBERphile Internet	01543 454840	www.cyberphile.co.uk	info@cyberphile.co.uk
Cyberscape	01253 724000	www.cyberscape.net	sales@cyberscape.net
Cygnet Internet Services Ltd	0181 8804650	www.cygnet.co.uk	info@cygnet.co.uk
Data Link Internet	01522 681100	www.data-link.net	sales@data-link.net
Datanet International	01252 810081	www.data.net.uk	info@data.net.uk
Demon Internet	0181 3711234	www.demon.net	sales@demon.net
DIALnet PLC	0990 665665	www.dialnet.co.uk	sales@dialnet.co.uk
Diamond Cable Communications	0800 003005	www.diamond.co.uk	info@diamond.co.uk
Direct Connection	0800 0720000	www.dircon.net	sales@dircon.net
Direct Net @ccess	01232 201555	www@d-n-a.net	info@d-n-a.net
Discovery	01203 364400	www.discover.co.uk	invent@discover.co.uk
Dolphin Internet Services	0181 9325000	www.dolphinet.co.uk	info@dolphinet.co.uk
Dorset Internet	01202 659991	www.lds.co.uk	sales@lds.co.uk
Easinet Ltd	0115 9469930	www.easinet.co.uk	sales@easinet.co.uk
Easynet Ltd	0171 6814444	www.easynet.net	postbox@easynet.net
Eclipse Networking Limited	01392 202345	www.eclipse.co.uk	sales@eclipse.co.uk
Ecosse Telecoms	0800 0267092	www.ecossetel.co.uk	netsales@ecossetel.co.uk
edNET	0131 4667003	www.ednet.co.uk	info@ednet.co.uk
Enablis	0800 607608	www.enablis.net	sales@enablis.net
Entanet	0500 368263	www.enta.net	info@enta.net
Enterprise plc	01624 677666	www.enterprise.net	sales@enterprise.net
EntWeb	0800 525470	www.entweb.co.uk	info@entweb.co.uk
Epinet Data Networks	01242 821000	www.epinet.co.uk	info@epinet.co.uk
Exconet	01268 453000	www.exconet.co.uk	sales@exconet.co.uk
ExNet	0181 2965577	www.exnet.com	info@exnet.com
FeNETre	01538 398298	www.fenetre.co.uk	sales@fenetre.co.uk
FlexNet	01638 711550	www.flexnet.co.uk	info@flexnet.co.uk
Foobar Internet	0116 2330033	www.foobar.net	sales@foobar.net

Provider name	Telephone	Web site	E-mail address
Force9	0800 0737800	www.force9.net	sales@force9.net
Fourth Level / Cybercity	0117 9854455	www.flevel.co.uk	sales@flevel.co.uk
Freedom2surf	0181 8812111	www.freedom2surf.net	sales@freedom2surf.net
Free.Net	0181 5683377	www.thefree.net	info@thefree.net
Frontier Internet Services	0171 5369090	www.ftech.net	info@ftech.net
Genesis Project Ltd	0500 822404	www.gpl.net	sales@gpl.net
Gifford Internet Services	0117 9397722	www.gifford.co.uk	admin@gifford.co.uk
Global Internet Ltd	0870 9098043	www.global.net.uk	info@global.net.uk
GMTnet Ltd	01509 269999	www.gmtnet.co.uk	sales@gmtnet.co.uk
GreenNet	0171 7131941	www.gn.apc.org	support@gn.apc.org
Griffin Internet	01332 606160	www.griffin.co.uk	info@griffin.co.uk
GX Networks	0181 9571250	www.gxn.net	enquiries@gxn.net
Hi-Net	0181 5326532	www.hi-net.co.uk	hi-net@higrade.com
Hiway	01635 573300	www.hiway.co.uk	info@inform.hiway.co.uk
I-Way Limited	0118 9580058	www.I-way.net.uk	info@I-way.net.uk
IBM Global Network	0800 973000	www.ibm.net	internet_europe@ie.ibm.com
IFB	01224 333300	www.ifb.net	info@ifb.net
Infotrade/MENET	0800 226600	www.infotrade.co.uk	enquiries@infotrade.co.uk
Insight-Media Communications Ltd	01942 209696	www.insight-media.co.uk	info@insight-media.co.uk
Inter-Computer Technology Ltd	0171 4869601	www.inctech.com	sales@inctech.com
InterAct	01753 776699	www.uv.net	sysop@uv.net
Interalpha	01703 363200	www.interalpha.net	enquiry@interalpha.co.uk
InteResource Ltd	0171 6008820	www.interesource.co.uk	jsl@interesource.co.uk
Internet Alliance Exchange	0800 0520523	www.iax.net	info@iax.net
Internet Central	01270 611000	www.netcentral.co.uk	sales@netcentral.co.uk
Internet Discovery	0181 6942240	www.idiscover.co.uk	sales@idiscover.co.uk
Internet Network Services	0800 467638	www.insnet.net	info@insnet.net

Provider name	Telephone	Web site	E-mail address
Internet Solutions for Business	01203 633177	www.business-solutions.net	sales@is4b.net
IntoNet Ltd	0181 9419195	www.intonet.co.uk	hq@intonet.co.uk
Ireland On-Line	00353 18551739	www.iol.ie	sales@iol.ie
ISPC	01628 639595	www.ispc.net	barryr@ispc.net
k-WEB	0500 751111	www.k-web.co.uk	info@helpdesk.k-web.co.uk
Karoo	01482 602742	www.karoo.net	info@karoo.net
KBnet	01234 402020	www.kbnet.co.uk	sales@kbnet.co.uk
Ke-Connect Internet Services	07000 668436	www.keme.co.uk	info@keme.net
KENTnet Internet Services	01622 844801	www.kentnet.co.uk	sales@kentnet.co.uk
LarkNet	01638 716423	www.larknet.co.uk	info@larknet.co.uk
LDS Technology	01202 659991	www.lds.co.uk	sales@lds.co.uk
LineOne	0800 111210	www.lineone.net	enquiries@lineone.net
London Web Communications Ltd	0181 3494500	www.londonweb.net	contact@londonweb.net
Luna Internet	01782 855655	www.luna.co.uk	john@luna.co.uk
MacLine	0181 4011111	www.macline.co.uk	orders@macline.co.uk
Madhouse Net	0800 0748283	www.madhouse.uk.com	info@madhouse.uk.com
Maidenet	01628 825757	www.maidenet.co.uk	guy@maidenet.co.uk
Manx Computer Bureau (MANNET)	01624 623841	www.mcb.net	postmaster@mcb.net
Mercia Internet Ltd	01827 69166	www.mercia.net	sales@mercia.net
MetroNet	0800 0741881	www.metronet.co.uk	info@metronet.co.uk
Mistral Internet	01273 747432	www.mistral.co.uk	info@mistral.co.uk
Moonlight Internet	01276 856868	www.moon-light.co.uk	sales@moon-light.co.uk
Moose	0181 9506633	www.moose.co.uk	info@moose.co.uk
MSN	0345 002000	www.msn.com	ukweb@microsoft-contact.co.uk
Multimedia Machine Ltd	01204 363688	www.mmm.co.uk	sales@mmm.co.uk
Net Online	0171 4477447	www.nol.co.uk	sales@nol.co.uk
NETCHANNEL	0171 5917000	www.netchannel.co.uk	info@netchannel.co.uk

Provider name	Telephone	Web site	E-mail address
Netcom	0870 5668008	www.netcom.net.uk	sales@corp.netcom.net.uk
NetDirect Internet	0800 7313311	www.netdirect.net.uk	info@netdirect.net.uk
NetKonect Communcations Ltd	01420 542777	www.netkonect.net	info@netkonect.net
Netmania Ltd	0181 2521199	www.netmania.co.uk	info@netmania.co.uk
NetMatters	0345 573377	www.netmatters.co.uk	info@netmatters.co.uk
NewNet Limited	01705 647400	www.newnet.co.uk/home	sales@newnet.co.uk
Nildram	0800 0720400	www.nildram.co.uk	sales@nildram.co.uk
North West Net	0161 9507777	www.nwnet.co.uk	sales@nwnet.co.uk
Northants Computer Centre	01604 622539	www.nccnet.co.uk	sales@nccnet.co.uk
On-line	0181 5586114	www.on-line.co.uk	sysop@mail.on-line.co.uk
Onyx Internet	0345 715715	www.onyxnet.co.uk	sales@onyxnet.co.uk
OrangeNet	0181 930 6270	www.orangenet.co.uk	sales@orangenet.co.uk
Oxford CommUnity Internet plc	01865 856000	www.community.co.uk	info@community.co.uk
Paradise Internet Network Services	01256 414863	www.pins.co.uk	sales@pins.co.uk
Paston Chase	01603 502061	www.paston.co.uk	sales@paston.co.uk
Pavilion Internet plc	01273 607072	www.pavilion.net	sales@pavilion.net
Pinnacle Internet	01293 613686	www.pncl.co.uk	info@pncl.co.uk
Pipemedia OnLine	01455 828218	www.pipemedia.co.uk	sales@pipemedia.net
Poptel	0171 9239465	www.poptel.net	info@poptel.net
Power Internet	01908 605188	www.powernet.com	info@powernet.co.uk
Powernet International	0500 011501	www.powernet-int.co.uk	sales@powernet-int.co.uk
Premiernet	01908 377707	www.premiernet.co.uk	info@home.premiernet.co.uk
Prestel On-line	0990 223300	www.prestel.co.uk	enquiry@netsales.prestel.co.uk
Primex	01908 643597	www.primex.co.uk	info@alpha.primex.co.uk
Pro-Net Internet Services	0181 2003565	www.pro-net.co.uk	sales@pro-net.co.uk
PSINet UK Ltd	01223 577167	www.uk.psi.net	sales@uk.psi.com
RedNet	01494 511640	www.red.net	marketing@red.net

Provider name	Telephone	Web site	E-mail address
Relay	0345 369999	www.relay.co.uk	enquiries@relay.co.uk
Research Machines	01865 826868	www.rmplc.co.uk	sales@rmplc.co.uk
Round One Media	01237 425100	www.rom.net	info@rom.net
SAQ Network Services	0800 801514	www.saqnet.co.uk	sales@saqnet.co.uk
Sci-fi.net	01925 838007	www.sci-fi.net	admin@sci-fi.net
Scotland Online	0800 0272027	www.scotland.net	sales@sol.co.uk
Scotnet	0141 5666377	www.scotnet.co.uk	info@scotnet.co.uk
Simnet	0800 0745547	www.simnet.co.uk	sales@simnet.co.uk
Skynet Internet Services	01604 452245	www.skynet.co.uk	sales@skynet.co.uk
SoftProg Net	0181 7880656	www.softprog.net	sales@softprog.net
Sonnet Internet Ltd	0171 8912000	www.sonnet.co.uk	enquire@sonnet.co.uk
Stayfree Internet	0116 2910909	www.stayfree.co.uk	sales@stayfree.co.uk
Supernet	01534 880044	www.itl.net	admin@itl.net
Surflink	0800 243777	www.surflink.co.uk	info@surflink.co.uk
Swank & Swagger	01179 042288	www.swagger.co.uk	enquire@swagger.co.uk
Talk-101	01925 245145	www.talk-101.com	sales@mail.talk-101.com
Taunton Cyber	01823 353771	www.taunton-cyber.co.uk	info@taunton-cyber.co.uk
Technocom plc	01753 714200	www.technocom.co.uk	sales@technocom.co.uk
Telinco	0800 5424343	www.telinco.net	sales@telinco.net
Thames Global Internet Services	01344 641627	www.tgis.co.uk	info@tgis.co.uk
The X-Stream Network	0870 730 6466	www.x-stream.com	info@x-stream.com
The Internet Business Ltd	01232 424190	www. tibus.net	info@tibus.net
The Internet in Nottingham	0115 9562222	www.innotts.co.uk	info@innotts.co.uk
The Internet Shop	01355 276600	www.inter-s.co.uk	enquiries@inter-s.co.uk
The Legend Internet	01274 743500	www.legend.co.uk	sales@legend.co.uk
The Web Factory (Thames Valley)	01344 867733	www.webfactory.co.uk	sales@webtv.co.uk
The Web Factory Ltd	01782 858585	www.webfactory.co.uk	sales@webfactory.co.uk
Timewarp	0161 9508855	www.timewarp.co.uk	sales@timewarp.co.uk
Total Connectivity Providers	01703 393392	www.tcp.co.uk	sales@tcp.co.uk

Provider name	Telephone	Web site	E-mail address
TRINET IMB LTD	01539 731000	www.trinetimb.com	info@trinetimb.com
Tweednet	01573 229933	www.calligrafix.co.uk	mike@calligrafix.co.uk
U-NET Limited	01925 484444	www.u-net.net	hi@u-net.com
UK2NET	0171 3940388	www.uk2net.com	sales@uk2net.com
UKIP	01772 908000	www.ukip.co.uk	internet@ukip.co.uk
UK Online Ltd	01749 333333	www.ukonline.co.uk	sales@ukonline.co.uk
UNINET	0800 7837499	www.uninet.co.uk	sales@uninet.co.uk
UNITE Solutions	01232 777338	www.unite.co.uk	solutions@unite.co.uk
UUNET PIPEX Dial	0500 474739	www.uunet.pipex.com	sales@dial.pipex.com
VAS-NET	01732 866529	www.vas-net.net	mail@vas-net.net
Virgin Net	0500 558800	www.virgin.net	advice@virgin.net
Voss Net plc	01753 737800	www.vossnet.co.uk	info@vossnet.co.uk
WaveNet	01253 794386	www.wavenet.co.uk	sales@wavenet.co.uk
Wave Rider Internet	0121 6033888	www.waverider.co.uk	Info@waverider.co.uk
WEBplus	0345 932758	www.webplus.co.uk	info@webplus.co.uk
Webscape	01963 370800	www.webscape.co.uk	webmaster@webscape.co.uk
Webtronix	0115 9568823	www.webtronix.co.uk	sales@webtronix.co.uk
West Dorset Internet	01305 871543	www.wdi.co.uk	tim@wdi.co.uk
Which? Online	0645 830240	www.which.net	ogunlarur@which.co.uk
WildNET Ltd	01604 365600	www.wildnet.co.uk	stuartj@wildnet.co.uk
WinNet	0181 9306688	www.win-uk.net	info@win-uk.net
Wirenet Amiga	01925 496482	www.wirenet.co.uk	sales@wirenet.co.uk
Wisper Bandwidth Plc	01788 569777	www.wisper.net	sales@wisper.net
WiSS	01248 602405	www.wiss.co.uk	sales@wiss.co.uk
Wyenet Internet Services	01989 762476	www.wyenet.co.uk	sales@wyenet.co.uk
Zen Internet Ltd	01706 713714	www.zen.co.uk	sales@zen.co.uk
ZetNet Services Ltd	01595 696667	www.zetnet.co.uk	info@zetnet.co.uk
Zoo Internet	0181 9617000	www.zoo.co.uk	support@zoo.co.uk
Zulu Internet	01494 758895	www.zulu.co.uk	simon@zulu.co.uk
Zynet Ltd	01392 209500	www.zynet.co.uk	sales@zynet.net

Useful Business Addresses

Accounting

Institute of Chartered Accountants
in England and Wales — **www.icaew.co.uk**

Institute of Chartered Accountants
in Ireland — **www.icai.ie/**

Institute of Chartered Accountants
in Scotland — **www.icas.org.uk**

Bankers

British Bankers Association — **www.bankfacts.org.uk**

Business Organisations

Association of British
Chambers of Commerce — **www.britishchambers.org.uk**

Business Enterprise Trust — **www.betrust.org**

Business in the Community — **www.bitc.org.uk**

The Centre for Tomorrow's Company — **www.ctomco.co.uk**

Confederation of British Industry — **www.cbi.org.uk**

Crafts Council — **www.craftscouncil.org.uk**

The Federation of Small Businesses — **www.fsb.co.uk**

The Institute of Directors — **www.iod.co.uk**

Royal Society of Arts — **www.rsa.org.uk**

The Small Business Bureau — **www.thebiz.co.uk/smallbus.htm**

Society of Association Executives — **www.martexco.uk/sae**

Credit References

Credit Protection Association — **www.cpa.co.uk**

Dun & Bradstreet — **www.dunandbrad.co.uk**

Development & Enterprise

Centre for Enterprise Education — **www.strath.ac.uk/
departments/enterprise**

Institute for Enterprise Education — **www.iee.vaxxine.com/iee**

National Foundation for Teaching
Entrepreneurship — **www.nftebiz.org**

Scottish Council Development
& Industry — **www.scdi.org.uk**

Scottish Enterprise   www.scotent.co.uk
Welsh Development Agency   www.wda.co.uk

Euro Information
Bank of England   www.bankofengland.co.uk
HM Treasury   www.hm-treasury.gov.uk
European Institutions   europa.eu.int/index.htm
European Commission   europa.eu.int/comm
European Central Bank   www.ecb.int
UK Inland Revenue   inlandrevenue.gov.uk

Exports
British Exporters' Association   www.bexa.co.uk
Department of Trade and Industry   www.dtiinfo1.dti.gov.uk
ECGD   www.open.gov.uk/ecgd/
Institute of Export   www.export.org.uk

Franchising
British Franchise Association Ltd   www.british-franchise.org.uk

Government Departments
Department of Trade and Industry   www.dtiinfo1.dti.gov.uk

Insurance
Association of British Insurers   www.abi.org.uk

Marketing
Institute of Marketing   www.cim.co.uk
Institute of Public Relations   www.ipr.org.uk
Market & Opinion Research International www.mori.com

Patents
Chartered Institute of Patent Agents   www.dircon.co.uk/cipa
Patent Office   www.patent.gov.uk

Venture Capital
The British Venture Capital Association   www.bvca.co.uk
Cubic Egg   www.cubicegg.com
KPMG   www.kpmg.co.uk
LINC   www.linc.co.uk

INDEX

WHAT'S ON THE CD-ROM?

In the back of this book you will find a CD-ROM containing a collection of information files and software to help you get the most from your Internet connection.

To move between the different sections you simply click the name of the section in the left hand menu that you wish to open. You'll also find coloured and/or underlined links which allow you to move from page to page within a section.

The CD-ROM is divided up into six sections.

Chapter-by-Chapter Reference

In this section there are pages devoted to specific chapters of *The UK Business Internet Starter Kit*, putting all the web sites mentioned just one click away as you read throught the book.

Software Directory

Here you'll find an index of all the software applications and utilities included on the CD, along with descriptions and installation details. Some of these programs are free. Others are shareware, meaning that you'll need to register them. Details of how to register are included with each item of software.

Here's a quick run-down of what there is, but remember to look on the CD-ROM itself for more details:

Browsing

Internet Explorer 5	Quick View Plus
Ad-Wiper	Unmozify
Online Meter	Websnake

Chat

Webphone	IRC Ferret

E-mail

Acorn Email	ESP Mail Check
Eudora Lite	Pegasus
PicMail	Email Ferret

FTP

CoffeeCupDirect FTP   WS_FTP Pro
Cute FTP   File Ferret

Image & Multimedia

Buttonz & Tilez   Cool Edit
Eye Dropper   GIF Movie Gear
Ignite   JPEG Optimizer
Net Graphics Studio   Web Graphics Optimizer
Photovision Pro   Smart Pix Manager
Thumbs Plus

Miscellaneous

Acroobat Reader   Card Check
Exploit Submission Wizard Ferret Family
Netcalendar   NikNak
SubmitWold Pro   Webseeker
Wincrypt   Winzip
YahooNews Ticker

WebDevelopment

Browerola   BrowserSizer
ButtonWiz   Button Generator
Cool Page   HomeSite
Hot Dog   Image Map Generator
IPRISM   Pretty HTML
Sheet Stylist   Web Gateway
WebFlex

Business Web Directory

A directory listing of some of the best information sites for businesses you
can find on the Web.

HTML Reference

This section offers examples and practical information to help you plan and
build your own Web site. You'll also find a useful Colour Chart to help you
plan your page presentation.

IAPs

Here is a list of Internet Access Providers whom you can contact if you wish to open a new account, or change an existing one.

Virgin

Everything you need to install Virgin Net with this easy-to-use software. For more information on connecting to Virgin Net turn to the pages at the back of the book.

How to Use the CD-ROM

Everything on the CD-ROM is viewable in a web browser. If your computer does not have one installed, then insert the CD-ROM in the drive (let's assume it is your d:drive) and click your way to the directory **d:\software\browsing\i.e5**. Find the file called **ie5setup.exe** and double-click on it. This will install Internet Explorer version 5 onto your computer.

Alternatively, you can install Virgin Net with Internet Explorer version 4 by clicking to **d:\virgin** and double-clicking on **setup.exe**.

One you have a web browser installed, simply double-click on **d:\index.htm**.

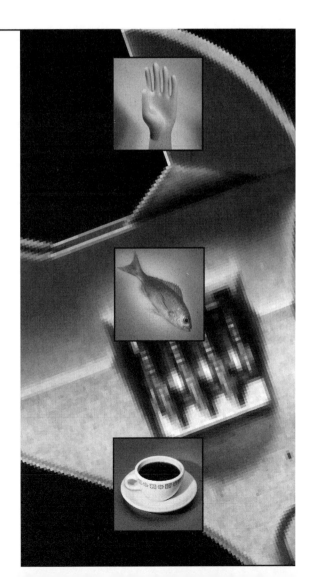

Welcome to Virgin Net

We're here to give you the best Internet service there is. That's it. Once you've tried it we hope you will stay with us for a long time. Exploring the **Internet** [1] can be a confusing experience at first. Virgin Net is here to provide a helping hand – we will guide you through the pitfalls and help you get the best from the Internet. Once you get online you'll find that we've provided you with a guide to some of the best things on the Internet, and a number of features of our own. Please feel free to contact us if you have any comments on how we might improve our service or if there are any new things you would like to see included.

If you feel yourself getting into trouble when registering, please call our local call rate helpline.

24-hour registration helpline: 0845 650 0000

Your calls may be monitored for training purposes.

1. Internet

Millions of computers storing billions of files accessed by tens of millions of people. But don't panic: we'll show you around the basics before turning you loose.

AND WE'LL ALWAYS BE CLOSE AT HAND TO HELP.

Virgin Net is simple to use. You don't need to know anything about the Internet

This section contains simple step-by-step instructions for getting on to the Internet, and will guide you through to a successful connection within a few minutes.

All you need is a PC or a Mac, a **modem**[1], an **ordinary telephone line**[2] and the installation pack on the CD.

Within minutes, you'll have access to the world's biggest reference library, CD collection, department store and news-stand. You'll be able to search for information, communicate with people all over the world, discuss your interests and share ideas.

1. Modem
A box of electronics that allows your computer to communicate through a telephone line. It's like a TV aerial tuned to Virgin Net, receiving all the things that you see on your screen. But unlike an aerial, your modem also sends your commands back.

2. Ordinary telephone line
Your computer is connected to Virgin Net by telephone. No matter where your computer is getting information from, you only pay for a local rate call. Remember: while you're connected, you can't use that line to make or receive calls.

What you will need

1. A **personal computer**[1]. You will need a PC running Windows 3.1 or **Windows 95**[2] or an Apple Mac running MacOS 7.1 or better.

2. A modem. Plug its phone lead into a working telephone socket, and, unless your computer has an internal modem built inside it, plug the other lead into the appropriate socket in the side or back of your computer.

3. The CD included with this book.

4. The following information:

• Your name, address and postcode.

• The make and model of your modem.

1. Personal computer
Detailed hardware requirements are provided at the back of this section.

2. Windows 95
If you are running Windows 95, you may also need your original Windows 95 CD or floppy disks.

Software pack

The Virgin Net software pack contains all the programs you need to connect to and use the Internet. Most of the information and entertainment you'll find on the Internet is linked by the **World Wide Web** [1]. You navigate through the World Wide Web using a browser. A browser is a program which knows how to play and display the many different types of pictures, sounds, movies or text files that you will find on the 'Web'. The browser is also your tool for moving around the Web, just using clicks of your mouse. It will also let you send and receive **e-mail** [2] and read and send messages to **newsgroups** [3]. The Virgin Net software pack includes both Microsoft Internet Explorer and Netscape Navigator. During this installation we will recommend which browser is appropriate for your computer.

1. World Wide Web
An easy way of finding most of the information on the Internet. The Web is made up of millions of linked pages of text and pictures, which you can display on your computer.

2. E-mail
Keep in touch with your friends and colleagues by sending electronic messages. It's cheaper than a phone call.

3. Newsgroups
Whatever your interest or hobby, you'll find people talking (in writing) about it in a newsgroup. Anyone can post messages to a newsgroup, and anyone can read them.

In addition to the browser

We will also install the following Virgin Net programs.

These are:

Global Chat
Lets you talk live to other people on the Net by typing messages.

Real Audio
Allows your browser to play sound files without downloading them first.

We also provide two optional extras, Cybersitter and Shockwave.

Full instructions can be found on the Help service once you are online.

Cybersitter
This program allows you to control your children's access to the Internet.

Shockwave
This program allows your browser to play animated graphics and movies.

How to install Virgin Net

First, make sure that you have shut down any other programs and applications that are running on your computer, except **Windows 95** [1] or Windows 3.1 or MacOS. Next, put the CD into your CD drive. The Installation program will do some tests on your computer, to see if you have disk space for the Virgin Net programs and test whether your machine can run them. If there's a problem, the Installation program will tell you exactly what it is. Some problems you can solve easily by following the on-screen instructions. If the problem is more serious, call our 24-hour helpline on 0845 650 0000. Before you call, take a note of the problem message from the Installation program as it will help our team guide you through the solution.

24-hour registration helpline: 0845 650 0000

1. Windows 95
During installation, you may be asked to insert your Windows 95 CD or floppy disks, so keep them handy. Virgin Net uses certain Windows 95 programs to connect your computer and modem to the Internet. These files may not have already been installed.
Remember: if you have any problems, simply call the 24-hour Virgin Net registration helpline on 0845 650 0000 for advice.

Window 95 and 98 users only

(If the installation starts automatically, you can skip straight to step 4.)

1. Select start on the Taskbar.

2. Select run in the Start menu.

3. If you are using a CD, type D:/virgin.net/setup

4. Click OK and follow the on-screen instructions.

Window 3.1 users only

1. Open program manager.

2. Select file from the Menubar.

3. Select run.

4. Type D:/virgin.net/setup.

5. Click OK and follow the on-screen instructions.

Mac users only

1. Double click on the Virgin Net icon in the desktop.

2. In the Virgin Net folder, click the Installer icon.

3. Follow the on-screen instructions.

Registration

Once installation is complete you are ready to register with Virgin Net. Before you start, be sure to check that your modem, telephone line and computer are all properly linked up and that the modem is switched on. Then just follow the simple on-screen registration instructions. The Registration program will make a local rate telephone call to Virgin Net using your modem, and then will ask you for your **name and address**[1]. The information you provide is used to set up your account. As soon as you have done this, Virgin Net will send you a unique Username and Password. Your Username will tell us who you are when you go online with Virgin Net. Your Password allows us to confirm that you are who you say you are. Please make a note of both your Username and your Password as you will need them every time you want to connect to Virgin Net. In addition, your Username will be used to set up your e-mail address on Virgin Net.

1. Name and address

This information is confidential and secure. Your details are sent by a direct link to our private computer, which is not connected to the Internet. The information you send cannot be intercepted or read by any other Internet user.

Problems with registration

If the Installation procedure has been successful, it should have taken you directly to our online registration screen. But if it hasn't, don't worry. First try this:

1. Check that your modem is turned on and plugged in correctly.

2. Check that your **telephone line** [1] is working properly. Do this by plugging in an ordinary telephone and dialling the special Virgin Net Registration number, **0645 50 54 40**. You should first hear the line ringing and then something that sounds a bit like a fax machine or static on the radio.

If after these checks you still cannot register, call:

24-hour registration helpline: 0845 650 0000.

1. Telephone line
Make sure that no one is on the phone before you try to connect to Virgin Net. It won't work and they're likely to hear a horrible screeching.

Whenever you want to connect to Virgin Net

All you need to do is:

1. First, make sure that your modem, telephone line and computer are properly connected.

2. Then turn your modem and computer on and **double-click**[1] the Virgin Net icon on your Windows 95/MacOS desktop or in the Virgin Net Program Group if you are using Windows 3.1.

3. If you are using Windows 95, you will need to confirm your Username and Password.

4. Finally, click the connect button. Your modem will connect you to Virgin Net by making a **local rate phone call**[2].

1. Double-click
Tap the left-hand mouse button twice, quickly. Usually used to start a program. Remember: once you're using your browser, you only need to click ONCE to jump to a new link.

2. Local rate phone call
Wherever you are in the country, your telephone connection to Virgin Net's computers is always charged as if you were making a local call.

Once the connection has successfully been made

The browser will **download**[1] on to your screen the Virgin Net **homepage**[2]. Your homepage is the first thing you see each time you connect to the Internet, and the Virgin Net homepage is designed clearly and simply to:

1. Help you to search for useful, entertaining or important information.

2. Give you direct links to the places we recommend.

3. Bring you up-to-the-minute news, sport and entertainment.

4. Let you download and play games or use your computer to connect to **websites**[3] containing recorded and even live sounds, such as **Virgin Radio**[4].

That's it. The rest is up to you. Remember, you're in charge. From now on, we're just here to help.

1. Download
Get information or files from a computer on the Internet and copy it on to your own computer.

2. Homepage
The place you'll begin your exploration of the Internet from. And don't worry if you ever get lost: one click of the **HOME** button on your browser will take you straight back there.

3. Websites
What a programme is to TV and a book is to a library, a website is to the Internet.

4. Virgin Radio
1215AM & 105.8FM. The world's greatest radio station, of course.

Help – and where to find it

We have made Virgin Net as simple and easy to use as possible.

Even so, we know that for newcomers the Internet can be a strange

and confusing place. That's why we've created a Help service that

will answer the **questions**[1] you're most likely to ask.

1. Questions
There are some questions that come up again and again. They're referred to as "Frequently Asked Questions" or FAQs. Before asking a question – either in Virgin Net or a newsgroup – it's a good idea to check to see if the answer is already in the relevant FAQ.

Electronic mail

Electronic mail, better known as e-mail, is so useful that many people get on to the Net just to use it. It's that good. Unlike old-fashioned 'snail mail', you don't need a stamp and it travels at the speed of light. Once you start using e-mail, you will be able to send messages and documents quickly, cheaply and at any time of the day or night to anyone in the world with an e-mail address.

To start using e-mail, press on the mail button on **the browser**[1]. This will open Outlook Express, the e-mail program. To receive e-mail, click on the send & receive button. Outlook Express will go to the **Virgin Net computers**[2], check to see if you have new mail waiting for you there and download any new messages onto your computer.

1. The browser
If you are using Netscape click GET MAIL to recieve an e-mail, TO MAIL to send one and RE: MAIL to reply.

2. Virgin Net computers
Giant, mysterious black cabinets covered in thousands of flashing lights and quietly leaking white coolant fumes. No? Actually they look pretty much like your machine, except a bit faster. Probably.

Electronic mail

New messages will appear in bold and you can read them by double-clicking on them. To send e-mail, click on the compose message button and an empty message window will appear. Type in the e-mail address of the person you want to write to, and then type your message. Send it by clicking on the send button. To reply directly to an e-mail that you have received, the simplest way is by clicking on the reply to author button. A window will open showing the original message with the sender's return e-mail address already filled in. Just type your reply and press the send button. To learn more about using e-mail, use the Virgin Net **Help service** [1], where we have prepared a full guide to using and getting the best out of e-mail.

1. Help service

We want to make using the Internet as easy as possible. And that means having the best help service you'll find anywhere. As well as our 24-hour helpline, we've prepared an online tutorial to take you through the basics, step by step. We've written reference pages that answer the most commonly asked questions. You can find the Help service on our homepage.

Detailed hardware requirements

PC requirements:

• Windows 95, Windows 98 or Windows 3.1

• 486dx processor or better (100MHz for IE4)

• 6Mb free hard disk space (75Mb for Internet Explorer)

• 14.4Kbps or faster modem

• 256 colour display monitor

Apple Mac requirements:

• MacOS System 7.1 or above

• 68040 processor or better

• 16Mb free hard disk space (24Mb recommended)

• 14.4Kbps or faster modem

• 256 colour display monitor